Order and Chaos

Order and Chaos

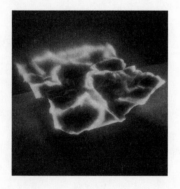

The Great Books Foundation

A nonprofit educational organization

Published and distributed by

 The Great Books Foundation

A nonprofit educational organization

35 East Wacker Drive, Suite 2300
Chicago, IL 60601-2298

Copyright © 1997 by The Great Books Foundation
Chicago, Illinois
ISBN 1-880323-78-8

First Printing
9 8 7 6 5 4 3 2 1 0

Library of Congress Cataloging-in-Publication Data
Order and chaos.
    p.   cm. — (The Great Books Foundation 50th anniversary series)
    Contents: The overcoat / Nikolai Gogol — Bhagavad-Gita :
selection — Troth / Gregor von Rezzori — The Bacchae / Euripides —
Everything that rises must converge / Flannery O'Connor — Poetry :
William Butler Yeats, Wallace Stevens, Robert Frost, Elizabeth Bishop —
Questions for The master and Margarita (Mikhail Bulgakov) —
Questions for Things fall apart (Chinua Achebe)
    ISBN 1-880323-78-8
    1. Literature — Collections. 2. Group reading. 3. Reader-response criticism.
I. Great Books Foundation (U.S.) II. Series.
    PN6014.073 1997
    808—dc21   97-31626

CONTENTS

PREFACE

"Why are both loving and killing the way to God in the Bhagavad-Gita?"
"Does civilization depend on a periodic, controlled indulgence in violence?"
"When does hierarchy in the workplace become a source of
chaos rather than order?"

Anyone who has been in a book discussion group has experienced the joy of new insight. Sometimes an idea or question occurs to us during the group meeting. Often, it is afterward—sometimes much later—that an idea we had overlooked unexpectedly strikes us with new force. A good group becomes a community of minds. We share perspectives, questions, insights, and surprises. Our fellow readers challenge and broaden our thinking as we probe deeply into characters and ideas. They help us resolve questions, and raise new ones, in a creative process that connects literature with life.

It is this kind of experience that makes book discussion groups worthwhile, and that the Great Books Foundation fosters for thousands of readers around the world.

The Great Books Foundation is a pioneer of book discussion groups that bring together dedicated readers who wish to continue to learn throughout their lives. The literature anthologies published by the Foundation have been the focus of many enlightening discussions among people of all educational backgrounds and walks of life. And the *shared inquiry* method practiced by Great Books groups has proven to be a powerful approach to literature that solves many practical concerns of new discussion groups: How can we maintain a flow of ideas? What kinds of questions should we discuss? How can we keep the discussion focused on the reading so that we use our time together to really get at the heart of a work—to learn from it and each other?

With the publication of its 50th Anniversary Series, the Great Books Foundation continues and expands upon its tradition of helping all readers engage in a meaningful exchange of ideas about outstanding works of literature.

ABOUT ORDER AND CHAOS

The reading selections in *Order and Chaos* have been chosen to stimulate lively shared inquiry discussions. This collection brings together works from around the world that speak to each other on a theme of universal human significance. In this volume you will find classic works from Eastern and Western traditions—a selection from the sacred Hindu work the Bhagavad-Gita, and the ancient Greek tragedy *The Bacchae*. Also included are a timeless story by Nikolai Gogol and modern fiction by Flannery O'Connor and Gregor von Rezzori. In addition to the prose selections, you will discuss poetry by W. B. Yeats, Wallace Stevens, Robert Frost, and Elizabeth Bishop.

These are carefully crafted works that readers will interpret in different ways. They portray characters whose lives and motivations are complex, embody concepts that go beyond simple analysis, and raise many questions to inspire extended reflection.

As an aid to reading and discussion, open-ended *interpretive questions* are included with each selection in the volume, and also for the recommended novels *The Master and Margarita* by Mikhail Bulgakov and *Things Fall Apart* by Chinua Achebe. A fundamental or *basic* interpretive question about the meaning of the selection is printed in boldface, followed by a list of related questions that will help you fully discuss the issue raised by the basic question. Passages for *textual analysis* that you may want to look at closely during discussion are suggested for each set of questions. Questions under the heading "For Further Reflection" can be used at the end of discussion to help your group consider the reading selection in a broader context.

ABOUT SHARED INQUIRY

The success of Great Books discussions depends not only on thought-provoking literature, but also on the shared inquiry method of discussion. A shared inquiry discussion begins with a basic interpretive question—a genuine question about the meaning of the selection that continues to be puzzling even after careful reading. As participants offer different possible answers to this question, the discussion leader or members of the group follow up on the ideas that are voiced, asking questions about how responses relate to the original question or to new ideas, and probing what specifically in the text prompted the response.

In shared inquiry discussion, readers think for themselves about the selection, and do not rely on critical or biographical sources outside the text for ideas about its meaning. Discussion remains focused on the text. Evidence for opinions is found in the selection. Because interpretive questions have no single "correct answer," participants are encouraged to entertain a range of ideas. The exchange of ideas is open and spontaneous, a common search for understanding that leads to closer, more illuminating reading.

Shared inquiry fosters a habit of critical questioning and thinking. It encourages patience in the face of complexity, and a respect for the opinions of others. As participants explore the work in depth, they try out ideas, reconsider simple answers, and synthesize interpretations. Over time, shared inquiry engenders a profound experience of intellectual intimacy as your group searches together for meaning in literature.

IMPROVING YOUR DISCUSSIONS

The selections in *Order and Chaos* will support six meetings of your discussion group, with each prose selection and the poetry group being the focus of a single meeting. Discussions usually last about two hours, and are guided by a member of the group who acts as leader. Since the leader has no special knowledge or qualification beyond a genuine curiosity about the text, any member of the group may lead discussion. The leader carefully prepares the interpretive questions that he or she wants to explore with the group, and is primarily responsible for continuing the process of questioning that maintains the flow of ideas.

To ensure a successful discussion, we encourage you to make it a policy to read the selection twice. A first reading will familiarize you with the plot and ideas of a selection; on a second reading you will read more reflectively and discover many aspects of the work that deepen your thinking about it. Allowing a few days to pass between your readings will also help you approach a second reading with greater insight.

Read the selection actively. Make marginal comments that you might want to refer to in discussion. While our interpretive questions can help you think about different aspects of the work, jotting down your own questions as you read is the best way to engage with the selection and bring a wealth of ideas and meaningful questions to discussion.

During discussion, expect a variety of answers to the basic question. Follow up carefully on these different ideas. Refer to and read from the text often—by way of explaining your answer, and to see if the rest of the group understands the author's words the same way you do. (You will often be surprised!) As your group looks closely at the text, many new ideas will arise.

While leaders in shared inquiry discussion strive to keep comments focused on the text and on the basic interpretive question the group is discussing, the entire group can share responsibility for politely refocusing comments that wander from the text into personal anecdotes or issues that begin to sidetrack discussion.

Remember that during shared inquiry discussion you are investigating differing perspectives on the reading, not on social issues. Talk should be about characters in the story, not about participants' own lives. By maintaining this focus, each discussion will be new and interesting, with each participant bringing a different perspective to bear on the text. After the work has been explored thoroughly on its own terms, your thinking about important issues of the day or in your own life will be enhanced. We have found that it is best to formally set aside a time—perhaps the last half-hour of discussion or over coffee afterward—for members of the group to share personal experiences and opinions that go beyond a discussion of the selection.

DISCUSSING THE POETRY SELECTIONS

Many book groups shy away from the challenge of discussing poetry, but the shared inquiry method will enable you to make poetry a very satisfying part of your discussion group. Poetry, by its very nature, communicates ideas through suggestion, allusion, and resonance. Because meaning in poetry resides in the interaction between author and reader, and is brought to light through the pooling of different perspectives and readers' responses, poems are ideal for shared inquiry discussion.

We suggest that you discuss the four poems in *Order and Chaos* in turn, rather than all together as a group. The accompanying interpretive questions will help you focus on each poem individually, and the questions marked "For Further Reflection" will help you consider common and differing elements of the poems.

It is helpful to read each poem aloud before beginning discussion. Because poetry is usually more densely constructed than prose and highly selective in detail, it often lends itself to what we call *textual analysis*—looking closely at particular lines, words, and images as an entryway to discussing the whole work. Having readers share their different associations with a word or image can often help broaden interpretations.

DISCUSSING THE NOVELS

Many novels might come to mind that relate to the theme of order and chaos. We have recommended *The Master and Margarita* and *Things Fall Apart* as particularly enriching novels on this theme, and have provided interpretive questions that can be a significant aid to the reader. Even readers familiar with these novels will find a shared inquiry discussion of them a fresh and rewarding experience.

Most shared inquiry groups discuss a novel at a single discussion; some prefer to spread the discussion over more than one session, especially for longer novels. Since it is usually not realistic to expect participants to read a novel twice in full before discussion, we recommend that you at least reread parts of the novel that seemed especially important to you or that raised a number of questions in your mind. Our passages for textual analysis suggest parts of the novel where reading twice might be most valuable. You might even begin your discussion, after posing a basic question, by looking closely at one or two short passages to get people talking about central ideas and offering a variety of opinions that can be probed and expanded into a discussion of the whole work.

HOW THE GREAT BOOKS FOUNDATION CAN HELP YOU

The Great Books Foundation can be a significant resource for you and your discussion group. Our staff conducts shared inquiry workshops throughout the country that will help you or your entire group conduct better discussions. Thousands of people—from elementary school teachers and college professors to those who just love books and ideas—have found our workshops to be an enjoyable experience that changes forever how they approach literature.

The Foundation publishes a variety of reading series that might interest you. We invite you to call us at 1-800-222-5870 or visit our Web site at http://www.greatbooks.org. We can help you start a book group, put you in touch with established Great Books groups in your area, or give you information about many special events—such as poetry weekends or week-long discussion institutes—sponsored by Great Books groups around the country.

Finally, we invite you to inquire about Junior Great Books for students in kindergarten through high school, to learn how you can help develop the next generation of book lovers and shared inquiry participants.

We hope you enjoy *Order and Chaos* and that it inaugurates many years of exciting discussions for your group. Great Books programs—for children as well as adults—are founded on the idea that readers discussing together can achieve insight and great pleasure from literature. We look forward, with you, to cultivating this idea through the next century.

*Footnotes by the author are not bracketed; footnotes by
the Great Books Foundation, an editor,
or a translator are [bracketed].*

THE OVERCOAT

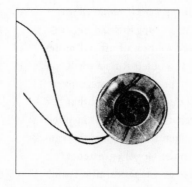

Nikolai Gogol

NIKOLAI GOGOL (1809–1852) was born in provincial Sorochintsy, Russia. A member of the petty Ukrainian gentry, he moved to St. Petersburg in 1828 in an attempt to establish himself in the civil service, and then as an actor, but without success. His first book, *Evenings on a Farm near Dikanka,* was published in 1831–32 to high praise. Gogol's next great success was *The Inspector General* (1836), a comedy satirizing corrupt Russian bureaucracy that produced a storm of official protest. Shortly after this, Gogol left Russia for Rome, where he lived (except for a few interruptions) until 1848. It was during this period that he wrote "The Overcoat"—a story that inspired Dostoevsky to exclaim that all Russian Realists had come "from under Gogol's greatcoat." Under the influence of a fanatical priest, and both mentally and physically weakened by his ascetic religious practices, Gogol burned the unpublished manuscripts of the second part of his epic novel, *Dead Souls,* ten days before he died of starvation.

ONCE, IN A DEPARTMENT. . . but better not mention which department. There is nothing touchier than departments, regiments, bureaus, in fact, any caste of officials. Things have reached the point where every individual takes an insult to himself as a slur on society as a whole. It seems that not long ago a complaint was lodged by the police inspector of I forget which town, in which he stated clearly that government institutions had been imperiled and his own sacred name taken in vain. In evidence he produced a huge volume, practically a novel, in which, every ten pages, a police inspector appears, and what's more, at times completely drunk. So, to stay out of trouble, let us refer to it just as *a department.*

And so, once, in *a department,* there worked a clerk. This clerk was nothing much to speak of: he was small, somewhat pockmarked, his hair was somewhat reddish, and he even looked somewhat blind. Moreover, he was getting thin on top, had wrinkled cheeks and a complexion that might be aptly described as hemorrhoidal. But that's the Petersburg climate for you.

As to his civil-service category (for first a man's standing should be established), he was what is called an eternal pen-pusher, a lowly ninth-class clerk, the usual butt of the jeers and jokes of those writers who have the congenial habit of biting those who cannot bite back.

The clerk's name was Shoenik. There is no doubt that this name derives from shoe, but we know nothing of how, why, or when. His father, his grandfather, and even his brother-in-law wore boots, having new soles put on them not more than three times a year.

His first name was Akaky, like his father's, which made him Akaky Akakievich. This may sound somewhat strange and contrived but it is not contrived at all, and, in view of the circumstances, any other name was unthinkable. If I am not mistaken, Akaky Akakievich was born on the night between the 22nd and the 23rd of March. His late mother, an excellent woman and the wife of a clerk, had made all the arrangements for the child's christening, and, while she was still confined to her bed, the godparents arrived: the worthy Ivan Yeroshkin, head clerk in the Senate, and Arina Whitetumkin, the wife of a police captain, a woman of rare virtue.

The new mother was given her pick of the following three names for her son: Mochius, Sossius, and that of the martyr, Hotzazat. "That won't do," Akaky's late mother thought. "Those names are . . . how shall I put it . . ." To please her, the godparents opened the calendar at another page and again three names came out: Strifilius, Dulius, and Varachasius.

"We're in a mess," the old woman said. "Who ever heard of such names? If it was something like Varadat or Varuch, I wouldn't object . . . but Strifilius and Varachasius . . ."

So they turned to yet another page and out came Pavsicachius and Vachtisius.

"Well, that's that," the mother said. "That settles it. He'll just have to be Akaky like his father."

So that's how Akaky Akakievich originated.

And when they christened the child it cried and twisted its

features into a sour expression as though it had a foreboding that it would become a ninth-class clerk.

Well, that's how it all happened, and it has been reported here just to show that the child couldn't have been called anything but Akaky.

No one remembers who helped him get his appointment to the department or when he started working there. Directors and all sorts of chiefs came and went, but he was always to be found at the same place, in the same position, and in the same capacity, that of copying clerk. Until, after a while, people began to believe that he must have been born just as he was, shabby frock coat, bald patch, and all.

In the office, not the slightest respect was shown him. The porters didn't get up when he passed. In fact, they didn't even raise their eyes, as if nothing but an ordinary fly had passed through the reception room. His chiefs were cold and despotic with him. Some head clerks would just thrust a paper under his nose without even saying, "Copy this," or "Here's a nice interesting little job for you," or some such pleasant remark as is current in well-bred offices. And Akaky Akakievich would take the paper without glancing up to see who had put it under his nose or whether the person was entitled to do so. And right away he would set about copying it.

The young clerks laughed at him and played tricks on him to the limit of their clerkish wit. They made up stories about him and told them in front of him. They said that his seventy-year-old landlady beat him and asked him when the wedding would be. They scattered scraps of paper which they said was snow over his head. But with all this going on, Akaky Akakievich never said a word and even acted as though no one were there. It didn't even affect his work, and in spite of their loud badgering he made no mistakes in his copying. Only when they tormented him unbearably, when they jogged his elbow and prevented him from getting on with his work, would he say:

"Let me be. Why do you do this to me? . . ."

And his words and the way he said them sounded strange. There was something touching about them. Once a young man who was new to the office started to tease him, following the crowd. Suddenly he stopped as if awakened from a trance and, after that, he couldn't stand the others, whom at first he had deemed decent people. And for a long time to come, during his gayest moments, he would suddenly see in his mind's eye the little, balding clerk and he would hear the words, "Let me be. Why do you do this to me?" and within those words rang the phrase, "I am your brother." And the young man would cover his face with his hands. Later in life he often shuddered, musing about the wickedness of man toward man and all the cruelty and vulgarity which are concealed under refined manners. And this, he decided, was also true of men who were considered upright and honorable.

It would be hard to find a man who so lived for his job. It would not be enough to say that he worked conscientiously—he worked with love. There, in his copying, he found an interesting, pleasant world for himself, and his delight was reflected in his face. He had his favorites among the letters of the alphabet and, when he came to them, he would chuckle, wink, and help them along with his lips so that they could almost be read on his face as they were formed by his pen.

Had he been rewarded in proportion with his zeal, he would, perhaps to his own surprise, have been promoted to fifth-class clerk. But all he got out of it was, as his witty colleagues put it, a pin for his buttonhole and hemorrhoids to sit on.

Still, it would be unfair to say that no attention had ever been paid him. One of the successive directors, a kindly man, who thought Akaky Akakievich should be rewarded for his long service, suggested that he be given something more interesting than ordinary copying. So he was asked to prepare an already drawn-up document for referral to another department. Actually, all he had to do was to give it a new heading and change some of the verbs from the first to the third person. But Akaky Akakievich found this work so complicated that he broke into a sweat and finally, mopping his brow, he said:

"Oh no, I would rather have something to copy instead."

After that they left him to his copying forever. And aside from it, it seemed, nothing existed for him.

He never gave a thought to his clothes. His frock coat, which was supposed to be green, had turned a sort of mealy reddish. Its collar was very low and very narrow so that his neck, which was really quite ordinary, looked incredibly long—like the spring necks of the head-shaking plaster kittens which foreign peddlers carry around on their heads on trays. And, somehow, there was always something stuck to Akaky Akakievich's frock coat, a wisp of hay, a little thread. Then too, he had a knack of passing under windows just when refuse happened to be thrown out and as a result was forever carrying around on his hat melon rinds and other such rubbish.

Never did he pay any attention to what was going on around him in the street. In this he was very different from the other members of the pen-pushing brotherhood, who are so keen-eyed and observant that they'll notice an undone strap on the bottom of someone's trousers, an observation that unfailingly molds their features into a sly sneer. But even when Akaky Akakievich's eyes were resting on something, he saw superimposed on it his own well-formed, neat handwriting. Perhaps it was only when, out of nowhere, a horse rested its head on his shoulder and sent a blast of wind down his cheek that he'd realize he was not in the middle of a line but in the middle of a street.

When he got home he would sit straight down to the table and quickly gulp his cabbage soup, followed by beef and onions. He never noticed the taste and ate it with flies and whatever else God happened to send along. When his stomach began to feel bloated, he would get up from the table, take out his inkwell, and copy papers he had brought with him from the office. And if there weren't any papers to copy for the office, he would make a copy for his own pleasure, especially if the document were unusual. Unusual, not for the beauty of its style, but because it was addressed to some new or important personage.

Even during those hours when light has completely disappeared from the gray Petersburg sky and the pen-pushing brotherhood have filled themselves with dinner of one sort or another, each as best he can according to his income and his preference; when everyone has rested from the scraping of pens in the office, from running around on their own and others' errands; when the restless human being has relaxed after the tasks, sometimes unnecessary, he sets himself; and the clerks hasten to give over the remaining hours to pleasure—the more enterprising among them rushes to the theater, another walks in the streets, allotting his time to the inspection of ladies' hats; another spends his evening paying compliments to some prettyish damsel, the queen of a small circle of clerks; another, the most frequent case, goes to visit a brother clerk, who lives somewhere on the third or fourth floor, in two small rooms with a hall of a kitchen and some little pretensions to fashion, a lamp or some other article bought at great sacrifice, such as going without dinner or outside pleasures—in brief, at the time when all clerks have dispersed among the lodgings of their friends to play a little game of whist, sipping tea from glasses and nibbling biscuits, inhaling the smoke from their long pipes, relaying, while the cards are dealt, some bit of gossip that has trickled down from high society, a thing which a Russian cannot do without whatever his circumstances, and even, when there's nothing else to talk about, telling once again the ancient joke about the commandant to whom it was reported that someone had hacked the tail off the horse of the monument to Peter the First—in a word, when everyone else was trying to have a good time, Akaky Akakievich was not even thinking of diverting himself.

No one had ever seen him at a party in the evening. Having written to his heart's content, he would go to bed, smiling in anticipation of the morrow, of what God would send him to copy.

Thus flowed the life of a man who, on a yearly salary of four hundred rubles, was content with his lot. And perhaps it would have flowed on to old age if it hadn't been for the various disasters which are scattered along life's paths, not only for ninth-class clerks, but even for eighth-, seventh-, sixth-class clerks, and all the way up to State Councilors, Privy Councilors, and even to those who counsel no one, not even themselves.

In Petersburg, there's a formidable enemy for all those who receive a salary in the neighborhood of four hundred rubles a year. The enemy is none other than our northern cold, although they say it's very healthy.

Between eight and nine in the morning, at just the time when the streets are filled with people walking to their offices, the cold starts to mete out indiscriminately such hard, stinging flicks on noses that the wretched clerks don't know where to put them. And when the cold pinches the brows and brings tears to the eyes of those in high positions, ninth-class clerks are completely defenseless. They can only wrap themselves in their threadbare overcoats and run as fast as they can the five or six blocks to the office. Once arrived, they have to stamp their feet in the vestibule until their abilities and talents, which have been frozen on the way, thaw out once again.

Akaky Akakievich had noticed that for some time the cold had been attacking his back and shoulders quite viciously, try as he might to sprint the prescribed distance. He finally began to wonder whether the fault did not lie with his overcoat. When he gave it a good looking-over in his room, he discovered that in two or three places—the shoulders and back—it had become very much like gauze. The cloth was worn so thin that it let the draft in, and, to make things worse, the lining had disintegrated.

It must be noted that Akaky Akakievich's overcoat had also been a butt of the clerks' jokes. They had even deprived it of its respectable name, referring to it as the old dressing gown. And, as far as that goes, it did have a strange shape. Its collar shrank with every year, since it was used to patch other areas. And the patching, which did not flatter the tailor, made the overcoat baggy and ugly.

Having located the trouble, Akaky Akakievich decided to take the cloak to Petrovich, a tailor who lived somewhere on the fourth floor, up a back stairs, and who, one-eyed and pock-marked as he was, was still quite good at repairing clerks' and other such people's trousers and frock coats, provided he happened to be sober and hadn't other things on his mind.

We shouldn't, of course, waste too many words on the tailor, but since it has become the fashion to give a thorough description of every character figuring in a story, there's nothing to be done but to give you Petrovich.

At first he was called just Grigory and was the serf of some gentleman or other. He began to call himself Petrovich when he received his freedom and took to drinking rather heavily on all holidays, on the big ones at first and then, without distinction, on all church holidays—on any day marked by a little cross on the calendar. In this he was true to the traditions of his forefathers, and when his wife nagged him about it, he called her impious and a German. Now that we've mentioned his wife, we'd better say a word or two about her, too. But unfortunately very little is known about her, except that Petrovich had a wife who wore a bonnet instead of a kerchief but was apparently no beauty, since, on meeting her, it occurred to no one but an occasional soldier to peek under that bonnet of hers, twitching his mustache and making gurgling sounds.

Going up the stairs leading to Petrovich's place, which, to be honest about it, were saturated with water and slops and exuded that ammonia smell which burns your eyes and which you'll always find on the back stairs of all Petersburg houses—going up those stairs, Akaky Akakievich was already conjecturing how much Petrovich would ask and making up his mind not to pay more than two rubles.

The door stood open because Petrovich's wife was cooking some fish or other and had made so much smoke in the kitchen that you couldn't even see the cockroaches. Akaky Akakievich went through the kitchen without even seeing Mrs. Petrovich and finally reached the other room, where he saw Petrovich sitting on a wide, unpainted wooden table, with his legs crossed under him like a Turkish pasha.

He was barefoot, as tailors at work usually are, and the first thing Akaky Akakievich saw was Petrovich's big toe, with its twisted nail thick and hard like a tortoiseshell. A skein of silk and cotton thread hung around Petrovich's neck. On his knees there was some old garment. For the past three minutes he had been trying to thread his needle, very irritated at the darkness of the room and even with the thread itself, muttering under his breath, "It won't go through, the pig, it's killing me, the bitch!" Akaky Akakievich was unhappy to find Petrovich so irritated. He preferred to negotiate when the tailor was a little under the weather, or, as his wife put it, "when the one-eyed buzzard had a load on." When caught in such a state, Petrovich usually gave way very readily on the price and would even thank Akaky Akakievich with respectful bows and all that. True, afterwards his wife would come whining that her husband had charged too little because he was drunk; but all you had to do was to add ten kopeks and it was a deal.

This time, however, Petrovich seemed to be sober and therefore curt, intractable, and likely to charge an outrageous price. Akaky Akakievich realized this and would have liked to beat a hasty retreat, but the die was cast. Petrovich had fixed his one eye on him, and Akaky Akakievich involuntarily came out with:

"Hello, Petrovich."

"Wish you good day, sir," said Petrovich and bent his eye toward Akaky Akakievich's hands to see what kind of spoil he had brought him.

"Well, Petrovich, I've come . . . see . . . the thing is . . . to . . ."

It should be realized that Akaky Akakievich used all sorts of prepositions, adverbs, and all those meaningless little parts of speech when he spoke. Moreover, if the matter were very involved, he generally didn't finish his sentences and opened them with the words: "This, really, is absolutely, I mean to say . . ." and then nothing more—he had forgotten that he hadn't said what he wanted to.

"What is it then?" Petrovich asked, looking over Akaky Akakievich's frock coat with his one eye; the collar, the sleeves, the back, the tails, the buttonholes, all of which he was already acquainted with, since, repairs and all, it was his own work. That's just what tailors do as soon as they see you.

"Well, it's like this, Petrovich . . . my cloak, well, the material . . . look, you can see, everywhere else it's very strong, well, it's a bit dusty and it looks rather shabby, but it's not really . . . look, it's just in one place it's a little . . . on the back here, and here too . . . it's a little worn . . . and here on this shoulder too, a little—and that's all. There's not much work . . ."

Petrovich took Akaky Akakievich's old dressing gown, as his colleagues called it, spread it out on the table and looked it over at length. Then he shook his head and, stretching out his hand, took from the windowsill a snuffbox embellished with the portrait of a general, though just what general it was impossible to tell since right where his face used to be there was now a dent glued over with a piece of paper. Taking some snuff, Petrovich spread the overcoat out on his hands, held it up against the light, and again shook his head. Then he turned the overcoat inside out, with the lining up, and shook his head again. Then, once more, he removed the snuffbox lid with its general under the piece of paper, and, stuffing snuff into his nose, closed the box, put it away, and finally said:

"No. It can't be mended. It's no use."

At these words, Akaky Akakievich's heart turned over.

"But why can't it be, Petrovich?" he said in the imploring

voice of a child. "Look, the only trouble is that it's worn around the shoulders. I'm sure you have some scraps of cloth . . ."

"As for scraps, I suppose I could find them," Petrovich said, "but I couldn't sew them on. The whole thing is rotten. It'd go to pieces the moment you touched it with a needle."

"Well, if it starts to go, you'll catch it with a patch . . ."

"But there's nothing for patches to hold to. It's too far gone. It's only cloth in name—a puff of wind and it'll disintegrate."

"Still, I'm sure you can make them hold just the same. Otherwise, really, Petrovich, see what I mean . . ."

"No," Petrovich said with finality, "nothing can be done with it. It's just no good. You'd better make yourself some bands out of it to wrap round your legs when it's cold and socks aren't enough to keep you warm. The Germans thought up those things to make money for themselves." (Petrovich liked to take a dig at the Germans whenever there was a chance.) "As to the overcoat, it looks as if you'll have to have a new one made."

At the word "new" Akaky Akakievich's vision became foggy and the whole room began to sway. The only thing he saw clearly was the general with the paper-covered face on the lid of Petrovich's snuffbox.

"What do you mean a *new* one?" he said, talking as if in a dream. "I haven't even got the money . . ."

"A new one," Petrovich repeated with savage calm.

"Well, but if I really had to have a new one, how would it be that . . ."

"That is, what will it cost?"

"Yes."

"Well, it will be over one hundred and fifty rubles," Petrovich said, pursing his lips meaningfully. He liked strong effects; he liked to perplex someone suddenly and then observe the grimace that his words produced.

"A hundred and fifty rubles for an overcoat!" shrieked the poor Akaky Akakievich, shrieked perhaps for the first time in his life, since he was always noted for his quietness.

"Yes, sir," said Petrovich, "but what an overcoat! And if it is to have marten on the collar and a silk-lined hood, that'll bring it up to two hundred."

"Please, Petrovich, please," Akaky Akakievich said beseechingly, not taking in Petrovich's words or noticing his dramatic effects, "mend it somehow, just enough to make it last a little longer."

"No sir, it won't work. It would be a waste of labor and money."

Akaky Akakievich left completely crushed. And when he left, Petrovich, instead of going back to his work, remained for a long time immobile, his lips pursed meaningfully. He was pleased with himself for having upheld his own honor as well as that of the entire tailoring profession.

Akaky Akakievich emerged into the street feeling as if he were in a dream. "So that's it," he repeated to himself. "I never suspected it would turn out this way . . ." And then, after a brief pause, he went on: "So that's it! Here's how it turns out in the end, and I, really, simply couldn't have foreseen it." After another, longer pause he added: "And so here we are! Here's how things stand. I in no way expected . . . but this is impossible . . . what a business!" Muttering thus, instead of going home, he went in the opposite direction, without having the slightest idea of what was going on.

As he was walking, a chimney sweep brushed his dirty side against him and blackened his whole shoulder; a whole bucketful of lime was showered over him from the top of a house under construction. But he noticed nothing, and only when he bumped into a watchman who, resting his halberd near him, was shaking some snuff out of a horn into his calloused palm, did he come to a little, and that only because the watchman said:

"Ya hafta knock my head off? Ya got the whole sidewalk, ain'tcha?"

This caused him to look about him and turn back toward home. Only then did he start to collect his thoughts and to see his real position clearly. He began to talk to himself, not in bits of phrases now but sensibly, as to a wise friend in whom he could confide.

"Oh no," he said, "this wasn't the moment to speak to Petrovich. Right now he's sort of . . . his wife obviously has given him a beating . . . that sort of thing. It'd be better if I went and saw him Sunday morning. After Saturday night, his one eye will be wandering and he'll be tired and in need of another drink, and his wife won't give him the money. So I'll slip him a quarter and that will make him more reasonable and so, for the overcoat . . ." Thus Akaky Akakievich tried to reassure himself, and persuaded himself to wait for Sunday.

When that day came, he waited at a distance until he saw Petrovich's wife leave the house and then went up. After his Saturday night libations, Petrovich's eye certainly was wandering. He hung his head and looked terribly sleepy. But, despite all that, as soon as he learned what Akaky Akakievich had come about, it was as if the devil had poked him.

"It can't be done," he said. "You must order a new one."

Here Akaky Akakievich pressed the quarter on him.

"Thank you," Petrovich said. "I'll drink a short one to you, sir. And as to the overcoat, you can stop worrying. It's worthless. But I'll make you a first-rate new one. That I'll see to."

Akaky Akakievich tried once more to bring the conversation around to mending, but Petrovich, instead of listening, said:

"I'll make you a new one, sir, and you can count on me to do my best. I may even make the collar fastened with silver-plated clasps for you."

At this point Akaky Akakievich saw that he'd have to have a new overcoat, and he became utterly depressed. Where was he going to get the money? There was of course the next holiday bonus. But the sum involved had long ago been allotted to other needs. He had to order new trousers, to pay the cobbler for replacing the tops on his boots. He owed the seamstress for three shirts and simply had to have two items of underwear which one cannot refer to in print. In fact, all the money, to the last kopek, was owed, and even if the director made an unexpectedly generous gesture and allotted him, instead of forty rubles, a whole forty-five or even fifty, the difference would be a drop in the ocean in the overcoat outlay.

It is true Akaky Akakievich knew that, on occasion, Petrovich slapped on heaven-knows-what exorbitant price, so that even his wife couldn't refrain from exclaiming:

"Have you gone mad, you fool! One day he accepts work for nothing, and the next, something gets into him and makes him ask for more than he's worth himself."

But he also knew that Petrovich would agree to make him a new overcoat for eighty rubles. Even so, where was he to find the eighty? He could perhaps scrape together half that sum. Even a little more. But where would he get the other half? . . . Let us, however, start with the first half and see where it was to come from.

Akaky Akakievich had a rule: whenever he spent one ruble, he slipped a copper into a little box with a slot in its side. Every six months, he counted the coppers and changed them for silver. He'd been doing this for a long time and, after all these years, had accumulated more than forty rubles. So this came to one half. But what about the remaining forty rubles?

Akaky Akakievich thought and thought and decided that he would have to reduce his regular expenses for an entire year at least. It would mean going without his evening tea, not burning candles at night, and, if he absolutely had to have light, going to his landlady's room and working by her candle. It would mean, when walking in the street, stepping as carefully as possible over the cobbles and paving stones, almost tiptoeing, so as not to wear out the soles of his boots too rapidly, and giving out his laundry as seldom as possible, and, so that it shouldn't get too soiled, undressing as soon as he got home and staying in just his thin cotton dressing gown, which, if time hadn't taken pity on it, would itself have collapsed long ago.

It must be admitted that, at first, he suffered somewhat from these restrictions. But then he became accustomed to them somehow, and things went smoothly again. He even got used to going hungry in the evenings, but then he was able to feed himself spiritually, carrying within him the eternal idea of his overcoat-to-be. It was as if his existence had become somehow fuller, as if he had married and another human being were there with him, as if he were no longer alone on life's road but walking by the side of a delightful companion. And that companion was none other than the overcoat itself, with its thick padding and strong lining that would last forever. In some way, he became more alive, even stronger-minded, like a man who has determined his ultimate goal in life.

From his face and actions all the marks of vacillation and indecision vanished.

At times there was even a fire in his eyes, and the boldest, wildest notions flashed through his head—perhaps he should really consider having marten put on the collar? The intensity of these thoughts almost distracted his attention from his work. Once he almost made a mistake, which caused him to exclaim—true, very softly—"Oof!" and to cross himself.

At least once each month he looked in on Petrovich to discuss the overcoat—the best place to buy the material, its color, its price . . . Then, on the way home, a little worried but always pleased, he mused about how, finally, all this buying would be over and the coat would be made.

Things went ahead faster than he had expected. Beyond all expectations, the director granted Akaky Akakievich not forty, nor forty-five, but a whole sixty rubles. Could he have had a premonition that Akaky Akakievich needed a new overcoat, or had it just happened by itself? Whatever it was, Akaky Akakievich wound up with an extra twenty rubles. This circumstance speeded matters up. Another two or three months of moderate hunger and he had almost all of the eighty rubles he needed. His heartbeat, generally very quiet, grew faster.

As soon as he could, he set out for the store with Petrovich. They bought excellent material, which is not surprising since they had been planning the move for all of six months, and a month had seldom gone by without Akaky Akakievich dropping into the shop to work out prices. Petrovich himself said that there was no better material to be had.

For the lining they chose calico, but so good and thick that, Petrovich said, it even looked better and glossier than silk. They did not buy marten because it was too expensive. Instead they got cat, the best available—cat which at a distance could always be taken for marten. Petrovich spent two full weeks on the overcoat because of all the quilting he had to do. He charged twelve rubles for his work—it was impossible to take less: it had been sewn with silk, with fine double seams, and Petrovich had gone over each seam again afterwards with his own teeth, squeezing out different patterns with them.

It was—well, it's hard to say exactly which day it was, but it was probably the most solemn day in Akaky Akakievich's life, the day Petrovich finally brought him the overcoat. He brought it in the morning, just before it was time to go to the office. There couldn't have been a better moment for the coat to arrive, because cold spells had been creeping in and threatened to become even more severe. Petrovich appeared with the coat, as befits a good tailor. He had an expression of importance on his face that Akaky Akakievich had never seen before. He looked very much aware of having performed an important act, an act that carried tailors over the chasm which separates those who merely put in linings and do repairs from those who create.

He took the overcoat out of the gigantic handkerchief—just fresh from the wash—in which he had wrapped it to deliver it. The handkerchief he folded neatly and put in his pocket, ready for use. Then he took the coat, looked at it with great pride and, holding it in both hands, threw it quite deftly around Akaky Akakievich's shoulders. He pulled and smoothed it down at the back, wrapped it around Akaky Akakievich, leaving it a little open at the front. Akaky Akakievich, a down-to-earth sort of man, wanted to try out the sleeves. Petrovich helped him to pull his arms through, and it turned out that with the sleeves, too, it was good. In a word, it was clear that the coat fitted perfectly.

Petrovich didn't fail to take advantage of the occasion to remark that it was only because he did without a signboard, lived in a small side street, and had known Akaky Akakievich for a long time that he had charged him so little. On Nevsky Avenue, nowadays, he said, they'd have taken seventy-five rubles for the work alone. Akaky Akakievich had no desire to debate the point with Petrovich—he was always rather awed by the big sums which Petrovich liked to mention to impress people. He paid up, thanked Petrovich, and left for the office wearing his new overcoat.

Petrovich followed him and stood for a long time in the street, gazing at the overcoat from a distance. Then he plunged into a curving side street, took a short cut, and reemerged on the street ahead of Akaky Akakievich, so that he could have another look at the coat from another angle.

Meanwhile, Akaky Akakievich walked on, bubbling with good spirits. Every second of every minute he felt the new overcoat on his shoulders, and several times he even let out a little chuckle of inward pleasure. Indeed, the overcoat presented him with a double advantage: it was warm and it was good. He didn't notice his trip at all and suddenly found himself before the office building. In the porter's lodge, he slipped off the overcoat, inspected it, and entrusted it to the porter's special care.

No one knows how, but it suddenly became general knowledge in the office that Akaky Akakievich had a new overcoat and that the old dressing gown no longer existed. Elbowing one another, they all rushed to the cloakroom to see the new coat. Then they proceeded to congratulate him. He smiled at first, but then the congratulations became too exuberant and he felt embarrassed. And when they surrounded him and started trying to persuade him that the very least he could do was to invite them over one evening to drink to the coat, Akaky Akakievich felt completely at a loss, didn't know what to do with himself, what to say or how to talk himself out of it. And a few minutes later, all red in the face, he was trying rather naively to convince them that it wasn't a new overcoat at all, that it wasn't much, that it was an old one.

In the end, a clerk, no lesser person than an assistant to the head clerk, probably wanting to show that he wasn't too proud to mingle with those beneath him, said:

"All right then, I'll do it instead of Akaky Akakievich. I invite you all over for a party. Come over to my place tonight. Incidentally, it happens to be my birthday today."

Naturally the clerks now congratulated the head clerk's assistant and happily accepted his invitation. Akaky Akakievich started to excuse himself, but he was told that it would be rude on his part, a disgrace, so he had to give way in the end. And later he was even rather pleased that he had accepted, since it would give him an opportunity to wear the new coat in the evening too.

Akaky Akakievich felt as if it were a holiday. He arrived home in the happiest frame of mind, took off the overcoat, hung it up very carefully on the wall, gave the material and the lining one more admiring inspection. Then he took out that ragged item known as the old dressing gown and put it next to the new overcoat, looked at it, and began to laugh, so great was the difference between the two. And long after that, while eating his dinner, he snorted every time he thought of the dressing gown. He felt very gay during his dinner, and afterwards he did no copying whatsoever. Instead he wallowed in luxury for a while, lying on his bed until dark. Then, without further dallying, he dressed, pulled on his new overcoat, and went out.

It is, alas, impossible to say just where the party-giving clerk lived. My memory is beginning to fail me badly and everything in Petersburg, streets and houses, has become so mixed up in my head that it's very difficult to extract anything from it and to present it in an orderly fashion. Be that as it may, it is a fact that the clerk in question lived in a better district of the city, which means not too close to Akaky Akakievich.

To start with, Akaky Akakievich had to pass through a maze of deserted, dimly lit streets, but, toward the clerk's house, the streets became lighter and livelier. More pedestrians began flashing by more often; there were some well-dressed ladies and men with beaver collars. And, instead of the drivers with their wooden, fretworked sledges studded with gilt nails, he came across smart coachmen in crimson velvet caps, in lacquered sledges, with bearskin lap rugs. He even saw some carriages darting past with decorated boxes, their wheels squeaking on the snow.

Akaky Akakievich gazed around him. For several years now he hadn't been out in the evening. He stopped before the small, lighted window of a shop, staring curiously at a picture of a pretty woman kicking off her shoe and thereby showing her whole leg, which was not bad at all; in the background, some man or other with side whiskers and a handsome Spanish goatee was sticking his head through a door leading to another room. Akaky Akakievich shook his head, snorted, smiled, and walked on. Why did he snort? Was it because he had come across something that, although completely strange to him, still aroused in him, as it would in anyone, a certain instinct—or did he think, as many clerks do, along the following lines: "Well, really, the French! If they are after something . . . that sort of thing . . . then, really! . . ." Maybe he didn't even think that. After all, one can't just creep into a man's soul and find out everything he's thinking.

At last he reached the house in which the head clerk's assistant lived. And he lived in style, on the second floor, with the staircase lighted by a lantern. In the hall, Akaky Akakievich found several rows of galoshes. Amidst the galoshes, a samovar was hissing and puffing steam. All around the walls hung overcoats and cloaks, some with beaver collars and others with velvet lapels. The noise and talk that could be heard through the partition became suddenly clear and resounding when the door opened and a servant came out with a tray of empty glasses, a cream jug, and a basket of cookies. It was clear that the clerks had arrived long before and had already drunk their first round of tea.

Akaky Akakievich hung his coat up and went in. In a flash, he took in the candles, the clerks, the pipes, the card tables, while his ears were filled with the hubbub of voices rising all around him and the banging of chairs being moved. Awkwardly, he paused in the middle of the room, trying to think what to do. But he had been noticed, and his arrival was greeted with a huge yell. Immediately everybody rushed out into the hall to have another look at his new overcoat. Akaky Akakievich felt a bit confused, but, being an uncomplicated man, he was rather pleased when everyone agreed that it was a good overcoat.

Soon, however, they abandoned him and his overcoat and turned their attention, as was to be expected, to the card tables.

The din, the voices, the presence of so many people—all this was unreal to Akaky Akakievich. He had no idea how to behave, where to put his hands, his feet, or, for that matter, his whole body. He sat down near a card table, stared at the cards, and peeked in turn into the faces of the players. In a little while he got bored and began to yawn, feeling rather sleepy—it was long past his usual bedtime. He wanted to take leave of the host, but they wouldn't let him go. He really had to toast his new overcoat with champagne, they insisted. They made Akaky Akakievich drink two glasses of champagne, after which he felt that the party was becoming gayer, but nevertheless he was quite unable to forget that it was now midnight and that he should have gone home long ago.

In spite of everything his host could think up to keep him, he went quietly out into the hall, found his overcoat, which to his annoyance was lying on the floor, shook it, carefully removed every speck he could find on it, put it on, and walked down the stairs and out into the street.

The street was still lighted. Some little stores, those meeting places for servants and people of every sort, were open, while others, although closed, still showed a long streak of light under their doors, which indicated that the company had not yet dispersed and that the menservants and maids were finishing up their gossip and their conversations, leaving their masters perplexed as to their whereabouts.

Akaky Akakievich walked along in such a gay mood that, who knows why, he almost darted after a lady who flashed by him like a streak of lightning, every part of her body astir with independent, fascinating motion. Still, he restrained himself immediately, went back to walking slowly, and even wondered where that compulsion to gallop had come from.

Soon there stretched out before him those deserted streets which, even in the daytime, are not so gay, and, now that it was night, looked even more desolate. Fewer street lamps were lit— obviously a smaller oil allowance was given out in this district. Then came wooden houses and fences; not a soul around, nothing but glistening snow and the black silhouettes of the low, sleeping hovels with their shuttered windows. He came to the spot where the street cut through a square so immense that the houses opposite were hardly visible beyond its sinister emptiness.

God knows where, far away on the edge of the world, he could see the glow of a brazier by a watchman's hut.

Akaky Akakievich's gay mood definitely waned. He could not suppress a shiver as he stepped out into the square, a foreboding of evil in his heart. He glanced behind him and to either side—it was like being in the middle of the sea. "No, it's better not to look," he thought, and walked on with his eyes shut. And when he opened them again to see if the other side of the square was close, he saw instead, standing there, almost in front of his nose, people with mustaches, although he couldn't make out exactly who or what. Then his vision became foggy and there was a beating in his chest.

"Why, here's my overcoat," one of the people thundered, grabbing him by the collar.

Akaky Akakievich was just going to shout out, "Help!" when another brought a fist about the size of a clerk's head up to his very mouth, and said:

"You just try and yell . . ."

Akaky Akakievich felt them pull off his coat, then he received a knee in the groin. He went down on his back, and after that he lay in the snow and felt nothing more.

When he came to a few minutes later and scrambled to his feet, there was no one around. He felt cold and, when he realized that the overcoat was gone, desperate. He let out a yell. But his voice didn't come close to reaching the other side of the square.

Frantic, he hollered all the way across the square as he scrambled straight toward the watchman's hut. The watchman was standing beside it, leaning on his halberd, and gazing out across the square, wondering who it could be running toward him and shouting. At last Akaky Akakievich reached him. Gasping for breath, he began shouting at him—what sort of a watchman did he think he was, hadn't he seen anything, and why the devil had he allowed them to rob a man? The watchman said he had seen no one except the two men who had stopped Akaky Akakievich in the middle of the square, who he had thought were friends of his, and that instead of hollering at the watchman, he'd better go and see the police inspector tomorrow and the inspector would find out who had taken the overcoat.

Akaky Akakievich hurried home; he was in a terrible state. The little hair he had left, on his temples and on the back of his head, was completely disheveled; there was snow all down one side of him and on his chest and all over his trousers. His old landlady, hearing his impatient banging on the door, jumped out of bed and, with only one shoe on, ran to open up, clutching her nightgown at the neck, probably out of modesty. When she saw the state Akaky Akakievich was in, she stepped back.

When he told her what had happened, she threw up her hands and said that he should go straight to the borough Police Commissioner, that the local police inspector could not be trusted, that he'd just make promises and give him the run-around. So it was best, she said, to go straight to the borough Commissioner. In fact, she even knew him because Anna, her former Finnish cook, had now got a job as a nanny at his house. And the landlady herself often saw him driving past their house. Moreover, she knew he went to church every Sunday and prayed and at the same time looked cheerful and was obviously a good man. Having heard her advice, Akaky Akakievich trudged off sadly to his room and somehow got through the night, though exactly how must be imagined by those who know how to put themselves in another man's place.

Early the next morning, he went to the borough Commissioner's. But it turned out that he was still asleep. He returned at ten and again was told that he was asleep. He went back at eleven and was told that the Commissioner was not home. He tried again during the dinner hour, but the secretaries in the reception room would not let him in and wanted to know what business had brought him. For once in his life Akaky Akakievich decided to show some character and told them curtly that he must see the Commissioner personally, that they'd better let him in since he was on official government business, that he would lodge a complaint against them, and that then they would see.

The secretaries didn't dare say anything to that, and one of them went to call the Commissioner. The Commissioner reacted very strangely to Akaky Akakievich's story of the robbery. Instead of concentrating on the main point, he asked Akaky Akakievich what he had been doing out so late, whether he had stopped off somewhere on his way, hadn't he been to a house of ill repute. Akaky Akakievich became very confused, and when he left he wasn't sure whether something would be done about his overcoat or not.

That day he did not go to his office for the first time in his life. The next day he appeared, looking very pale and wearing his old dressing gown, which now seemed shabbier than ever. His account of the theft of his overcoat touched many of the clerks, although, even now, there were some who poked fun at him. They decided on the spot to take up a collection for him, but they collected next to nothing because the department employees had already had to donate money for a portrait of the Director and to subscribe to some book or other, on the suggestion of the section chief, who was a friend of the author's. So the sum turned out to be the merest trifle.

Someone, moved by compassion, decided to help Akaky Akakievich by giving him good advice. He told him that he had better not go to his local inspector because, even supposing the inspector wanted to impress his superiors and managed to recover the coat, Akaky Akakievich would still find it difficult to obtain it at the police station unless he could present irrefutable proof of ownership. The best thing was to go through a certain important personage who, by writing and contacting the right people, would set things moving faster. So Akaky Akakievich decided to seek an audience with the important personage.

Even to this day, it is not known exactly what position the important personage held or what his duties consisted of. All we need to know is that this important personage had become important quite recently and that formerly he had been an unimportant person. And even his present position was unimportant compared with other, more important ones. But there is always a category of people for whom somebody who is unimportant to others is an important personage. And the personage in question used various devices to play up his importance: for instance, he made the civil servants of lower categories come out to meet him on the stairs before he'd even reached his office; and a subordinate could not approach him directly but had to go through proper channels. That's the way things are in Holy Russia—everyone tries to ape his superior.

They say that one ninth-class clerk, when he was named section chief in a small office, immediately had a partition put up to make a separate room, which he called the conference room. He stationed an usher at the door who had to open it for all those who came in, although the conference room had hardly enough space for a writing table, even without visitors. The audiences and the manner of our important personage were impressive and stately, but quite uncomplicated. The key to his system was severity. He liked to say, "Severity, severity, severity," and as he uttered the word for the third time, he usually looked very meaningfully into the face of the person he was talking to. True, it was not too clear what need there was for all this severity since the ten-odd employees who made up the whole administrative apparatus of his office were quite frightened enough as it was. Seeing him coming, they would leave their work and stand to attention until he had crossed the room. His usual communication with his inferiors was full of severity and consisted almost entirely of three phrases: "How dare you!" "Who do you think you're talking to?" and "Do you appreciate who I am?" Actually, he was a kindly man, a good friend and obliging, but promotion to a high rank had gone to his head, knocked him completely off balance, and he just didn't know how to act. When he happened to be with equals, he was still a decent fellow and, in a way, by no means stupid. But whenever he found himself among those who were below him—even a single rank—he became impossible. He fell silent and was quite pitiable, because even he himself realized that he could have been having a much better time. Sometimes he was obviously longing to join some group in a lively conversation, but he would be stopped by the thought that he would be going too far, putting himself on familiar terms and thereby losing face. And so he remained eternally in silent, aloof isolation, only occasionally uttering some monosyllabic sounds, and, as a result, he acquired a reputation as a deadly bore.

It was to this important personage that Akaky Akakievich presented himself, and at a most unpropitious moment to boot. That is, very unpropitious for him, although quite suitable for the important personage. The latter was in his office talking gaily to a childhood friend who had recently come to Petersburg and whom he hadn't seen for many years. This was the moment when they announced that there was a man named Shoenik to see him.

"Who's he?" the personage wanted to know.

"Some clerk," they told him.

"I see. Let him wait. I am not available now."

Here it should be noted that the important personage was greatly exaggerating. He was available. He and his friend had talked over everything imaginable. For some time now the conversation had been interlaced with lengthy silences, and they weren't doing much more than slapping each other on the thigh and saying:

"So that's how it is, Ivan Abramovich."

"Yes, indeed, Stepan Varlamovich!"

Still Akaky Akakievich had to wait, so that his friend, who had left the government service long ago and now lived in the country, could see what a long time employees had to wait in his reception room.

At last, when they had talked and had sat silent facing each other for as long as they could stand it, when they had smoked a cigar reclining in comfortable armchairs with sloping backs, the important personage, as if he had just recalled it, said to his secretary who was standing at the door with papers for a report:

"Wait a minute. Wasn't there a clerk waiting? Tell him to come in."

Seeing Akaky Akakievich's humble appearance and his wretched old frock coat, he turned abruptly to face him and said: "What do you want?"

He spoke in the hard, sharp voice which he had deliberately developed by practicing at home before a mirror an entire week before he had taken over his present exalted position.

Akaky Akakievich, who had felt properly subdued even before this, felt decidedly embarrassed. He did his best, as far as he could control his tongue, to explain what had happened. Of course, he added even more than his usual share of phrases like "that is to say" and "so to speak." The overcoat, he explained, was completely new and had been cruelly taken away from him, and he had turned to the important personage, that is to say, come to him, in the hope that he would, so to speak, intercede for him somehow, that is to say, write to the Superintendent of Police or, so to speak, to someone, and find the overcoat.

For some unimaginable reason the important personage found his manner too familiar.

"My dear sir," he answered sharply, "don't you know the proper channels? Do you realize whom you're addressing and what the proper procedure should be? You should first have handed in a petition to the office. It would have gone to the head clerk. From him it would have reached the section head, who would have approached my secretary, and only then would the secretary have presented it to me. . . ."

"But, Your Excellency," said Akaky Akakievich, trying to gather what little composure he had and feeling at the same time that he was sweating terribly, "I, Your Excellency, ventured to trouble you because secretaries, that is to say . . . are, so to speak, an unreliable lot. . . ."

"What, what, what?" demanded the important personage. "Where did you pick up such an attitude? Where did you get such ideas? What is this insubordination that is spreading among young people against their chiefs and superiors?"

The important personage, apparently, had not noticed that Akaky Akakievich was well over fifty. Thus, surely, if he could be called young at all it would only be relative, that is, to someone of seventy.

"Do you realize to whom you are talking? Do you appreciate who I am? Do you really realize, do you, I'm asking you?"

Here he stamped his foot and raised his voice to such a pitch that there was no need to be an Akaky Akakievich to be frightened.

And Akaky Akakievich froze completely. He staggered, his whole body shook, and he was quite unable to keep his feet. If a messenger hadn't rushed over and supported him, he would have collapsed onto the floor. They carried him out almost unconscious.

And the important personage, pleased to see that his dramatic effect had exceeded his expectations, and completely delighted with the idea that a word from him could knock a man unconscious, glanced at his friend to see what he thought of it all and was pleased to see that the friend looked somewhat at a loss and that fear had extended to him too.

Akaky Akakievich remembered nothing about getting downstairs and out into the street. He could feel neither hand nor foot. In all his life he had never been so severely reprimanded by a high official, and not a direct chief of his at that. He walked open-mouthed through a blizzard, again and again stumbling off the sidewalk. The wind, according to Petersburg custom, blew at him from all four sides at once, out of every side street. In no time it had blown him a sore throat, and he got himself home at last quite unable to say a word. His throat was swollen and he went straight to bed. That's how severe the effects of an adequate reprimand can be.

The next day he was found to have a high fever. Thanks to the generous assistance of the Petersburg climate, the illness progressed beyond all expectations. A doctor came, felt his pulse, found there was nothing he could do, and prescribed a poultice. That was done so that the patient would not be deprived of the beneficial aid of medicine. The doctor added, however, that, by the way, the patient had another day and a half to go, after which he would be what is called kaput. Then, turning to the landlady, the doctor said:

"And you, my good woman, I'd not waste my time if I were you. I'd order him the coffin right away. A pine one. The oak ones, I imagine, would be too expensive for him."

Whether Akaky Akakievich heard what for him were fateful words, and, if he heard, whether they had a shattering effect on him and whether he was sorry to lose his wretched life, are matters of conjecture. He was feverish and delirious the whole time. Apparitions, each stranger than the last, kept crowding before him. He saw Petrovich and ordered an overcoat containing some sort of concealed traps to catch the thieves who were hiding under his bed, so that every minute he kept calling his landlady to come and pull out the one who had even slipped under his blanket. Next, he would ask why his old dressing gown was hanging there in front of him when he had a new overcoat. Then he would find himself standing before the important personage, listening to the reprimand and repeating over and over: "I am sorry, Your Excellency, I am sorry."

Then he began to swear, using the most frightful words, which caused his old landlady to cross herself in horror; never in her life had she heard anything like it from him, and what made it even worse was that they came pouring out on the heels of the phrase, "Your Excellency." After that he talked complete nonsense, and it was impossible to make out anything he was saying, except that his disconnected words kept groping for that lost overcoat of his. Then, at last, poor Akaky Akakievich gave up the ghost.

They did not bother to seal his room or his belongings because there were no heirs and, moreover, very little to inherit—namely, a bundle of goose quills, a quire of white government paper, three pairs of socks, a few buttons that had come off his trousers, and the old dressing-gown coat already mentioned. God knows whom they went to; even the reporter of this story did not care enough to find out.

They took Akaky Akakievich away and buried him. And Petersburg went on without him exactly as if he had never existed. A creature had vanished, disappeared. He had had no one to protect him. No one had ever paid him the slightest attention. Not even that which a naturalist pays to a common fly which he mounts on a pin and looks at through his microscope. True, this creature, who had meekly borne the office jokes and gone quietly to his grave, had had, toward the end of his life, a cherished visitor—the overcoat, which for a brief moment had brightened his wretched existence. Then a crushing blow had finished everything, a blow such as befalls the powerful of the earth. . . .

A few days after his death, a messenger from his office was sent to his lodgings with an order summoning him to report immediately; the chief was asking for him. But the messenger had to return alone and to report that Akaky Akakievich could not come.

"Why not?" he was asked.

"Because," the messenger said, "he died. They buried him four days ago."

That is how the department found out about Akaky Akakievich's death, and the next day a new clerk sat in his place: he was much taller and his handwriting was not as straight. In fact, his letters slanted considerably.

But who would have imagined that that was not the end of Akaky Akakievich, that he was fated to live on and make his presence felt for a few days after his death as if in compensation for having spent his life unnoticed by anyone? But that's the way it happened, and our little story gains an unexpectedly fantastic ending. Rumors suddenly started to fly around Petersburg that a ghost was haunting the streets at night in the vicinity of the Kalinkin Bridge. The ghost, which looked like a little clerk, was purportedly searching for a stolen overcoat and used this pretext to pull the coats off the shoulders of everyone he met without regard for rank or title. And it made no difference what kind of coat it was—cat, beaver, fox, bearskin, in fact any of the furs and skins people have thought up to cover their own skins with.

One of the department employees saw the ghost with his own eyes and instantly recognized Akaky Akakievich. However, he was so terrified that he dashed off as fast as his legs would carry him and so didn't get a good look; he only saw from a distance that the ghost was shaking his finger at him. Complaints kept pouring in, and not only from petty employees, which would have been understandable. One and all, even Privy Councilors, were catching chills in their backs and shoulders from having their overcoats peeled off. The police were ordered to catch the ghost at any cost, dead or alive, and to punish him with due severity as a warning to others. And what's more, they nearly succeeded.

To be precise, a watchman caught the ghost red-handed, grabbed it by the collar, in Kiryushkin Alley, as it was trying to pull the coat off a retired musician who, in his day, used to tootle on the flute. Grabbing it, he called for help from two colleagues of his and asked them to hold on to it for just a minute. He had, he said, to get his snuffbox out of his boot so that he could bring some feeling back to his nose, which had been frostbitten six times in his life. But it was evidently snuff that even a ghost couldn't stand. The man, closing his right nostril with his finger, had hardly sniffed up half a fistful into the left when the ghost sneezed so violently that the three watchmen were blinded by the resulting shower. They all raised their fists to wipe their eyes and, when they could see again, the ghost had vanished. They even wondered whether they had really held him at all. After that, watchmen were so afraid of the ghost that they felt reluctant to interfere with live robbers and contented themselves with shouting from a distance: "Hey you! On your way!"

And the clerk's ghost began to haunt the streets well beyond the Kalinkin Bridge, spreading terror among the meek.

However, we have completely neglected the important personage, who really, in a sense, was the cause of the fantastic direction that this story—which, by the way, is completely true—has taken. First of all, it is only fair to say that shortly after poor Akaky Akakievich, reduced to a pulp, had left his office, the important personage felt a twinge of regret. Compassion was not foreign to him—many good impulses stirred his heart, although his position usually prevented them

from coming to the surface. As soon as his visiting friend had
left the office, his thoughts returned to Akaky Akakievich. And
after that, almost every day, he saw in his mind's eye the blood-
less face of the little clerk who had been unable to take a proper
reprimand. This thought was so disturbing that a week later he
went so far as to send a clerk from his office to see how Akaky
Akakievich was doing and to find out whether, in fact, there was
any way to help him. And when he heard the news that Akaky
Akakievich had died suddenly of a fever, it was almost a blow
to him, even made him feel guilty and spoiled his mood for the
whole day.

Trying to rid himself of these thoughts, to forget the whole
unpleasant business, he went to a party at a friend's house.
There he found himself in respectable company and, what's
more, among people nearly all of whom were of the same standing so that there was absolutely nothing to oppress him. A great
change came over him. He let himself go, chatted pleas-
antly, was amiable, in a word, spent a very pleasant evening.
At supper, he drank a couple of glasses of champagne, a
well-recommended prescription for inducing good spirits. The
champagne gave him an inclination for something special, and
so he decided not to go home but instead to pay a little visit to
a certain well-known lady named Karolina Ivanovna, a lady, it
seems, of German extraction, toward whom he felt very
friendly. It should be said that the important personage was no
longer a young man, that he was a good husband, the respected
father of a family. His two sons, one of whom already had a
civil-service post, and his sweet-faced sixteen-year-old daughter,
who had a slightly hooked but nevertheless pretty little nose,
greeted him every day with a *"Bonjour,* Papa." His wife, a
youngish woman and not unattractive at that, gave him her
hand to kiss and then kissed his. But although the important
personage was quite content with these displays of family affection, he considered it the proper thing to do to have, for
friendship's sake, a lady friend in another part of the city. This
lady friend was not a bit prettier or younger than his wife, but

the world is full of such puzzling things and it is not our business to judge them.

So the important personage came down the steps, stepped into his sledge, and said to the coachman:

"To Karolina Ivanovna's."

Wrapping his warm, luxurious fur coat around him, he sat back in his seat. He was in that state so cherished by Russians, in which without your having to make any effort, thoughts, each one pleasanter than the last, slip into your head by themselves.

Perfectly content, he went over all the most pleasant moments at the party, over the clever retorts that had caused that select gathering to laugh. He even repeated many of them under his breath and, still finding them funny, laughed heartily at them all over again, which was natural enough. However, he kept being bothered by gusts of wind which would suddenly blow, God knows from where or for what reason, cutting his face, throwing lumps of snow into it, filling the cape of his coat like a sail, and throwing it over his head, so that he had to extricate himself from it again and again.

Suddenly the important personage felt someone grab him violently from behind. He turned around and saw a small man in a worn-out frock coat. Terrified, he recognized Akaky Akakievich, his face as white as the snow and looking altogether very ghostly indeed. Fear took over completely when the important personage saw the ghost's mouth twist and, sending a whiff of the grave into his face, utter the following words:

"I've caught you at last. I've got you by the collar now! It's the coat I need. You did nothing about mine and hollered at me to boot. Now I'll take yours!"

The poor important personage almost died. He may have displayed force of character in the office and, in general, toward his inferiors, so that after one glance at his strong face and manly figure, people would say, "Quite a man," but now, like many other mighty-looking people, he was so frightened that he began to think, and not without reason, that he was about to have an attack of something or other. He was even very helpful in peeling off his coat, after which he shouted to the coachman in a ferocious tone:

"Home! As fast as you can!"

The coachman, hearing the ferocious tone which the important personage used in critical moments and which was sometimes accompanied with something even more drastic, instinctively ducked his head and cracked his whip, so that they tore away like a streak. In a little over six minutes the important personage was in front of his house. Instead of being at Karolina Ivanovna's, he was somehow staggering to his room, pale, terrified, and coatless. There he spent such a restless night that the next morning, at breakfast, his daughter said:

"You look terribly pale this morning, Papa."

But Papa was silent, and he didn't say a word to anyone about what had happened to him, or where he had been, or where he had intended to go. This incident made a deep impression upon him. From then on his subordinates heard far less often: "How dare you!" and "Do you know whom you're talking to?" And even when he did use these expressions, it was after listening to what others had to say.

But even more remarkable—after that night, Akaky Akakievich's ghost was never seen again. The important personage's overcoat must have fitted him snugly. At any rate, one no longer heard of coats being torn from people's shoulders. However, many busybodies wouldn't let the matter rest there and maintained that the ghost was still haunting certain distant parts of the city. And, sure enough, a watchman in the Kolomna district caught a glimpse of the ghost behind a house. But he was rather a frail watchman. (Once an ordinary, but mature, piglet, rushing out of a private house, knocked him off his feet to the huge delight of a bunch of cabbies, whom he fined two kopeks each for their lack of respect—then he spent the proceeds on tobacco.) So, being rather frail, the watchman didn't dare to arrest the ghost. Instead he followed it in the darkness until at last it stopped suddenly, turned to face him, and asked:

"You looking for trouble?"

And it shook a huge fist at him, much larger than any you'll find among the living.

"No," the watchman said, turning away.

This ghost, however, was a much taller one and wore an enormous mustache. It walked off, it seems, in the direction of the Obukhov Bridge and soon dissolved into the gloom of night. ∾

INTERPRETIVE QUESTIONS
FOR DISCUSSION

Why does the overcoat awaken Akaky to the world around him, making him "more alive, even stronger-minded"?

1. Why does everyone treat Akaky disrespectfully and make him the butt of jeers and jokes? Why does Akaky usually never say a word when the young clerks laugh at and play tricks on him?

2. Why does Akaky walk through the streets without paying the slightest attention to what is going on around him? Why does he see "his own well-formed, neat handwriting" superimposed on everything? (7)

3. When Akaky is forced to admit that he needs a new overcoat, why does he repeat in a dreamlike stupor, "So that's it! Here's how it turns out in the end, and I, really, simply couldn't have foreseen it"? (14)

4. Why does the thought of the overcoat-to-be make Akaky's existence "somehow fuller, as if he had married and another human being were there with him"? Why do "all the marks of vacillation and indecision" vanish from his face? (17)

5. Why does Petrovich, along with Akaky, find dignity through the creation of the overcoat? (18)

6. Why doesn't Akaky do any copying on the night after he first wears his overcoat?

7. Why do all of Akaky's fellow workers make such a fuss about his new overcoat? Why does the assistant head clerk insist that Akaky toast his new overcoat with champagne?

8. Why after the party must Akaky restrain himself from galloping after a lady? Why does he find her body, "astir with independent . . . motion," fascinating? (23)

Suggested textual analysis
Pages 16–19: beginning, "Akaky Akakievich had a rule:"
and ending, "and entrusted it to the porter's special care."

Why does Akaky's ghost become an overcoat thief, spreading terror throughout St. Petersburg?

1. Why does no one want to help Akaky find his stolen overcoat?

2. Why does the loss of his new overcoat make Akaky assertive, so that for the first time in his life he decides to "show some character"? (25)

3. Why is the story told so that Akaky sickens and dies after he is reprimanded by the important personage?

4. Why does Akaky use violent language on his deathbed? Why does he both swear and apologize in his final delirium?

5. Why does Akaky's ghost tear off the overcoats of the meek as well as the high ranking?

6. Why does the narrator assure us that the story of the ghost is completely true? (33)

7. Why is Akaky's ghost satisfied after taking the coat of the important personage?

8. Why does the important personage's encounter with the ghost of Akaky cause him to treat his subordinates with more kindness and respect?

Suggested textual analysis
Pages 31–36: beginning, "Whether Akaky Akakievich heard,"
and ending, "after listening to what others had to say."

Are we meant to think that Akaky would have been better off had he not obtained the new overcoat?

1. Why does Akaky love his work, finding an "interesting, pleasant world for himself" in copying the words of others? (6)

2. Why are we told that Akaky would often copy a paper for his own pleasure, especially if it were unusual for being addressed to some new or important personage?

3. Is Akaky saintly or pathetic for dutifully continuing to work when he is badgered by the young clerks?

4. Why do Akaky's words "Let me be. Why do you do this to me? . . . " impress upon the new man in the office how badly he has treated the lowly clerk? Why does the author say that upon hearing Akaky's words, the new man seems as if "awakened from a trance"? (5–6)

5. Why does the author want us to both pity and laugh at Akaky?

6. Why is Akaky allowed only a "brief moment" of happiness with his overcoat? (32)

7. Does Akaky's short reign of terror mean that he, too, has become part of the general "wickedness of man toward man"? (6)

8. Why does the story end with the sighting of a second ghost? Why does the second ghost have a huge fist and a mustache, much like the thief who stole Akaky's overcoat?

Suggested textual analysis
Pages 5–8: beginning, "In the office," and ending, "new or important personage."

FOR FURTHER REFLECTION

1. When does hierarchy in the workplace become a source of chaos rather than order?

2. Which Akaky is better for society—the oblivious, contented Akaky, or the avenging ghost who through his assertiveness makes people behave more humanely?

3. Is the boredom and pointlessness in people's lives just as significant a cause of social unrest as injustice?

4. Are some people natural victims?

5. Can people control whether or not they are liked by others?

6. Do you admire Akaky for finding contentment in a limited, unambitious life?

BHAGAVAD-GITA

(selection)

BHAGAVAD-GITA ("Song of the Lord"),
considered by most Hindus to be their most
important text, is a religious poem consisting
of 700 Sanskrit verses divided into eighteen
chapters. It was probably written in the first or
second century A.D. and forms part of Book VI
of the great Indian epic the *Mahabharata*.
Composed beginning about 300 B.C. and added
to until about A.D. 300, the *Mahabharata* is the
longest poem in history, containing altogether
about 100,000 couplets interspersed with short
prose passages. The Bhagavad-Gita is written
in the form of a dialogue between Lord Krishna,
the earthly incarnation of the god Vishnu,
and the warrior Arjuna. The dialogue between
Prince Arjuna and his friend and charioteer
Krishna takes place on the holy field of
Kurukshetra, just as the great battle of the
Mahabharata is about to begin.

THE SORROW OF ARJUNA

DHRITARASHTRA: Tell me, Sanjaya, what my sons and the sons of Pandu did, when they gathered on the sacred field of Kurukshetra eager for battle?[1]

[In the following verses, Sanjaya describes how Duryodhana, seeing the opposing army of Pandavas in array, went to Drona, his teacher, and expressed his fear that their own army was the weaker of the two, although numerically larger. He named the leading warriors on either side. This is one of the catalogue passages to be found in nearly all epics. It need not be translated in full.

---

1. [Dhritarashtra is King Pandu's brother and successor. He educated King Pandu's five sons (the Pandavas) including Arjuna, as well as his own 100 sons. It is the greed of Dhritarashtra's son, Duryodhana, that is the cause of the war between the two noble families. Sanjaya is Dhritarashtra's minister and charioteer. As they sit together in the palace, Sanjaya, by a clairvoyant power, describes to his blind master everything he sees and hears on the distant battlefield.]

In order to raise Duryodhana's failing courage, Bhisma, the commander-in-chief, sounded his conch-shell horn. But this was ill-advised—for the enemy chieftains immediately blew their horns in reply, and made much more noise. The trumpeting "resounded through heaven and earth," we are told.

Arjuna now addresses Krishna, his friend and charioteer.]

ARJUNA: Krishna the changeless,
  Halt my chariot
  There where the warriors,
  Bold for the battle,
  Face their foemen.
  Between the armies
  There let me see them,
  The men I must fight with,
  Gathered together
  Now at the bidding
  Of him their leader,
  Blind Dhritarashtra's
  Evil offspring:
  Such are my foes
  In the war that is coming.

SANJAYA (*to Dhritarashtra*): Then Krishna, subduer of the senses, thus requested by Arjuna, the conqueror of sloth,[2] drove that most splendid of chariots into a place between the two armies, confronting Bhisma, Drona, and all those other rulers of the earth. And he said: "O Prince, behold the assembled Kurus!"

Then the prince looked on the array, and in both armies he recognized fathers and grandfathers, teachers, uncles, sons, brothers, grandsons, fathers-in-law, dear friends, and many other familiar faces.

---

2. [Arjuna is traditionally supposed to have lived entirely without sleep. We may take this to mean that he had overcome all forms of laziness. —TRANS.]

When Kunti's son saw all those ranks of kinsmen he was filled with deep compassion, and he spoke despairingly, as follows:

ARJUNA: Krishna, Krishna,
Now as I look on
These my kinsmen
Arrayed for battle,
My limbs are weakened,
My mouth is parching,
My body trembles,
My hair stands upright,
My skin seems burning,
The bow Gandiva
Slips from my hand,
My brain is whirling
Round and round,
I can stand no longer:
Krishna, I see such
Omens of evil!
What can we hope from
This killing of kinsmen?
What do I want with
Victory, empire,
Or their enjoyment?
O Govinda,[3]
How can I care for
Power or pleasure,
My own life, even,
When all these others,
Teachers, fathers,
Grandfathers, uncles,
Sons and brothers,
Husbands of sisters,

---

3. [One of the names of Sri Krishna, meaning Giver of Enlightenment. —TRANS.]

Grandsons and cousins,
For whose sake only
I could enjoy them
Stand here ready
To risk blood and wealth
In war against us?

Knower of all things,
Though they should slay me
How could I harm them?
I cannot wish it:
Never, never,
Not though it won me
The throne of the three worlds;
How much the less for
Earthly lordship!

Krishna, hearing
The prayers of all men,
Tell me how can
We hope to be happy
Slaying the sons
Of Dhritarashtra?
Evil they may be,
Worst of the wicked,
Yet if we kill them
Our sin is greater.
How could we dare spill
The blood that unites us?
Where is joy in
The killing of kinsmen?

Foul their hearts are
With greed, and blinded:
They see no evil
In breaking of blood bonds,

See no sin
In treason to comrades.
But we, clear-sighted,
Scanning the ruin
Of families scattered,
Should we not shun
This crime, O Krishna?

We know what fate falls
On families broken:
The rites are forgotten,
Vice rots the remnant
Defiling the women,
And from their corruption
Comes mixing of castes:
The curse of confusion
Degrades the victims
And damns the destroyers.
The rice and the water
No longer are offered;
The ancestors also
Must fall dishonored
From home in heaven.

Such is the crime
Of the killers of kinsmen:
The ancient, the sacred,
Is broken, forgotten.
Such is the doom
Of the lost, without caste-rites:
Darkness and doubting
And hell forever.

What is this crime
I am planning, O Krishna?
Murder most hateful,

Murder of brothers!
Am I indeed
So greedy for greatness?

Rather than this
Let the evil children
Of Dhritarashtra
Come with their weapons
Against me in battle:
I shall not struggle,
I shall not strike them.
Now let them kill me,
That will be better.

SANJAYA: Having spoken thus, Arjuna threw aside his arrows
and his bow in the midst of the battlefield. He sat down
on the seat of the chariot, and his heart was overcome with
sorrow.

THE YOGA OF KNOWLEDGE

SANJAYA: Then his eyes filled with tears, and his heart grieved
and was bewildered with pity. And Sri Krishna spoke to him,
saying:

SRI KRISHNA: Arjuna, is this hour of battle the time for scruples
and fancies? Are they worthy of you, who seek enlightenment? Any brave man who merely hopes for fame or heaven
would despise them.

What is this weakness? It is beneath you. Is it for nothing
men call you the foe-consumer? Shake off this cowardice,
Arjuna. Stand up.

ARJUNA: Bhisma and Drona are noble and ancient, worthy of the deepest reverence. How can I greet them with arrows, in battle? If I kill them, how can I ever enjoy my wealth, or any other pleasure? It will be cursed with bloodguilt. I would much rather spare them, and eat the bread of a beggar.

Which will be worse, to win this war, or to lose it? I scarcely know. Even the sons of Dhritarashtra stand in the enemy ranks. If we kill them, none of us will wish to live.

Is this real compassion that I feel, or only a delusion? My mind gropes about in darkness. I cannot see where my duty lies. Krishna, I beg you, tell me frankly and clearly what I ought to do. I am your disciple. I put myself into your hands. Show me the way.

Not this world's kingdom,
Supreme, unchallenged,
No, nor the throne
Of the gods in heaven,
Could ease this sorrow
That numbs my senses!

SANJAYA: When Arjuna, the foe-consuming, the never-slothful, had spoken thus to Govinda, ruler of the senses, he added: "I will not fight," and was silent.

Then to him who thus sorrowed between the two armies, the ruler of the senses spoke, smiling:

SRI KRISHNA: Your words are wise, Arjuna, but your sorrow is for nothing. The truly wise mourn neither for the living nor for the dead.

There was never a time when I did not exist, nor you, nor any of these kings. Nor is there any future in which we shall cease to be.

Just as the dweller in this body passes through childhood, youth, and old age, so at death he merely passes into another kind of body. The wise are not deceived by that.

Feelings of heat and cold, pleasure and pain, are caused by the contact of the senses with their objects. They come and they go, never lasting long. You must accept them.

A serene spirit accepts pleasure and pain with an even mind, and is unmoved by either. He alone is worthy of immortality.

That which is nonexistent can never come into being, and that which is can never cease to be. Those who have known the inmost Reality know also the nature of *is* and *is not*.

That Reality which pervades the universe is indestructible. No one has power to change the Changeless.

Bodies are said to die, but That which possesses the body is eternal. It cannot be limited, or destroyed. Therefore you must fight.

Some say this Atman[4]
Is slain, and others
Call It the slayer:
They know nothing.
How can It slay
Or who shall slay It?

Know this Atman
Unborn, undying,
Never ceasing,
Never beginning,
Deathless, birthless,
Unchanging forever.
How can It die
The death of the body?

Knowing It birthless,
Knowing It deathless,
Knowing It endless,

---

4. [The Godhead that is within every being. —TRANS.]

Forever unchanging,
Dream not you do
The deed of the killer,
Dream not the power
Is yours to command it.

Worn-out garments
Are shed by the body:
Worn-out bodies
Are shed by the dweller
Within the body.
New bodies are donned
By the dweller, like garments.

Not wounded by weapons,
Not burned by fire,
Not dried by the wind,
Not wetted by water:
Such is the Atman,
Not dried, not wetted,
Not burned, not wounded,
Innermost element,
Everywhere, always,
Being of beings,
Changeless, eternal,
Forever and ever.

This Atman cannot be manifested to the senses, or thought
about by the mind. It is not subject to modification. Since you
know this, you should not grieve.

But if you should suppose this Atman to be subject to constant birth and death, even then you ought not to be sorry.

Death is certain for the born. Rebirth is certain for the
dead. You should not grieve for what is unavoidable.

Before birth, beings are not manifest to our human senses. In the interim between birth and death, they are manifest. At death they return to the unmanifest again. What is there in all this to grieve over?

There are some who have actually looked upon the Atman, and understood It, in all Its wonder. Others can only speak of It as wonderful beyond their understanding. Others know of Its wonder by hearsay. And there are others who are told about It and do not understand a word.

He Who dwells within all living bodies remains forever indestructible. Therefore, you should never mourn for anyone.

Even if you consider this from the standpoint of your own caste-duty, you ought not to hesitate; for, to a warrior, there is nothing nobler than a righteous war. Happy are the warriors to whom a battle such as this comes: it opens a door to heaven.

But if you refuse to fight this righteous war, you will be turning aside from your duty. You will be a sinner, and disgraced. People will speak ill of you throughout the ages. To a man who values his honor, that is surely worse than death. The warrior-chiefs will believe it was fear that drove you from the battle; you will be despised by those who have admired you so long. Your enemies, also, will slander your courage. They will use the words which should never be spoken. What could be harder to bear than that?

Die, and you win heaven. Conquer, and you enjoy the earth. Stand up now, son of Kunti, and resolve to fight. Realize that pleasure and pain, gain and loss, victory and defeat, are all one and the same: then go into battle. Do this and you cannot commit any sin.

I have explained to you the true nature of the Atman. Now listen to the method of Karma Yoga.[5] If you can understand

---

5. [*Karma:* (1) work, a deed; (2) effect of a deed; (3) law of causation governing action and its effects in the physical and psychological plane. *Yoga:* (1) union with God; (2) a prescribed path of spiritual life. The various yogas are, therefore, different paths to union with God. Karma Yoga is the path of selfless, God-dedicated action. —TRANS.]

and follow it, you will be able to break the chains of desire which bind you to your actions.

In this yoga, even the abortive attempt is not wasted. Nor can it produce a contrary result. Even a little practice of this yoga will save you from the terrible wheel of rebirth and death.

In this yoga, the will is directed singly toward one ideal. When a man lacks this discrimination, his will wanders in all directions, after innumerable aims. Those who lack discrimination may quote the letter of the scripture, but they are really denying its inner truth. They are full of worldly desires, and hungry for the rewards of heaven. They use beautiful figures of speech. They teach elaborate rituals which are supposed to obtain pleasure and power for those who perform them. But, actually, they understand nothing except the law of Karma, that chains men to rebirth.

Those whose discrimination is stolen away by such talk grow deeply attached to pleasure and power. And so they are unable to develop that concentration of the will which leads a man to absorption in God.

The Vedas[6] teach us about the three gunas[7] and their functions. You, Arjuna, must overcome the three gunas. You must be free from the pairs of opposites.[8] Poise your mind in tranquillity. Take care neither to acquire nor to hoard. Be established in the consciousness of the Atman, always.

When the whole country is flooded, the reservoir becomes superfluous. So, to the illumined seer, the Vedas are all superfluous.

---

6. [Revealed scriptures of the Hindus. The reference here is to the ritualistic portion of the Vedas.—TRANS.]

7. [The three components of the world of matter (*prakriti*). They are *sattwa* (tension or harmony, goodness), *raja* (activity, passion), and *tamas* (inertia, darkness).]

8. [Heat and cold, pleasure and pain, etc. The seeming contradictions of the relative world. —TRANS.]

You have the right to work, but for the work's sake only. You have no right to the fruits of work. Desire for the fruits of work must never be your motive in working. Never give way to laziness, either.

Perform every action with your heart fixed on the Supreme Lord. Renounce attachment to the fruits. Be even-tempered in success and failure; for it is this evenness of temper which is meant by yoga.

Work done with anxiety about results is far inferior to work done without such anxiety, in the calm of self-surrender. Seek refuge in the knowledge of Brahman.[9] They who work selfishly for results are miserable.

In the calm of self-surrender you can free yourself from the bondage of virtue and vice during this very life. Devote yourself, therefore, to reaching union with Brahman. To unite the heart with Brahman and then to act: that is the secret of nonattached work. In the calm of self-surrender, the seers renounce the fruits of their actions, and so reach enlightenment. Then they are free from the bondage of rebirth, and pass to that state which is beyond all evil.

When your intellect has cleared itself of its delusions, you will become indifferent to the results of all action, present or future. At present, your intellect is bewildered by conflicting interpretations of the scriptures. When it can rest, steady and undistracted, in contemplation of the Atman, then you will reach union with the Atman.

ARJUNA: Krishna, how can one identify a man who is firmly established and absorbed in Brahman? In what manner does an illumined soul speak? How does he sit? How does he walk?

SRI KRISHNA: He knows bliss in the Atman
And wants nothing else.

---

9. [The Godhead. —TRANS.]

Cravings torment the heart:
He renounces cravings.
I call him illumined.

Not shaken by adversity,
Not hankering after happiness:
Free from fear, free from anger,
Free from the things of desire.
I call him a seer, and illumined.
The bonds of his flesh are broken.
He is lucky, and does not rejoice:
He is unlucky, and does not weep.
I call him illumined.

The tortoise can draw in his legs:
The seer can draw in his senses.
I call him illumined.

The abstinent run away from what they desire
But carry their desires with them.
When a man enters Reality,
He leaves his desires behind him.

Even a mind that knows the path
Can be dragged from the path:
The senses are so unruly.
But he controls the senses
And recollects the mind.
And fixes it on me.
I call him illumined.

Thinking about sense-objects
Will attach you to sense-objects;
Grow attached, and you become addicted;
Thwart your addiction, it turns to anger;
Be angry, and you confuse your mind;

Confuse your mind, you forget the lesson of experience;
Forget experience, you lose discrimination;
Lose discrimination, and you miss life's only purpose.

When he has no lust, no hatred,
A man walks safely among the things of lust and hatred.
To obey the Atman
Is his peaceful joy:
Sorrow melts
Into that clear peace:
His quiet mind
Is soon established in peace.

The uncontrolled mind
Does not guess that the Atman is present:
How can it meditate?
Without meditation, where is peace?
Without peace, where is happiness?

The wind turns a ship
From its course upon the waters:
The wandering winds of the senses
Cast man's mind adrift
And turn his better judgment from its course.
When a man can still the senses
I call him illumined.
The recollected mind is awake
In the knowledge of the Atman
Which is dark night to the ignorant:
The ignorant are awake in their sense-life
Which they think is daylight:
To the seer it is darkness.

Water flows continually into the ocean
But the ocean is never disturbed:

Desire flows into the mind of the seer
But he is never disturbed.
The seer knows peace:
The man who stirs up his own lusts
Can never know peace.
He knows peace who has forgotten desire.
He lives without craving:
Free from ego, free from pride.

This is the state of enlightenment in Brahman:
A man does not fall back from it
Into delusion.
Even at the moment of death
He is alive in that enlightenment:
Brahman and he are one.

KARMA YOGA

ARJUNA: But, Krishna, if you consider knowledge of Brahman superior to any sort of action, why are you telling me to do these terrible deeds?

Your statements seem to contradict each other. They confuse my mind. Tell me one definite way of reaching the highest good.

SRI KRISHNA: I have already told you that, in this world, aspirants may find enlightenment by two different paths. For the contemplative is the path of knowledge: for the active is the path of selfless action.

Freedom from activity is never achieved by abstaining from action. Nobody can become perfect by merely ceasing to act. In fact, nobody can ever rest from his activity[10] even for a moment. All are helplessly forced to act, by the gunas.

---

10. [Here "activity" includes mental action, conscious and subconscious.—TRANS.]

A man who renounces certain physical actions but still lets his mind dwell on the objects of his sensual desire, is deceiving himself. He can only be called a hypocrite. The truly admirable man controls his senses by the power of his will. All his actions are disinterested. All are directed along the path to union with Brahman.

Activity is better than inertia. Act, but with self-control. If you are lazy, you cannot even sustain your own body.

The world is imprisoned in its own activity, except when actions are performed as worship of God. Therefore you must perform every action sacramentally, and be free from all attachments to results.

In the beginning
The Lord of beings
Created all men,
To each his duty.
"Do this," He said,
"And you shall prosper.
Duty well done
Fulfills desire
Like Kamadhenu[11]
The wish-fulfiller."
"Doing of duty
Honors the devas:[12]
To you the devas
In turn will be gracious:
Each honoring other,
Man reaches the Highest.
Please the devas:
Your prayer will be granted."
But he who enjoys the devas' bounty
Showing no thanks,
He thieves from the devas.

---

11. [A legendary cow, mentioned in the *Mahabharata*. —TRANS.]

12. [The inhabitants of heaven. —TRANS.]

Pious men eat
What the gods leave over
After the offering:
Thus they are sinless.
But those ungodly
Cooking good food
For the greed of their stomachs
Sin as they eat it.
Food quickens the life-sperm:
Food grows from the rainfall
Called down out of heaven
By sacrifice offered:
Sacrifice speaks
Through the act of the ritual.
This is the ritual
Taught by the sacred
Scriptures that spring
From the lips of the Changeless:
Know therefore that Brahman
The all-pervading
Is dwelling forever
Within this ritual.

If a man plays no part
In the acts thus appointed
His living is evil
His joy is in lusting.
Know this, O Prince:
His life is for nothing.

But when a man has found delight and satisfaction and
peace in the Atman, then he is no longer obliged to perform
any kind of action. He has nothing to gain in this world
by action, and nothing to lose by refraining from action. He
is independent of everybody and everything. Do your duty,
always; but without attachment. That is how a man reaches

the ultimate Truth; by working without anxiety about results. In fact, Janaka[13] and many others reached enlightenment, simply because they did their duty in this spirit. Your motive in working should be to set others, by your example, on the path of duty.

Whatever a great man does, ordinary people will imitate; they follow his example. Consider me: I am not bound by any sort of duty. There is nothing, in all the three worlds, which I do not already possess; nothing I have yet to acquire. But I go on working, nevertheless. If I did not continue to work untiringly as I do, mankind would still follow me, no matter where I led them. Suppose I were to stop? They would all be lost. The result would be caste-mixture and universal destruction.

The ignorant work
For the fruit of their action:
The wise must work also
Without desire
Pointing man's feet
To the path of his duty.

Let the wise beware
Lest they bewilder
The minds of the ignorant
Hungry for action:
Let them show by example
How work is holy
When the heart of the worker
Is fixed on the Highest.

Every action is really performed by the gunas. Man, deluded by his egoism, thinks: "I am the doer." But he who has the true insight into the operations of the gunas and their

13. [A royal saint mentioned in the Upanishads.—TRANS.]

various functions, knows that when senses attach themselves to objects, gunas are merely attaching themselves to gunas. Knowing this, he does not become attached to his actions.

The illumined soul must not create confusion in the minds of the ignorant by refraining from work. The ignorant, in their delusion, identify the Atman with the gunas. They become tied to the senses and the action of the senses.

Shake off this fever of ignorance. Stop hoping for worldly rewards. Fix your mind on the Atman. Be free from the sense of ego. Dedicate all your actions to me. Then go forward and fight.

If a man keeps following my teaching with faith in his heart, and does not make mental reservations, he will be released from the bondage of his karma. But those who scorn my teaching, and do not follow it, are lost. They are without spiritual discrimination. All their knowledge is a delusion.

Even a wise man acts according to the tendencies of his own nature. All living creatures follow their tendencies. What use is any external restraint? The attraction and aversion which the senses feel for different objects are natural. But you must not give way to such feelings; they are obstacles.

It is better to do your own duty, however imperfectly, than to assume the duties of another person, however successfully. Prefer to die doing your own duty: the duty of another will bring you into great spiritual danger.

ARJUNA: Krishna, what is it that makes a man do evil, even against his own will; under compulsion, as it were?

SRI KRISHNA: The rajo-guna has two faces,
Rage and lust: the ravenous, the deadly:
Recognize these: they are your enemies.
Smoke hides fire,
Dust hides a mirror,
The womb hides the embryo:
By lust the Atman is hidden.

Lust hides the Atman in its hungry flames,
The wise man's faithful foe.
Intellect, senses and mind
Are fuel to its fire:
Thus it deludes
The dweller in the body,
Bewildering his judgment.

Therefore, Arjuna, you must first control your senses, then kill this evil thing which obstructs discriminative knowledge and realization of the Atman.

The senses are said to be higher than the sense-objects. The mind is higher than the senses. The intelligent will is higher than the mind. What is higher than the intelligent will? The Atman Itself.

You must know Him who is above the intelligent will. Get control of the mind through spiritual discrimination. Then destroy your elusive enemy, who wears the form of lust.

RENUNCIATION THROUGH KNOWLEDGE

SRI KRISHNA: Foe-consumer,
Now I have shown you
Yoga that leads
To the truth undying.
I taught this yoga
First to Vivaswat,
Vivaswat taught it
In turn to Manu,
Next Ikshaku
Learnt it from Manu,
And so the sages
In royal succession
Carried it onward

From teacher to teacher,
Till at length it was lost,
Throughout ages forgotten.

ARJUNA: Vivaswat was born long before you. How am I to
believe that you were the first to teach this yoga?

SRI KRISHNA: You and I, Arjuna,
Have lived many lives.
I remember them all:
You do not remember.

I am the birthless, the deathless,
Lord of all that breathes.
I seem to be born:
It is only seeming,
Only my Maya.
I am still master
Of my Prakriti,[14]
The power that makes me.

When goodness grows weak,
When evil increases,
I make myself a body.

In every age I come back
To deliver the holy,
To destroy the sin of the sinner,
To establish righteousness.

He who knows the nature
Of my task and my holy birth

---

14. [While both *maya* and *prakriti* refer to the creative power of Brahman, *prakriti*,
    or matter, is the primeval stuff, not the world of matter perceived by the senses.
    Maya is both the origin of the world and the illusory appearance of the world.]

Is not reborn
When he leaves this body:
He comes to me.

Flying from fear,
From lust and anger,
He hides in me
His refuge, his safety:
Burnt clean in the blaze of my being,
In me many find home.

Whatever wish men bring me in worship,
That wish I grant them.
Whatever path men travel
Is my path:
No matter where they walk
It leads to me.

Most men worship the gods because they want success in their worldly undertakings. This kind of material success can be gained very quickly, here on earth.

I established the four castes, which correspond to the different types of guna and karma. I am their author; nevertheless, you must realize that I am beyond action and changeless. Action does not contaminate me. I have no desire at all for the fruits of action. A man who understands my nature in this respect will never become the slave of his own activity. Because they understood this, the ancient seekers for liberation could safely engage in action. You, too, must do your work in the spirit of those early seers.

What is action? What is inaction? Even the wise are puzzled by this question. Therefore, I will tell you what action is. When you know that, you will be free from all impurity. You must learn what kind of work to do, what kind of work to avoid, and how to reach a state of calm detachment from your work. The real nature of action is hard to understand.

He who sees the inaction that is in action, and the action that is in inaction, is wise indeed. Even when he is engaged in action he remains poised in the tranquillity of the Atman.

The seers say truly
That he is wise
Who acts without lust or scheming
For the fruit of the act:
His act falls from him,
Its chain is broken,
Melted in the flame of my knowledge.
Turning his face from the fruit,
He needs nothing:
The Atman is enough.
He acts, and is beyond action.

Not hoping, not lusting,
Bridling body and mind,
He calls nothing his own:
He acts, and earns no evil.

What God's Will gives
He takes, and is contented.
Pain follows pleasure,
He is not troubled:
Gain follows loss,
He is indifferent:
Of whom should he be jealous?
He acts, and is not bound by his action.

When the bonds are broken
His illumined heart
Beats in Brahman:
His every action
Is worship of Brahman:
Can such acts bring evil?

Brahman is the ritual,
Brahman is the offering,
Brahman is he who offers
To the fire that is Brahman.
If a man sees Brahman
In every action,
He will find Brahman.[15]

Some yogis merely worship the devas. Others are able, by the grace of the Atman, to meditate on the identity of the Atman with Brahman. For these, the Atman is the offering, and Brahman the sacrificial fire into which It is offered.

Some withdraw all their senses from contact with exterior sense-objects. For these, hearing and other senses are the offering, and self-discipline the sacrificial fire. Others allow their minds and senses to wander unchecked, and try to see Brahman within all exterior sense-objects. For these, sound and the other sense-objects are the offering, and sense-enjoyment the sacrificial fire.

Some renounce all the actions of the senses, and all the functions of the vital force. For these, such actions and functions are the offering, and the practice of self-control is the sacrificial fire, kindled by knowledge of the Atman.

Then there are others whose way of worship is to renounce sense-objects and material possessions. Others set themselves austerities and spiritual disciplines: that is their way of worship. Others worship through the practice of Raja Yoga.[16] Others who are earnest seekers for perfection and men of

---

15. [This verse is chanted by all Hindu monks as a grace before meals. In this case "the fire" is regarded as the fire of hunger. —TRANS.]

16. [The path of Raja Yoga is said to have eight steps: (1) practice of the moral virtues; (2) regular habits of purity, contentment, study, austerity, and self-surrender to God; (3) posture; (4) control of the vital energy by breathing exercises; (5) withdrawal of the mind from sense-objects; (6) concentration; (7) meditation; (8) absorption in the consciousness of God. —TRANS.]

strict vows, study and meditate on the truths of the scriptures. That is their way of worship.

Others are intent on controlling the vital energy; so they practice breathing exercises—inhalation, exhalation, and the stoppage of the breath. Others mortify their flesh by fasting, to weaken their sensual desires, and thus achieve self-control.

All these understand the meaning of sacrificial worship. Through worship, their sins are consumed away. They eat the food which has been blessed in the sacrifice. Thus they obtain immortality and reach eternal Brahman. He who does not worship God cannot be happy even in this world. What, then, can he expect from any other?

All these, and many other forms of worship are prescribed by the scriptures.

All of them involve the doing of some kind of action. When you fully understand this, you will be made free in Brahman.

The form of worship which consists in contemplating Brahman is superior to ritualistic worship with material offerings.

The reward of all action is to be found in enlightenment.

Those illumined souls who have realized the Truth will instruct you in the knowledge of Brahman, if you will prostrate yourself before them, question them and serve them as a disciple.

When you have reached enlightenment, ignorance will delude you no longer. In the light of that knowledge you will see the entire creation within your own Atman and in me.

And though you were the foulest of sinners,
This knowledge alone would carry you
Like a raft, over all your sin.

The blazing fire turns wood to ashes:
The fire of knowledge turns all karmas to ashes.

On earth there is no purifier
As great as this knowledge,
When a man is made perfect in yoga,
He knows its truth within his heart.
The man of faith,
Whose heart is devoted,
Whose senses are mastered:
He finds Brahman.
Enlightened, he passes
At once to the highest,
The peace beyond passion.

The ignorant, the faithless, the doubter
Goes to his destruction.
How shall he enjoy
This world, or the next,
Or any happiness?

When a man can act without desire,
Through practice of yoga;
When his doubts are torn to shreds,
Because he knows Brahman;
When his heart is poised
In the being of the Atman
No bonds can bind him.

Still I can see it:
A doubt that lingers
Deep in your heart
Brought forth by delusion.
You doubt the truth
Of the living Atman.

Where is your sword
Discrimination?

Draw it and slash
Delusion to pieces.
Then arise
O son of Bharata:
Take your stand
In Karma Yoga.

THE YOGA OF RENUNCIATION

ARJUNA: You speak so highly of the renunciation of action; yet you ask me to follow the yoga of action. Now tell me definitely: which of these is better?

SRI KRISHNA: Action rightly renounced brings freedom:
Action rightly performed brings freedom:
Both are better
Than mere shunning of action.

When a man lacks lust and hatred,
His renunciation does not waver.
He neither longs for one thing
Nor loathes its opposite:
The chains of his delusion
Are soon cast off.

The yoga of action, say the ignorant,
Is different from the yoga of the knowledge of Brahman.

The wise see knowledge and action as one:
They see truly.
Take either path
And tread it to the end:
The end is the same.

There the followers of action
Meet the seekers after knowledge
In equal freedom.

It is hard to renounce action
Without following the yoga of action.
This yoga purifies
The man of meditation,
Bringing him soon to Brahman.

When the heart is made pure by that yoga,
When the body is obedient,
When the senses are mastered,
When man knows that his Atman
Is the Atman in all creatures,
Then let him act,
Untainted by action.

The illumined soul
Whose heart is Brahman's heart
Thinks always: "I am doing nothing."
No matter what he sees,
Hears, touches, smells, eats;
No matter whether he is moving,
Sleeping, breathing, speaking,
Excreting, or grasping something with his hand,
Or opening his eyes,
Or closing his eyes:
This he knows always:
"I am not seeing, I am not hearing:
It is the senses that see and hear
And touch the things of the senses."

He puts aside desire,
Offering the act to Brahman.

The lotus leaf rests unwetted on water:
He rests on action, untouched by action.

To the follower of the yoga of action,
The body and the mind,
The sense organs and the intellect
Are instruments only:
He knows himself other than the instrument
And thus his heart grows pure.

United with Brahman,
Cut free from the fruit of the act,
A man finds peace
In the work of the spirit.
Without Brahman,
Man is a prisoner,
Enslaved by action,
Dragged onward by desire.

Happy is that dweller
In the city of nine gates[17]
Whose discrimination
Has cut him free from his act:
He is not involved in action,
He does not involve others.

Do not say:
"God gave us this delusion."
You dream you are the doer,
You dream that action is done,
You dream that action bears fruit.
It is your ignorance,
It is the world's delusion
That gives you these dreams.

17. [The human body. —TRANS.]

The Lord is everywhere
And always perfect:
What does He care for man's sin
Or the righteousness of man?

The Atman is the light:
The light is covered by darkness:
This darkness is delusion:
That is why we dream.

When the light of the Atman
Drives out our darkness
That light shines forth from us,
A sun in splendor,
The revealed Brahman.

The devoted dwell with Him,
They know Him always
There in the heart,
Where action is not.
He is all their aim.
Made free by His Knowledge
From past uncleanness
Of deed or of thought,
They find the place of freedom,
The place of no return.[18]

Seeing all things equal,
The enlightened may look
On the Brahmin, learned and gentle,
On the cow, on the elephant,
On the dog, on the eater of dogs.

---

18. [The state in which one is no longer subject to rebirth, because illumination
has been attained. —TRANS.]

74

Absorbed in Brahman
He overcomes the world
Even here, alive in the world.
Brahman is one,
Changeless, untouched by evil:
What home have we but Him?

The enlightened, the Brahman-abiding,
Calm-hearted, unbewildered,
Is neither elated by the pleasant
Nor saddened by the unpleasant.

His mind is dead
To the touch of the external:
It is alive
To the bliss of the Atman,
Because his heart knows Brahman
His happiness is forever.

When senses touch objects
The pleasures therefrom
Are like wombs that bear sorrow.
They begin, they are ended:
They bring no delight to the wise.

Already, here on earth,
Before his departure,
Let man be the master
Of every impulse
Lust-begotten
Or fathered by anger:
Thus he finds Brahman,
Thus he is happy.

Only that yogi
Whose joy is inward,

Inward his peace,
And his vision inward
Shall come to Brahman
And know Nirvana.[19]

All consumed
Are their imperfections,
Doubts are dispelled,
Their senses mastered,
Their every action
Is wed to the welfare
Of fellow creatures:
Such are the seers
Who enter Brahman
And know Nirvana.

Self-controlled,
Cut free from desire,
Curbing the heart
And knowing the Atman,
Man finds Nirvana
That is in Brahman,
Here and hereafter.

Shutting off sense
From what is outward,
Fixing the gaze
At the root of the eyebrows,
Checking the breath-stream
In and outgoing
Within the nostrils,
Holding the senses,
Holding the intellect,
Holding the mind fast,

---

19. [The state of union with Brahman. —TRANS.]

He who seeks freedom,
Thrusts fear aside,
Thrusts aside anger
And puts off desire:
Truly that man
Is made free forever.

When thus he knows me
The end, the author
Of every offering
And all austerity,
Lord of the worlds
And the friend of all men:
O Son of Kunti
Shall he not enter
The peace of my presence?

THE VISION OF GOD IN HIS UNIVERSAL FORM

ARJUNA: By your grace, you have taught me the truth about the Atman. Your words are mystic and sublime. They have dispelled my ignorance.

From you, whose eyes are like the lotus flowers, I have learnt in detail of the origin and dissolution of creatures, and of your own infinite glory.

O Supreme Lord, you are as you describe yourself to be: I do not doubt that. Nevertheless, I long to behold your divine Form.

If you find me worthy of that vision, then reveal to me, O Master of yogis, your changeless Atman.

SRI KRISHNA: Behold, O Prince, my divine forms, hundreds upon thousands, various in kind, various in color and in shape.

Behold the Adityas, and the Vasus, and the Rudras, and the Aswins, and the Maruts.[20] Behold many wonders, O Descendant of Bharata, that no man has seen before.

O conqueror of sloth, this very day you shall behold the whole universe with all things animate and inert made one within this body of mine. And whatever else you desire to see, that you shall see also.

But you cannot see me thus with those human eyes. Therefore, I give you divine sight. Behold—this is my yoga power.

SANJAYA: Then, O King, when he had spoken these words, Sri Krishna, Master of all yogis, revealed to Arjuna his transcendent, divine Form, speaking from innumerable mouths, seeing with a myriad eyes, of many marvelous aspects, adorned with countless divine ornaments, brandishing all kinds of heavenly weapons, wearing celestial garlands and the raiment of paradise, anointed with perfumes of heavenly fragrance, full of revelations, resplendent, boundless, of ubiquitous regard.

Suppose a thousand suns should rise together into the sky: such is the glory of the Shape of Infinite God.

Then the son of Pandu beheld the entire universe, in all its multitudinous diversity, lodged as one being within the body of the God of gods.

Then was Arjuna, that lord of mighty riches, overcome with wonder. His hair stood erect. He bowed low before God in adoration, and clasped his hands, and spoke:

ARJUNA: Ah, my God, I see all gods within your body;
Each in his degree, the multitude of creatures;
See Lord Brahma throned upon the lotus;
See all the sages, and the holy serpents.

Universal Form, I see you without limit,
Infinite of arms, eyes, mouths and bellies—
See, and find no end, midst, or beginning.

---

20. [Various classes of celestial beings. —TRANS.]

Crowned with diadems, you wield the mace and discus,
Shining every way—the eyes shrink from your splendor
Brilliant like the sun; like fire, blazing, boundless.

You are all we know, supreme, beyond man's measure,
This world's sure-set plinth and refuge never shaken,
Guardian of eternal law, life's Soul undying.
Birthless, deathless; yours the strength titanic,
Million-armed, the sun and moon your eyeballs,
Fiery-faced, you blast the world to ashes,

Fill the sky's four corners, span the chasm
Sundering heaven from earth. Superb and awful
Is your Form that makes the three worlds tremble.

Into you, the companies of devas
Enter with clasped hands, in dread and wonder.
Crying "Peace," the Rishis and the Siddhas
Sing your praise with hymns of adoration.

Adityas and Rudras, Sadhyas, Viswas, Aswins,
Maruts and Vasus, the hosts of the Gandharvas,
Yakshas, Asuras, Ushmapas and Siddhas—
All of them gaze upon you in amazement.

At the sight of this, your Shape stupendous
Full of mouths and eyes, feet, thighs and bellies,
Terrible with fangs, O mighty master,
All the worlds are fear-struck, even as I am.

When I see you, Vishnu, omnipresent,
Shouldering the sky, in hues of rainbow,
With your mouths agape and flame-eyes staring—
All my peace is gone; my heart is troubled.

Now with frightful tusks your mouths are gnashing,
Flaring like the fires of Doomsday morning—
North, south, east and west seem all confounded—
Lord of devas, world's abode, have mercy!

Dhritarashtra's offspring, many a monarch,
Bhisma, Drona, and the son of Karna,
There they go—with our own warriors also—
Hurrying to your jaws, wide-fanged and hideous—
See where mangled heads lie crushed between them!

Swift as many rivers streaming to the ocean,
Rush the heroes to your fiery gullets:
Mothlike, to meet the flame of their destruction,
Headlong these plunge into you, and perish.

Licking with your burning tongues, devouring
All the worlds, you probe the heights of heaven
With intolerable beams, O Vishnu.

Tell me who you are, and were from the beginning,
You of aspect grim, O God of gods, be gracious.
Take my homage, Lord. From me your ways are hidden.

SRI KRISHNA: I am come as Time, the waster of the peoples,
Ready for that hour that ripens to their ruin.
All these hosts must die; strike, stay your hand—no matter.

Therefore, strike. Win kingdom, wealth and glory.
Arjuna, arise, O ambidextrous bowman.
Seem to slay. By me these men are slain already.

You but smite the dead, the doom-devoted heroes,
Jayadratha, Drona, Bhisma, Karna.
Fight, and have no fear. The foe is yours to conquer.

SANJAYA: After Arjuna had heard these words of the Lord
Krishna, he folded his palms and bowed down, trembling.
Prostrating himself, with great fear, he addressed Krishna
once more, in a choking voice:

ARJUNA: Well it is the world delights to do you honor!
At the sight of you, O master of the senses,
Demons scatter every way in terror,
And the hosts of Siddhas bow adoring.

Mightiest, how should they indeed withhold their homage?
O Prime Cause of all, even Brahma the Beginner—
Deathless, world's abode, the Lord of devas,
You are what is not, what is, and what transcends them.

You are first and highest in heaven, O ancient Spirit.
It is within you the cosmos rests in safety.
You are known and knower, goal of all our striving.
Endless in your change, you body forth creation.

Lord of fire and death, of wind and moon and waters,
Father of the born, and this world's father's Father.
Hail, all hail to you—a thousand salutations.

Take our salutations, Lord, from every quarter,
Infinite of might and boundless in your glory,
You are all that is, since everywhere we find you.

Carelessly I called you "Krishna" and "my comrade,"
Took undying God for friend and fellow mortal,
Overbold with love, unconscious of your greatness.

Often I would jest, familiar, as we feasted
Midst the throng, or walked, or lay at rest together:
Did my words offend? Forgive me, Lord Eternal.

Author of this world, the unmoved and the moving,
You alone are fit for worship, you the highest.
Where in the three worlds shall any find your equal?

Therefore I bow down, prostrate and ask for pardon:
Now forgive me, God, as friend forgives his comrade,
Father forgives son, and man his dearest lover.

I have seen what no man ever saw before me:
Deep is my delight, but still my dread is greater.
Show me now your other Form, O Lord, be gracious.

Thousand-membered, Universal Being,
Show me now the Shape I knew of old, the four-armed,[21]
With your diadem and mace, the discus-bearer.

SRI KRISHNA: This my Form of fire, worldwide, supreme, primeval,
　　Manifest by yoga power, alone of all men,
　　Arjuna, I showed to you because I love you.

Neither through sacrifice, nor study of the Vedas,
Nor strict austerities, nor alms, nor rituals,
Shall this my Shape be viewed by any mortal,
Other than you, O hero of the Pandus.

Now you need fear no more, nor be bewildered,
Seeing me so terrible. Be glad, take courage.
Look, here am I, transformed, as first you knew me.

---

21. [The only explanation of this passage seems to be that Arjuna is asking Sri Krishna
to assume the shape of his chosen deity, Vishnu—since it cannot mean that Krishna
had four arms while in his human shape. If this interpretation is correct, we may
assume that God took on the four-armed shape of Vishnu for a moment, before
reappearing as Krishna. As has been stated elsewhere, Krishna was regarded as an
incarnation of Vishnu. —TRANS.]

SANJAYA: Having spoken thus to Arjuna, Krishna appeared in his own shape. The Great-Souled One, assuming once more his mild and pleasing form, brought peace to him in his terror.

ARJUNA: O Krishna, now I see your pleasant human form, I am myself again.

SRI KRISHNA: That Shape of mine which you have seen is very difficult to behold. Even the devas themselves are always longing to see it. Neither by study of the Vedas, nor by austerities, nor by almsgiving, nor by rituals can I be seen as you have seen me. But by single-minded and intense devotion, that Form of mine may be completely known, and seen, and entered into, O Consumer of the foe.

Whosoever works for me alone, makes me his only goal and is devoted to me, free from attachment, and without hatred toward any creature—that man, O Prince, shall enter into me.

THE YOGA OF DEVOTION

ARJUNA: Some worship you with steadfast love. Others worship God the unmanifest and changeless. Which kind of devotee has the greater understanding of yoga?

SRI KRISHNA: Those whose minds are fixed on me in steadfast love, worshiping me with absolute faith. I consider them to have the greater understanding of yoga.

As for those others, the devotees of God the unmanifest, indefinable, and changeless, they worship that which is omnipresent, constant, eternal, beyond thought's compass, never to be moved. They hold all the senses in check. They are

tranquil-minded, and devoted to the welfare of humanity.
They see the Atman in every creature. They also will certainly
come to me.

But the devotees of the unmanifest have a harder task,
because the unmanifest is very difficult for embodied souls to
realize.

Quickly I come
To those who offer me
Every action,
Worship me only,
Their dearest delight,
With devotion undaunted.

Because they love me
These are my bondsmen
And I shall save them
From mortal sorrow
And all the waves
Of Life's deathly ocean.

Be absorbed in me,
Lodge your mind in me:
Thus you shall dwell in me,
Do not doubt it,
Here and hereafter.

If you cannot become absorbed in me, then try to reach me
by repeated concentration. If you lack the strength to con-
centrate, then devote yourself to works which will please me.
For, by working for my sake only, you will achieve perfection.
If you cannot even do this, then surrender yourself to me
altogether. Control the lusts of your heart, and renounce the
fruits of every action.

Concentration which is practiced with discernment is certainly better than the mechanical repetition of a ritual or a

prayer. Absorption in God—to live with Him and be one with Him always—is even better than concentration. But renunciation brings instant peace to the spirit.

A man should not hate any living creature. Let him be friendly and compassionate to all. He must free himself from the delusion of "I" and "mine." He must accept pleasure and pain with equal tranquillity. He must be forgiving, ever-contented, self-controlled, united constantly with me in his meditation. His resolve must be unshakable. He must be dedicated to me in intellect and in mind. Such a devotee is dear to me.

He neither molests his fellow men, nor allows himself to become disturbed by the world. He is no longer swayed by joy and envy, anxiety and fear. Therefore he is dear to me.

He is pure, and independent of the body's desire. He is able to deal with the unexpected: prepared for everything, unperturbed by anything. He is neither vain nor anxious about the results of his actions. Such a devotee is dear to me.

He does not desire or rejoice in what is pleasant. He does not dread what is unpleasant, or grieve over it. He remains unmoved by good or evil fortune. Such a devotee is dear to me.

His attitude is the same toward friend and foe. He is indifferent to honor and insult, heat and cold, pleasure and pain. He is free from attachment. He values praise and blame equally. He can control his speech. He is content with whatever he gets. His home is everywhere and nowhere. His mind is fixed upon me, and his heart is full of devotion. He is dear to me.

This true wisdom I have taught will lead you to immortality. The faithful practice it with devotion, taking me for their highest aim. To me they surrender heart and mind. They are exceedingly dear to me.

DEVOTION TO THE SUPREME SPIRIT

SRI KRISHNA: There is a fig tree
   In ancient story,
   The giant Aswattha,
   The everlasting,
   Rooted in heaven,
   Its branches earthward:
   Each of its leaves
   Is a song of the Vedas,
   And he who knows it
   Knows all the Vedas.

   Downward and upward
   Its branches bending
   Are fed by the gunas,
   The buds it puts forth
   Are the things of the senses,
   Roots it has also
   Reaching downward
   Into this world,
   The roots of man's action.

   What its form is,
   Its end and beginning,
   Its very nature,
   Can never be known here.

Therefore, a man should contemplate Brahman until he has sharpened the axe of his nonattachment. With this axe, he must cut through the firmly rooted Aswattha tree. Then he must try to realize that state from which there is no return to future births. Let him take refuge in that Primal Being, from whom all this seeming activity streams forth forever.

When men have thrown off their ignorance, they are free from pride and delusion. They have conquered the evil of worldly attachment. They live in constant union with the Atman. All craving has left them. They are no longer at the mercy of opposing sense-reactions. Thus they reach that state which is beyond all change.

This is my Infinite Being; shall the sun lend it
Any light—or the moon, or fire? For it shines
Self-luminous always: and he who attains me
Will never be reborn.

Part of myself is the God within every creature,
Keeps that nature eternal, yet seems to be separate,
Putting on mind and senses five, the garment
Made of Prakriti.

When the Lord puts on a body, or casts it from him,
He enters or departs, taking the mind and senses
Away with him, as the wind steals perfume
Out of the flowers.

Watching over the ear and the eye, and presiding
There behind touch, and taste, and smell, he is also
Within the mind: he enjoys and suffers
The things of the senses.

Dwelling in flesh, or departing, or one with the gunas,
Knowing their moods and motions, he is invisible
Always to the ignorant, but his sages see him
With the eye of wisdom.

Yogis who have gained tranquillity through the practice of spiritual disciplines, behold him in their own consciousness. But those who lack tranquillity and discernment will not find him, even though they may try hard to do so.

The light that lives in the sun.
Lighting all the world,
The light of the moon,
The light that is in fire:
Know that light to be mine.

My energy enters the earth,
Sustaining all that lives:
I become the moon,
Giver of water and sap,
To feed the plants and the trees.

Flame of life in all,
I consume the many foods,
Turning them into strength
That upholds the body.

I am in all hearts,
I give and take away
Knowledge and memory:
I am all that the Vedas tell,
I am the teacher,
The knower of Vedanta.

There are two kinds of personality in this world, the mortal and the immortal. The personality of all creatures is mortal. The personality of God is said to be immortal. It is the same forever. But there is one other than these; the Impersonal Being who is called the supreme Atman. He is the unchanging Lord who pervades and supports the three worlds. And since I, the Atman, transcend the mortal and even the immortal, I am known in this world and in the Vedas as the supreme Reality.

He who is free from delusion, and knows me as the supreme Reality, knows all that can be known. Therefore he adores me with his whole heart.

This is the most sacred of all the truths I have taught you. He who has realized it becomes truly wise. The purpose of his life is fulfilled.

THE YOGA OF RENUNCIATION

ARJUNA: I want to learn the truth about renunciation and non-attachment. What is the difference between these two principles?

SRI KRISHNA: The sages tell us that renunciation means the complete giving-up of all actions which are motivated by desire. And they say that nonattachment means abandonment of the fruits of action.

Some philosophers declare that all kinds of action should be given up, because action always contains a certain measure of evil. Others say that acts of sacrifice, almsgiving, and austerity should not be given up. Now you shall hear the truth of this matter.

Acts of sacrifice, almsgiving, and austerity should not be given up: their performance is necessary. For sacrifice, almsgiving, and austerity are a means of purification to those who rightly understand them. But even these acts must be performed without attachment or regard for their fruits. Such is my final and considered judgment.

Renunciation is said to be of three kinds. If a man, in his ignorance, renounces those actions which the scriptures ordain, his renunciation is inspired by tamas. If he abstains from any action merely because it is disagreeable, or because he fears it will cause him bodily pain, his renunciation is inspired by rajas. He will not obtain any spiritual benefit from such renunciation. But when a man performs an action which is sanctioned by the scriptures, and does it for duty's sake only, renouncing all attachment and desire for its fruits, then his renunciation is inspired by sattwa.

When a man is endowed with spiritual discrimination and illumined by knowledge of the Atman, all his doubts are dispelled. He does not shrink from doing what is disagreeable to him, nor does he long to do what is agreeable. No human being can give up action altogether, but he who gives up the fruits of action is said to be nonattached.

To those who have not yet renounced the ego and its desires, action bears three kinds of fruit—pleasant, unpleasant, and a mixture of both. They will be reaped in due season. But those who have renounced ego and desire will reap no fruit at all, either in this world or in the next.

All our action
Has five partakers:
So say the scriptures
That teach us wisdom
To break the bondage
Earned by our action:
Listen and learn them.

First, this body;
Then ego, the doer;
The organs of sense
And the many motions
Of Life in the body;
Lastly, the devas
In spirit presiding.[22]

Whatever the action,
Excellent, evil;
Whether of speech,
Of mind, or of body:
These are its causers.

---

22. [According to Hindu mythology, each sense organ has a presiding deity. —TRANS.]

Falsely he sees,
And with small discernment,
Who sees this Atman
The doer of action:
His mind is not purged
In the work of the spirit.

But he whose mind dwells
Beyond attachment,
Untainted by ego,
No act shall bind him
With any bond:
Though he slay these thousands
He is no slayer.

There are three things which motivate action: knowledge,
the knower, and that which is known. There are three con-
stituents of action: the instrument, the purpose, and the doer.
Sankhya[23] philosophy declares that knowledge, action, and
doer are of three kinds only, according to the guna which pre-
dominates in each. Listen, this is their nature.

There is that knowledge
From sattwa proceeding
Which knows one Being
Deathless in every creature,
Entire amidst all division.

The knowledge that is rajas
Knows nothing but difference:
Many souls in many creatures,
All various, each
Apart from his fellow.

23. [The system of philosophy compiled by Kapila, an early-sixth-century Hindu
philosopher. —TRANS.]

The knowledge that is tamas
Knows no reason:
Its sight distorted
Takes the part for the whole,
Misreading Nature.

The act of sacred duty,
Done without attachment,
Not as pleasure desired,
Not as hated compulsion,
By him who has no care
For the fruit of his action:
That act is of sattwa.

The act of weary toil
Done in despite of nature
Under the whip of lust
And the will of the ego:
That act is of rajas.

The act undertaken
In the hour of delusion
Without count of cost,
Squandering strength and treasure,
Heedless of harm to another,
By him who does not question
His power to perform it:
That act is of tamas.

The doer without desire,
Who does not boast of his deed,
Who is ardent, enduring,
Untouched by triumph,
In failure untroubled:
He is a man of sattwa.

The doer with desire,
Hot for the prize of vainglory,
Brutal, greedy and foul,
In triumph too quick to rejoice,
In failure despairing:
He is a man of rajas.

The indifferent doer
Whose heart is not in his deed,
Stupid and stubborn,
A cheat, and malicious,
The idle lover of delay,
Easily dejected:
He is a man of tamas.

There are three kinds of conscience and three kinds of determination, according to the predominance of each guna. Now listen: I will explain them fully, one by one.

A man's conscience has the nature of sattwa when it can distinguish between the paths of renunciation and worldly desire. Then it knows what actions are right or wrong, what is safe and what is dangerous, what binds the embodied spirit and what sets it free. But when the conscience cannot distinguish truly between right and wrong, or know what should and what should not be done, then it has the nature of rajas. And when the conscience is so thickly wrapped in ignorance that it mistakes wrong for right and sees everything distorted, then it has the nature of tamas.

Determination inspired by sattwa never wavers. It is strengthened by the practice of yoga. A man who has this kind of determination gains absolute control over his mind, vital energy, and senses. Rajas, on the other hand, inspires that kind of determination with which a man follows the object of his desire, or seeks wealth, or does a duty, looking for reward and personal advantage. As for the determination inspired by tamas, it is nothing but obstinacy. It makes a man stubbornly refuse to shake off his dullness, fear, grief, low spirits, or vanity.

And now, Arjuna, I will tell you about the three kinds of happiness:

Who knows the Atman
Knows that happiness
Born of pure knowledge:
The joy of sattwa.
Deep his delight
After strict self-schooling:
Sour toil at first
But at last what sweetness,
The end of sorrow.

Senses also
Have joy in their marriage
With things of the senses,
Sweet at first
But at last how bitter:
Steeped in rajas,
That pleasure is poison.
Bred of tamas
Is brutish contentment
In stupor and sloth
And obstinate error:
Its end, its beginning
Alike are delusion.

There is no creature, either on earth or among the devas in heaven, who is free from these three gunas which come forth from Prakriti.

Seer and leader,
Provider and server:[24]
Each has the duty
Ordained by his nature
Born of the gunas.
The seer's duty,
Ordained by his nature,
Is to be tranquil
In mind and in spirit,
Self-controlled,
Austere and stainless,
Upright, forbearing;
To follow wisdom,
To know the Atman,
Firm of faith
In the truth that is Brahman.

The leader's duty,
Ordained by his nature,
Is to be bold,
Unflinching and fearless,
Subtle of skill
And openhanded,
Great-hearted in battle,
A resolute ruler.

Others are born
To the tasks of providing:
These are the traders,
The cultivators,
The breeders of cattle.

---

24. [The four Hindu castes are: Brahmins (the priests), Kshatriyas (the warriors), Vaishyas (the merchants), and Sudras (the servants). Here the caste-names are used with a more psychological significance, and have been translated accordingly. —Trans.]

To work for all men,
Such is the duty
Ordained for the servers:
This is their nature.
All mankind
Is born for perfection
And each shall attain it
Will he but follow
His nature's duty.

Now you shall hear how a man may become perfect, if he devotes himself to the work which is natural to him. A man will reach perfection if he does his duty as an act of worship to the Lord, who is the source of the universe, prompting all action, everywhere present.

A man's own natural duty, even if it seems imperfectly done, is better than work not naturally his own even if this is well performed. When a man acts according to the law of his nature, he cannot be sinning. Therefore, no one should give up his natural work, even though he does it imperfectly. For all action is involved in imperfection, like fire in smoke.

When a man has achieved nonattachment, self-mastery, and freedom from desire through renunciation, he reaches union with Brahman, who is beyond all action.

Learn from me now,
O son of Kunti,
How man made perfect
Is one with Brahman,
The goal of wisdom.
When the mind and the heart
Are freed from delusion,
United with Brahman,
When steady will
Has subdued the senses,

When sight and taste
And sound are abandoned
Without regretting,
Without aversion;
When man seeks solitude,
Eats but little,
Curbing his speech,
His mind and his body,
Ever engaged
In his meditation
On Brahman the truth,
And full of compassion;
When he casts from him
Vanity, violence,
Pride, lust, anger
And all his possessions,
Totally free
From the sense of ego
And tranquil of heart:
That man is ready
For oneness with Brahman.
And he who dwells
United with Brahman,
Calm in mind,
Not grieving, not craving,
Regarding all men
With equal acceptance:
He loves me most dearly.

To love is to know me,
My innermost nature,
The truth that I am:
Through this knowledge he enters
At once to my Being.

All that he does
Is offered before me
In utter surrender:
My grace is upon him,
He finds the eternal,
The place unchanging.

Mentally resign all your action to me. Regard me as your dearest loved one. Know me to be your only refuge. Be united always in heart and consciousness with me.

United with me, you shall overcome all difficulties by my grace. But if your heart is full of conceit, and you do not heed me, you are lost. If, in your vanity, you say: "I will not fight," your resolve is vain. Your own nature will drive you to the act. For you yourself have created the karma that binds you. You are helpless in its power. And you will do that very thing which your ignorance seeks to avoid.

The Lord lives in the heart of every creature. He turns them round and round upon the wheel of his Maya. Take refuge utterly in him. By his grace you will find supreme peace, and the state which is beyond all change.

Now I have taught you that wisdom which is the secret of secrets. Ponder it carefully. Then act as you think best. These are the last words that I shall say to you, the deepest of all truths. I speak for your own good. You are the friend I chose and love.

Give me your whole heart,
Love and adore me,
Worship me always,
Bow to me only,
And you shall find me:
This is my promise
Who love you dearly.

Lay down all duties
In me, your refuge.
Fear no longer,
For I will save you
From sin and from bondage.

You must never tell this holy truth to anyone who lacks
self-control and devotion, or who despises his teacher and
mocks at me. But the man who loves me, and teaches my
devotees this supreme truth of the Gita, will certainly come
to me. No one can do me a higher service than this. No one
on earth can be dearer to me.

And if any man meditates upon this sacred discourse of
ours, I shall consider that he has worshiped me in spirit. Even
if a man simply listens to these words with faith, and does not
doubt them, he will be freed from his sins and reach the
heaven of the righteous.

Have you listened carefully, Arjuna, to everything I have
told you? Have I dispelled the delusions of your ignorance?

ARJUNA: By your grace, O Lord, my delusions have been
    dispelled.
My mind stands firm. Its doubts are ended. I will do your
    bidding.

SANJAYA: Such were the words that thrilled my heart, that
    marvelous discourse,
Heard from the lips of the high-souled Prince and the great
    Lord Krishna,
Not with these earthly ears, but by mystic grace of Vyasa,
Thus I learned that yoga supreme from the Master of yogis.
Ever and ever again I rejoice, O King, and remember
Sacred and wonderful truths that Krishna told to his comrade.
Ever again, O King, I am glad and remember rejoicing

That most splendid of forms put on by Krishna, the Sweet
　　One.
Where Lord Krishna is, and Arjuna, great among archers,
There, I know, is goodness and peace, and triumph and glory.

OM. Peace. Peace. Peace.

INTERPRETIVE QUESTIONS
FOR DISCUSSION

Why does Krishna insist that Arjuna disregard his compassion for his kinsmen and fight?

1. Why does Arjuna suspect that his compassion may not be real, that it may be a "delusion"? (51)

2. Are we meant to think, as Krishna suggests, that cowardice and vanity are at the root of Arjuna's refusal to fight? (50, 98)

3. Why does Krishna focus first on the immortality of the individual soul in order to convince Arjuna to fight? (51–52) Why is it only after explaining the indestructibility of the Atman that Krishna raises the issue of Arjuna's caste-duty? (54)

4. Why is Arjuna absolved of the guilt for killing his kinsmen in battle if he acts without concern for either victory or defeat? (54, 67, 91)

5. Why does Krishna call on Arjuna to overcome his pity for his kinsmen, but later declare that man should be "friendly and compassionate to all"? (50, 85)

6. Why are both loving and killing the way to God? Are we meant to think that Krishna is indifferent to human suffering?

7. Why must Arjuna go against his sense of what is moral in order to obey Krishna's injunction to do his duty?

8. What does Krishna mean when he says, "When a man acts according to the law of his nature, he cannot be sinning"? (96)

9. According to the Bhagavad-Gita, why is it better to perform one's own duty imperfectly rather than the duty of another perfectly? (63, 96)

Suggested textual analysis
Pages 50–56: beginning, "Then his eyes filled with tears," and ending, "then you will reach union with the Atman."

Why does Krishna say that those whose minds are fixed on him "in steadfast love," worshiping him "with absolute faith," have the greater understanding of yoga?

1. Is Krishna referring to the yoga of knowledge when he says that "the devotees of God the unmanifest . . . have a harder task"? (83–84) What is meant by "God the unmanifest"?

2. Are we meant to think that the yoga of devotion is superior to both the yoga of selfless action and the yoga of knowledge or renunciation? Are we meant to think it is easier? (83–84)

3. What does Krishna mean when he says that the "wise see knowledge and action as one"? (71)

4. What does Krishna mean when he says that the yoga of action "purifies / The man of meditation"? (72)

5. According to the Bhagavad-Gita, can a person follow any one of the three yogas, regardless of his or her caste? (83–85, 95–96)

6. Is Krishna recommending that Arjuna follow the path of selfless action or all three paths in order to attain union with Brahman and freedom? Is the text saying that the three paths are interdependent?

7. Do the followers of the path of devotion worship a personal God? Why does Krishna invite Arjuna to regard him as his "dearest loved one"? (98)

8. Why is it only through the yoga of devotion that Krishna's universal "Form . . . may be completely known, and seen"? (83)

Suggested textual analysis
Pages 83–85: beginning, "Some worship you with steadfast love," and ending, "They are exceedingly dear to me."

Why does Arjuna need the vision of Krishna at his most "terrible"—as well as Krishna's arguments—in order to be freed from his bewilderment, and resolve to fight?

1. If Arjuna does not doubt Krishna's supremacy, why does he long to behold Krishna's divine form? (77)

2. Is it fear of Krishna's grim, devouring aspect that moves Arjuna to accept his duty and fight? (80–81)

3. What does Arjuna mean when he tells Krishna, "From me your ways are hidden"? (80) Does this admission signal that Arjuna has arrived at a greater understanding of yoga?

4. After revealing himself to Arjuna in his transcendent form, why does Krishna call upon Arjuna to win "kingdom, wealth and glory"—and yet elsewhere claim that honor and dishonor are delusion? (80)

5. According to Krishna, how can a person discriminate between an action motivated by desire (or ego, or attachment) and an action motivated by duty? (91–93)

6. Why is the changeless Brahman, revealed by Krishna to be "wide-fanged and hideous," said to be "untouched by evil"? (80, 75)

7. Having seen Krishna in all his dreadful glory, is Arjuna moved to love as well as to revere the great Lord? (97–99)

8. To adore Krishna, the supreme Reality, with one's whole heart—why does Krishna identify this as the "most sacred of all the truths" he has taught Arjuna? (89)

9. Does the Bhagavad-Gita suggest that no one can attain union with Brahman without suffering or struggle? (94, 96–97)

Suggested textual analysis
Pages 78–82: beginning, "Then, O King, when he had spoken these words," and ending, "Look, here am I, transformed, as first you knew me."

FOR FURTHER REFLECTION

1. Do you agree with the Bhagavad-Gita's teaching that ego or "desire" is the source of human evil?

2. Could the Bhagavad-Gita, with its emphasis on performing one's duty as prescribed by caste and without hope for worldly rewards, form the basis for a more harmonious society than our own?

3. Can one live a life of calm detachment, as recommended in the Bhagavad-Gita, while maintaining normal, loving human relationships?

4. Does the Bhagavad-Gita set an impossible ideal for human behavior?

5. Is the problem of human suffering at the heart of all the great world religions?

6. Does one need spiritual devotion to lead a life of right action and to achieve internal harmony?

7. Does the Bhagavad-Gita provide a justification for war?

TROTH

Gregor von Rezzori

GREGOR VON REZZORI (1914–) was born in the Bukovina, a forested region of Rumania in the Carpathian Mountains that was once part of the Austro-Hungarian Empire. He attended the University of Vienna and for a time lived in Bucharest. After World War II, Rezzori resided in West Germany, where he supported himself by writing and by working in the fields of radio broadcasting and filmmaking. Among Rezzori's works translated into English are the novels *The Hussar* (1960), *The Death of My Brother Abel* (1985), *The Orient Express* (1992), and a memoir, *The Snows of Yesteryear* (1989). "Troth" was written in English in 1969 and is included in his 1981 autobiographical novel, *Memoirs of an Anti-Semite*.

THE BIG SOMETHING falling from the floor above my
grandmother's apartment cast a sudden shadow on the window
before it bumped on the cobblestones, and my grandmother's
gouty claw reached for the little bell beyond the flowery field
of playing cards she had laid out on the table for her game of
patience and shook it violently. Decades of strained impatience
made her movement awkward, and the thin silver sound seemed
to mock her intention to reach the deaf ears of old Marie.
Nevertheless, as in a vaudeville gag, the door opened instantly
and old Marie appeared, trembling with age and the suppressed
contradictions of nearly fifty years of service to a most complicated family.

"Yes, please?"

My grandmother majestically stretched her tortoise neck as if
it still were encircled by half a dozen rows of pearls and turned
her head toward the window. "Something fell down from the
upper floor. The Jews must have put their feather beds in the
windows to air or something of that kind. Go and have a look."

Old Marie pushed her head out of the window and then brought it back into the room. "Please," she said triumphantly. "That's no feather bed. It is the young Raubitschek girl."

I spent part of my youth in this apartment house, which was in a drowsy residential section of Vienna. When I met the "old Raubitscheks" on the stairs, I greeted them with the same polite reserve they used in saluting my grandmother, whose recognition was a delightful mixture of joviality and distance. Never a word was exchanged. They were educated people, though. Papa Raubitschek being a professor at the University of Vienna, famous artists came to their apartment, and every Wednesday evening the remote sounds of chamber music reached my grandmother's apartment and would make her—she was very sensitive to noise—say contemptuously, "They are playing Beethoven's 'Allergique' again or something equally horrid." Because so many Jews were successful in musical endeavors, my grandmother no longer quite considered it one of the fine arts.

Whether those chamber-music concerts got on the nerves not only of my grandmother but also of Minka Raubitschek I am unable to say. However, she was a high-spirited girl with a strong and stubborn will, and on the occasion I have just mentioned, during a quarrel with her mother, she jumped out of the window. "Exaggerated" was my grandmother's comment. "As those young Jewish intellectuals usually are." Fortunately she didn't do herself much harm. She broke a hip and was slightly lame thereafter, that was all. In later years, when I had been accepted into the circle of her friends, we used to put a mountain climber's cord around her waist and let her down the steep stairs to the ladies' room of the Kärntnerbar. This was necessary not only because of her lame hip but also because her sense of equilibrium was impaired by too many whiskeys. She used to thank us with bits of cultural-historical information. "Do you realize where you are, you drunken swine? This place was designed by Adolf Loos, an architect as important as Frank Lloyd Wright. It is one of the early masterpieces of modern architecture—a room that would normally not be big enough for a dozen ignoramuses of your kind shelters half a hundred. If that isn't progress . . ."

As the grandson of an architect who had done his share to make Vienna's monuments conform to the taste of the fin-de-siècle, I should have given particular consideration to such remarks of Minka Raubitschek's. Her tastes were exquisite and her knowledge was profound. But at the time I was merely reminded of my grandmother. "It is disgusting," my grandmother would say, "how very much like your father you have become. He is a perfect barbarian, with his monomaniacal passion for shooting. But when I think that I gave my daughters Renan to read in order to have them take up spiritualism . . ."

The two neuralgic points in my grandmother's existence were the marriage of her eldest daughter, my mother, with my father and the "exaggerated ideas" of my unmarried aunts. My grandmother never set foot in the back rooms of her apartment, which, after the death of my grandfather, were occupied by her two spinster daughters; for there, every Wednesday evening, accompanied by the remote sounds of the Raubitschek chamber music, the meetings of the esoteric community of Mr. Malik took place. Mr. Malik was an engineer with supernatural powers that enabled him to massage the souls out of the bodies of ladies who had metaphysical talents so that the emptied vessel could be filled with some free soul of a dead person not yet reborn, who would then use the mouth of the medium to utter mystical nonsense, the theosophical interpretation of which was left to my aunts. The soul massaged out of the body remained attached to it by an astral navel cord, and when the free soul, who came like a guest into your body for the duration of the séance, had left, Mr. Malik would massage your waiting soul along that very same astral navel cord back into your body, and you would be yourself again. In later years, when we were letting Minka down to the ladies' room of the Kärntnerbar, I had great success with what I had learned of Mr. Malik's teachings. "It's only her cursed *materia* that descends," I would explain. "Her soul stays with us and her whiskey."

The presumably free, not yet reborn soul of Mr. Malik will perhaps forgive me. I was only eighteen years old when I thus profaned his messages, and all during my childhood nobody had done much to make me take him very seriously. "I am sure that man is not an engineer at all but just a cheap crook," my grandmother used to say. "Probably a Jew who has changed his name."

The suspicion that somebody could have changed his name already made him a Jew—provided, of course, he was not an Englishman, like charming Mr. Wood, who one beautiful day became Lord Halifax. But that was quite another thing. It was typically Jewish to change your name, for Jews quite understandably did not want to be taken for what they were. Since their names usually made it quite clear what they were, they had to change them, for camouflage. Had we been Jews, we should certainly have done the same, because it must be painful to be a Jew. Even well-bred people would make you feel it—either by their reserve or by an exaggerated politeness and coy friendliness. But fortunately we were not Jews, so, though we could see their point, we considered it a piece of insolence when they changed their names and pretended to be like us. Part of the certain esteem my grandmother had for the Raubitscheks came from the fact that they had not changed their name. Jews who changed their names, like Mr. Malik, were crooks and swindlers. Their camouflage was but a falsehood to which they were driven by their disgusting greed for profit and their repulsive social climbing. This was particularly the case with the so-called Polish Jews—the prototype of the greedy, pushing little Jew one met so often in the Bukovina.[1] There were crowds of them; you could not take a step without running into swarms. The elder ones and very old ones, particularly the very poor, were humbly what they were—submissive men in black caftans and large-brimmed hats, with curls at their temples, and in their eyes a sort of melting look which the sadness of many thousands

1. [In 1919, the Austro-Hungarian Empire, or Dual Monarchy, ruled by the Habsburgs, came to an end, and the modern state of Austria was founded. The Bukovina, formerly a part of the empire, was ceded to Rumania.]

of years seemed to have bestowed. Their eyes were like dark ponds. Some of them were even beautiful in their melancholy. They had spun-silver prophets' heads, with which the butcher's face of Mr. Malik would have compared very unfavorably, and when they looked at you, humbly stepping aside to let you pass, it was like a sigh for not only themselves but all the burden of human existence which they knew so well. But the young ones, and especially the ones who were better off, or even rich, showed an embarrassing self-confidence. They wore elegant clothes and drove dandified roadsters, and their girls smelled of scent and sparkled with jewelry. Some of them even had dogs and walked them on leashes, just as my aunts did. When they spoke to one another, it was in a pushing, impatient way, even when they had just met. They asked direct personal questions and looked around for someone more worth knowing. They were not humble at all.

My father likewise hated Jews, all of them, even the old and humble ones. It was an ancient, traditional, and deep-rooted hatred, which he did not need to explain; any motivation, no matter how absurd, would justify it. Of course, nobody seriously believed that the Jews wanted to rule the world merely because their prophets had promised it to them (even though they were supposedly getting richer and more powerful, especially in America). But, of course, other stories were considered humbug: for instance an evil conspiracy, such as was described in the *Protocols of the Elders of Zion,* or their stealing communion wafers or committing ritual murders of innocent children (despite the still unexplained disappearance of little Esther Solymossian). Those were fairy tales that you told to a chambermaid when she said she couldn't stand it here anymore and would much rather go and work for a Jewish family, where she would be better treated and better paid. Then, of course, you casually reminded her that the Jews *had,* after all, crucified our Savior. But our kind of people, the educated kind, did not require such heavy arguments to look upon Jews as second-class people. We just didn't like them, or at least liked them less than other fellow human beings. This was as natural as liking cats less than dogs or bedbugs less than bees; and we amused ourselves by offering the most absurd justifications.

For instance, it was well known that it's bad luck to run into a Jew when you go hunting. Now, my father did little else but go hunting; and since there were so many Jews in the Bukovina that it was impossible to go hunting without promptly running into several of them, he had this annoyance almost every day. It made him suffer, like an ingrown toenail. There were violent scenes between him and my mother because she attracted crowds of Jews to our house. She used to give our cast-off clothing to rag-picking peddlers—Jews, needless to say, so-called *handalés*. You couldn't sell them the clothes—my father was the first to realize this. But it was better to throw the stuff away than to support the Jews in their dirty business, thus possibly helping them in their despicable social climbing. For the Jews dealt in secondhand clothes in order to emigrate to America. They arrived there as Yossel Tuttmann or Moishe Wassershtrom and soon earned enough dollars to change their names. Wassershtrom became Wondraschek, of course, and eventually von Draschek, and finally they'd come back to Europe as Barons von Dracheneck and buy themselves a hunting ground in the Tirol or Styria. And this was a personal affront to my father, for he could not afford a hunting ground in Styria, and thus he believed that all his privileges had been usurped by the Jews. More than anything, he felt it was their fault that he, as an Old Austrian, was forced to remain in the Bukovina and become a Rumanian, which made him too a kind of second-class human being.

He felt exiled in the Bukovina—or rather, as a pioneer, betrayed and deserted. He counted himself among the colonial officials of the former realm of the Austro-Hungarian Dual Monarchy; and it was the task of such officials to protect Europe against the wild hordes who kept breaking in from the East. "Civilization fertilizer" was his bitterly mocking term for the function he ascribed to himself and his kind: they were supposed to settle in the borderland, form a bulwark of Western civilization, and show a bold front to Eastern chaos. He had come to the Bukovina as a young man, after growing up in Graz during the most glorious era of the Dual Monarchy; and everything that had become sad and dreary and hidebound after the collapse of 1918 was, he felt, represented in the land where he had been cast away.

The Bukovina is probably one of the most beautiful areas in the world. But for my father—aside from one tip of the forest Carpathians where he hunted—it was a landscape without character. He even went so far as to deny that I had any character, because I passionately loved the Bukovina. "No wonder," he said with undisguised scorn. "You were simply born into corruption—I mean, the corruption of character. If these borderlands didn't constantly pose the danger of corroding character, then they wouldn't have needed our kind of people as civilization fertilizer."

In my boyhood, I found it very difficult to reach any precise notion of what "character" really was. For my father— he repeated it often enough—Styria had a distinct character. Naturally, I had to assume that this was connected to its "mountainous character," which was always brought up in Austrian books on local history and geography. *A propos,* instead of "character" or the lack thereof, they occasionally talked about "backbone." "The boy simply has no backbone," I had once been forced to hear when refusing to own up to some prank. Styria had character because of its mountain backbone. Now, the Bukovina did have a mountainous backbone, too, although not quite such a spectacular one as the Hohe Tauern. But rocky peaks did loom here and there from the green cones of the forest Carpathians, and the poetic gentleness of the flowery slopes was all too deceptive in obscuring the wildness of the deep forests in which they were embedded. If the word "character" signified what I sensed about it, then these tremendous, wind-swept black forests had at least as much character as the glacier-crowned massifs of Styria.

Even my father had to admit that hunting in the Bukovina was better, more adventurous, more primeval than in Styria. Nevertheless, he dreamed of a hunting ground in Styria and shrugged his shoulders when he was sharply reminded that owners of hunting grounds in Styria dreamed of having a hunting ground in the Carpathians. When I finally asked him what character was, he replied without hesitating: "Troth, more than anything else."

Now I thought I understood him. "Troth" was a much clearer fetish than the throat-scratching concept of "character." Since earliest childhood I had been taught to idolize this notion of loyalty, or troth. It was obvious: my father could not love the Bukovina, because he had become a Rumanian citizen after its defection from the Dual Monarchy. He had been compelled to commit an act of disloyalty, like the engineer Malik, who had changed his name. Only in my father's case, the conflict was tragic: through loyalty to the hunt, he had been forced to be disloyal to his flag. And what that meant was urgently brought home to me.

In those years, the first great war was still close by. Traces and evidence of it survived throughout the countryside: shot-up farms, barbed-wire entanglements, ditches and dugouts in the heart of the woods, the wasteland of villages over which the Russian offensives had rolled. When I viewed such things, I was seized with a strange excitement, a mixture of fear and yearning, which—projected out of myself into the world comprising my experiences back then—I found mirrored in certain evening moods. In the oppressively hopeless dove-blue of the twilights, as in the dramatics of blood-red and sulphur-yellow sunsets, I experienced the shock that the war had brought to my parents' lives. Under such skies, the flag of our allegiance had sunk in the tumult of battle and amid the croaking of ravens over the field of warriors. It was the golden flag with the black, two-headed eagle of the Holy Roman Empire which had been carried on by Imperial Austria. And anyone who had not died in the battle around that flag had betrayed his troth and was now living on without character.

With the mind of a child, always open to thrilling sublimity, I kept reviving the catastrophe of that destruction and that unwilling disloyalty over and over again. This alone explained the oddly empty grief of the people in my immediate surroundings, their resigned and only ironically reflective stance: their deadness, which allowed them to continue existing in an everyday rut that was barely aglow with the melancholy of golden memories, kept them going even though they seemed not to care about the present. My father and mother in the Bukovina were as old and as much a part of a previous era as my grandmother and my crotchety maiden aunts in Vienna. Their dogs had gray heads and trembled when they walked, like Marie. They lived only when they talked about bygone days. The golden glow of their memories came solely from that sunken golden flag.

This sunkenness even explained the melancholy of the landscape in which I grew up. Beautifully canopied by the silky blue of a usually serene sky, the woodland was afflicted with melancholy, the melancholy of eastern vastnesses, creeping in everywhere: into the dove-blue of twilight hours as into the summer heat brooding over the fruit-bearing earth, into the submission of the peasants and the Jews to God's will, into the gentle flutes of shepherds from the meadowed slopes of the Carpathians. These flutes died out when the wintry winds began whistling from the steppes and high deserts of Asia, which suddenly shifted close to us. The Jews and peasants then pulled up their shoulders and curled into themselves even more humbly; the earth turned to stone beneath the frost; and the twilight hours were no longer ambiguous stages of the universe, leading to mute and colorful celestial dramas: they now were a deeper freezing and darkening over a grayish-white, skeletal world. This was a landscape of catastrophe: the proper setting for a destruction growing from a mythically ancient dichotomy. For not only *one* empire had gone under with the sinking of that golden flag. Not only we—or, as we said, "our people"— had carried it, but also our adversaries, the Imperial Russians. Not only our emperor had gone down with the flag, but their emperor too.

The myth at the source of this tragedy had been drummed into me like a litany. It was the myth of the Holy Roman Empire of the Caesars, which had split apart. The black eagle in the golden field of the sunken flag had two crowned heads rising from his breast—shielded with coats of arms—because the empire had two capitals and two heads: Rome, and Byzantium, the Constantinople of the Emperor Constantine. A breach of troth was at the beginning of this myth: the defection of a part from a unified whole. Two empires arose from one and soon were bloodily fighting one another. For each considered itself the true descendant of the original one great imperium. Each symbolized this claim in the same flag. Under this flag, Eastern Rome and Western Rome unpeacefully divided the world, until one of the Asian storms that had menaced Western civilization since time immemorial broke loose once again, and Byzantium decayed and ultimately fell into the hands of the pagans.

Western Rome too had gone through dark and disorderly times, which were historically conjured away, as it were, under the term "Dark Ages" and inadequately bedizened with monarchical figures like Alaric and Odoacer. We leaped across centuries in order to come up all the more sensationally with the figure of light: Charlemagne, whom the Germans call Karl the Great, the reviver of the idea of Holy Empire and the founder of the Roman Empire of the German Nation. I cannot evoke my boyhood without his image. A bronze replica of a mounted statue of him stood on my father's desk, and I often gazed at that replica in deep meditation. The thought that after more than a millennium his slippers and gloves still belonged among the imperial treasures filled me with awe.

Nevertheless, I was puzzled by one enigma: how could Charlemagne, who was a Frank, after all, and thus, strictly speaking, a Frenchman (and, as a French governess furiously assured me, still viewed as a Frenchman by the French)—how could he be the new founder of an Empire of the German Nation? Needless to say, my father had explanations at hand which, while not dispelling my qualms, did divert me from them. In a higher sense, he maintained, one could think of Karl the Great as a German emperor because his descendance was thoroughly German. Germans, with the glorious Stauffers in the lead, had worn his crown and given the Holy Roman Empire an eternally German stamp. Besides, my father added, not quite logically, in medieval times (which had now lightened from the "Dark Ages" to the "High Middle Ages," the epoch of cathedrals and many-towered cities, of knights and ladies, of minstrels, inspired master stonecutters, and altarpiece painters)—in those times, such distinctions had been meaningless. People didn't have national sentiments in the modern sense. You just followed a flag, that was all. Either you were born lowly and were a serf belonging to a lord—you followed him blindly wherever he went, and you never thought beyond your own parish—or else you were born into knighthood and served some count or prince as a true liegeman, which might expand your horizon by a few provinces; but in the end it was all the same. It made no difference whatsoever which of the many nations of this imperium these lords belonged to with their little flags and their liegemen and serfs; it made no difference what language they spoke or what costume they wore. For they were all vassals and subjects of the emperor and the empire.

This was comprehensible because it was graphic. The world seemed well ordered to me. The empire was the epitome of order. From the emperor at the top down through the great vassals and their liegemen with their subliegemen and serfs, it was all as hieratically articulated as a pyramid. This could be enacted. This could be represented in the parades of my tin soldiers. This could also be grasped abstractly. Its mechanism was simple. One person protected the other, the higher one always the lower one; and one served the other, the lower one always the higher one above him. And thus up and down the ladder, like the hierarchy of angels under the Almighty's Heavenly Throne. And that was why the empire was holy, said my father. It was God's state on earth. Not just purely and simply a political construction, a state constitution that offered uniform protection, uniform leadership and administration, to a gigantic territory that was inhabited by many nations and threatened by many dangers. It was more than that: it was an idea and ideal; an ordered image of the world, of human society striving to make God's will come true. The divine right of the emperor was not as it would be today, an arbitrary usurping by power-drunk demagogues mounted on a pedestal made up of interwoven interests—financial, mercantile, and political. Oh no! It was the very symbol of what God wanted the state to be. And this state was held together not by material interests alone but by the ethical principle of troth, loyalty, allegiance, the allegiance of vassals, the unconditional obedience that the liegemen had sworn to their lord and his flag, just as we, the immediate liegemen of the Habsburgs, had sworn allegiance to the Austrian Imperial house and to the flag of the empire with the two-headed eagle in the golden field.

Usually at this point my mother got up and left the room. Whereupon my father felt obliged to help me, as a small boy, to understand things better. He explained to me that in spite of the fact that we were of Italian descent and had become subjects of Rumania, we were still Austrians, and that living in the Bukovina meant a sort of unfaithfulness forced on us by unlucky circumstances—one of which was that shooting in the Bukovina was much better than in Styria. Still, as Austrians, we should have stuck to our flag. Unfortunately that flag didn't exist anymore; the imperial flag of Austria had been replaced by the vulgar flag of the new republic, with which, fortunately, we had nothing to do. The old imperial flag was the flag of the emperors of the House of Habsburg, who for six hundred years had been the emperors of the Holy Roman Empire, founded by Charlemagne. For six hundred years, the emperors of the House of Habsburg had worn his crown and defended the world of

Christendom against another storm from Asia: the Turks. Under the House of Habsburg most of the nations of southeastern Europe had united in that noble task. That's how we, as Italians, had become Austrians, though we had neither come to Austria in the time of Charlemagne nor come in order, as true defenders of Christendom, to fight the Turks, but arrived only in the middle of the eighteenth century as bureaucrats from Sicily. But never mind. Nobody asked you where you were born. They asked only how you were born, and whether you were brave and just and faithful to your liege lord's flag. If you had been brave and just and faithful to your liege lord's flag, you got a coat of arms that obliged you to be even more brave and just and faithful to your flag. As the son of a knight who had his coat of arms—and we had had one already in Sicily, before we came to Austria—you first served as a page, preferably of a queen. Later, you became a squire and ran next to the horse of a knight, carrying his shield. Then you became a knight yourself, and when you weren't fighting for your liege lord and for chivalry in general, you went hunting and shooting. Now, as there were very few queens whom you could serve as a page, and even fewer knights whose shield you could carry as a squire, you were brought up to become a nobleman just by hunting and shooting, and the only way you could fight for chivalry was to stay where you were and at least see that the Jews did not get hunting grounds everywhere, even in the Bukovina. So, in spite of the fact that we were Austrians— though of Italian origin and subjects of Rumania—and my father's father had done his share, as an architect, to give Vienna its lovely neoclassic, and neo-Gothic, and neo-Renaissance appearance, my father never again set foot in Austria, where he had no hunting ground to defend.

But it was agreed that I should be brought up in Austria, and this I resented very much, because I loved the Bukovina. It seems to be the lot of every good childhood to be lonesome, and I was lonesome in both places. In Vienna I was lonesome as a little boy who came from a now remote country of the Balkans and lived with old people and fools. At home, in the Bukovina, I was lonesome as the little snob with a foreign education who tried to avoid contact with others of his age. As a matter of fact, this was not at all my intention. It was the logical consequence of the isolation into which the monomania of my father and the nostalgia of my mother had maneuvered us.

My mother too felt the Bukovina as a sort of exile, but simply as a woman who, with an unloved husband, lives far from those she loves. As my father's monomaniacal passion for shooting estranged him more and more from family life, my mother's various unfulfilled desires found an outlet in a no less monomaniacal love for me, her child. She watched over every step I took and every breath I drew. Between her terror that I would get pneumonia from running too fast and the suspicion that a contact with the gardener's children could give me lice, or that through the friendliness of a Rumanian officer who had put me in the saddle of his horse I would get syphilis, I did not develop into a very social youngster. In wintertime, on the big public skating rink, I found myself lonely in a corner, cutting my circles and loops into the ice, an enormous woolen shawl wrapped six times around my neck, while all around a whirl of hilarious liveliness filled the sparkling winter day.

The majority of the young skaters were Jews. Among them were some extremely pretty girls, with whom, one by one, I clandestinely fell in love, suffering not only from the overprotectiveness of my mother but from guilt. My mother came to fetch me every day and, in spite of my violent protests, had me wrapped in blankets and furs in order to protect my frail health after the exhausting exercise. My departure became a public amusement so humiliating that I did not dare to look the Jewish girls in the eye even when my mother had not yet turned up. At the same time I felt guilty because my tender feelings were a betrayal of everything that in the geography of my inner world formed the moral massifs, the mountainous backbone, so to speak—the Carpathians, without which that inner landscape would have had no character. Of course, there were some people who, with a dirty smirk, would say, "A Jewess is no Jew." But those were swine. For our kind it was impossible to fall in love with a Jewish girl. It meant being unfaithful to our flag. Love makes you long for intimacy, it leads to the most direct of all human relationships, and it was unthinkable to get into a human relationship with Jews. Jews were human beings, too; that could not be denied. But we did not have intimate relationships with other people, either, just because they were human beings. My father would not have anything to do with Rumanians, because they considered him part of a minority more or less equal with the Jews; nor with Poles, because they usually hated Austrians; nor would he have anything to do with other former Austrians who had stayed on in the Bukovina for mere personal interests, and not for a noble purpose like his, and who therefore had been unfaithful to their flag. That did not mean that we wouldn't regard them as human beings and behave like educated people when we came in contact with them. We answered every greeting more or less politely, with the same mixture of joviality and distance with which my grandmother in Vienna greeted the Raubitscheks, and, when it was inevitable, even shook hands with them, and, should the occasion have demanded it, we would presumably have done the same with the Jews of the Bukovina, the Polish Jews, unless they pretended they could come shooting with us. But that did not mean that we wished to enjoy a closer relationship either with them or with the Jews in general. As a matter of fact, it was not really true that we hated Jews. It was more a *façon de parler*. Hatred, too, is a direct human relationship. If there had been a real hatred for the Jews, it would have been just as much as loving them. No, Jews were simply people of another star—the star of David and Zion. It might be a shining star, but for us, unfortunately, it shone under the horizon. Therefore, falling in love with a Jewish girl could not be considered a pardonable perversion, like, for instance, that of a sodomite. It was *the* incomprehensible, a sudden gap in one's mind, worse than treason and breach of troth. I had good reason to be ashamed.

I would soon have some more, and better, reasons. Thanks to a few lessons from a skating teacher at the Wiener Eislaufverein, my circles and loops had very much improved. I was even capable of doing a few jumps. Home again in the Bukovina, I performed them in my corner of the skating rink. This aroused the curiosity of a group of sturdy youngsters—Jews, of course—who had formed a sort of wild hockey team. One day I found myself encircled by them. I felt a trifle uncomfortable, for they were tough and I did not know what they wanted. So I pretended not to notice their nearness and continued to perform a tidy eight with a Dutch jump at the conclusion of each circle. This went on for a while, till finally the biggest of them said, "Not bad, what you're doing. How about playing on our team?"

"No, thank you very much," I said.

"Why not? Because we're Jews?"

I did not answer and they came nearer.

"Well, what are you?" another of them asked. "A Rumanian? A Pole?"

"Neither the one nor the other."

"Well, then, what? A German?"

"No," I said. I felt an Austrian; that is: I was no German.

"But you speak German. So what the hell are you? A Jew, maybe?"

Why I did not answer I did not know at that moment. It was not cowardice, for it was obvious they meant me no harm. I did not like them very much; they were not my kind, and they were Jews. But I did not dislike them, either, and that made it worse. They had asked me to join their team, and here I stood and lacked the courage to say simply, "I would have liked to play with you, but I can't, because you are Jews and I am not, and I don't need to say any more. However, I thank you for having asked me." I did not fear hurting their feelings. What I feared was that open words of that kind could have meant the direct contact of which I was afraid. A direct human relationship could have resulted—esteem or hatred, either one, would have meant the same. I didn't answer.

"Well, speak, baby," one of them said and came so near that our noses nearly touched. "Are you a Jew or aren't you?"

I still kept silent, and finally the first one said, "Oh, leave him alone. He's only a stuck-up pissing goy." He threw the puck into the field, and they leaped after it, he with them, and there I stood alone again in my corner, with my beautifully tidy eights, and the huge shawl around my neck.

I believe that must have happened in the winter of 1927. I was thirteen or fourteen years old. In order to have the vagaries of my adolescence corrected, my benevolent and crazy parents, after a slight effort to have me tamed by a couple of relatives, put me in a Styrian boarding school renowned for its severe methods of education. To it I owe—along with the ever since vainly fought habit of smoking cigarettes and a profound knowledge of the pornographic folklore of the German and English languages—the insight that all public education's task is to vulgarize the genius of young people in such a way that only natures of extraordinarily strong neurotic tendencies are enabled to escape banality. The holidays I spent, usually, in the Bukovina, grateful for the utter loneliness that received me there, luckily freed for a few short summer weeks from the company of schoolmates in whose minds and muscles manhood fermented and from teachers deformed by their profession into baroque monstrosities. I passed my time hunting with my father in the Carpathian forests and walking the streets of Czernowitz and Sadagura, just watching and listening to what was going on. I don't know how I ever managed to pass my final examinations, for my midyear reports were catastrophic. My father, when he got the good news, sent me a cable with the single word *"Ahi!"*—an exclamation of Bukovinan Jews expressing unusual astonishment at the unexpected. Later, he explained that, in point of fact, the exclamation was a survival from the days of chivalry. Yiddish, he said, was mainly Middle High German, with Hebrew and Polish elements. For example, take the Yiddish expression "nebbish," which was nothing but the "squire" (*neb-ich:* "near I") who runs with the knight, carrying his shield. *"Ahi!"* was what the knights shouted when, at a tournament, they put their lances under their armpits and ran against one another.

This explanation was given to me not without a trace of embarrassment, for it was rather uncomfortable to think that the language of our models for a noble attitude of life should be faithfully preserved only by the Jews. Therefore my father did not fail to add that a certain decline of forms, as well as of habits and even of costumes, of the upper classes to the lower ones is the rule. The caftan of the rabbis, for instance, and their fur-lined caps and boots were actually the costume of Polish noblemen in medieval times, and a Jewish wedding preserved many a custom that originated in the court ceremonies of the dukes of Burgundy. It is about the only cultural-historical lesson put into my mind between my fourteenth and my seventeenth year that remains there today.

The diploma of a *Gymnasium* is a poor substitute for the rites of initiation with which primitive societies make a young male understand that he has become a man; yet in my youth nobody hesitated to take it as such. When I went back to Vienna, in order to follow in the footsteps of my late grandpapa and study architecture, I was merely a boy of seventeen, but I enjoyed all the liberties of a grown man, with none of the responsibilities. I could go to bed when and with whom I pleased, drink liquor to my heart's content and the revolt of my intestines, and spend my money and time as economically or wastefully as I felt like. My parents were not rich; my father's passion for hunting was expensive and soon devoured what the war had left of a former certain opulence. Yet, in the Bukovina, my monthly allowance would have sufficed to keep a Jewish family of seven from urgent need. Anyhow, I was not forced to begin my studies under the mental pressure of lack of time. But all this did not alter my solitude, which by now had become not only a habit but a deliberate, proud attitude. I did not have a single friend, and I did not long for one. With girls I was extremely clumsy and shy. Besides, my mother, fearing that I would abuse my new status and fall into debauchery, had arranged that I again live with my grandmother. Though my mother knew very well that the old lady was too much of a recluse to keep an eye on a young man, she counted on my aunts, whose theosophical preoccupations and love for dogs were evidence of a high morality that would perhaps keep me from immediately getting lost in a swamp of vices.

It was at this time I learned that we had done Mr. Malik an injustice by calling him a Jew. On the contrary, he was a man of high moral standards. A very important free and yet not reborn soul who had followed his invitation and slipped into the emptied vessel of the body of his sister, Miss Weingruber, a highly gifted medium, revealed to the esoteric community that great things were in preparation. The universe was a big system of perpetual perfection. Everything in it had but the sole wish to dematerialize more and more and finally become pure spirit and unite with God. *Materia* was the contrary of God. It was a burden given as a curse to the fallen angels, a curse put upon their souls, which were longing to be light and free again. Death did not mean you would be freed. When you died, your soul was suspended for a while outside the dimension perceivable to us and, in a sort of metaphysical extra course, was taught what was good and what was evil, and particularly to understand what it had done that was good or bad in the existence it had just left. If, in the former life, it had done much good, it was allowed to slip into a new existence less burdened with *materia*. If it had done a medium amount of good or evil, it had to come back to the same world in another existence and carry the same amount of *materia* and live again, trying to do better. If, on the other hand, it had done a great deal of wrong, it was condemned to a lower form of existence, even more burdened with *materia,* and slipped into a body that was not just flesh and bones, like ours, but—let us say—of stone or iron. Your soul, doing better and better each time, finally dematerialized into pure spirit and united with God.

Not only human souls were under the curse of *materia* but also your pet dog's, as a slightly lower form, and everything else—even the cobblestones on which Minka Raubitschek had broken her hip. And each creature or inanimate object was given the chance of doing good or evil and of dematerializing or materializing accordingly. And, of course, the stars and the planets on which you lived too had their chance, and when all the beings of a lower-grade star had done very well, the star itself potentialized and became a star of a higher category, with thinner *materia* and better souls on it. And this was going to happen to our globe.

My aunts were full of joy and expectation telling me about all this. By the good behavior of those who lived for the spirit, they said, our world had slowly potentialized and dematerialized and was now on the verge of potentializing into a nearly butterfly-like world. For there were very high-class souls—people like Buddha, Plato, and Jesus Christ—who deliberately took on the burden of *materia* in order to teach the others what was good or evil. Each of them was announced by some soul of a high category materialized for this very purpose. And as Jesus Christ had been announced by John the Baptist, Mr. Malik had come to announce the arrival of another dematerializer. His name was Adolf Hitler, and one could already see what enthusiasm he had created in Germany by spiritualizing the Germans and cleansing Germany of the low, materialistic Jews. Mr. Malik was no Jew, in spite of the fact that he had changed his name (as had Mr. Hitler, whose real name was Schicklgruber—and he certainly was no Jew, either); he had done this for a different reason, for Malik was the name given to him in the outer world—the name of his spirit. The name given to his material burden, which he had voluntarily undertaken to carry, was Weingruber. He and his sister were actually one high-category soul divided in two and inhabiting two bodies.

The potentialization of the world could already be felt in my grandmother's home by the fact that it, too, had to a certain extent been cleansed of Jews. No longer were the séances of the esoteric community accompanied by the chamber music of the Raubitscheks, for on the same day both Professor Raubitschek and his wife died of Spanish flu—a typical Jewish extravagance, as my grandmother said, because there was no epidemic, as in 1918, when many people died of it; therefore there was no cause to do it out of season, so to speak. Anyhow, they both died and left their daughter alone, and—alas!—what had been gained by their disappearance was largely spoiled by the scandalous behavior of Minka Raubitschek. Not only did she have an official lover, whose roadster often stood parked in front of the house all night, but other gentlemen were seen going into the Raubitschek apartment and coming out the morning after. Instead of chamber music on Wednesday evenings, one could hear the noises of carousing nearly every night.

I rather liked Minka. She was friendly when we met on the staircase. Her voice was full and warm, and her smile beautiful. She looked Spanish, with her shining black hair and large black eyes. Her skin was lovely, and she used a lipstick of a most provokingly vivid red. She dressed well, and even her slight limping had a certain charm; she did not try to hide it but limped ahead courageously and decidedly. On Sunday mornings, I was invited by my grandmother to breakfast in her room. From the window I could follow the spectacle of Minka's being called for by her official lover, a tall, fair, athletic chap, for their weekend outing. He was obviously an ice-hockey player. Sometimes he got into his roadster wearing his hockey uniform, vividly striped in red and white and yellow. Minka carried his sticks, kneepads, and shoulder pads. It all looked very smart and gay, and made me feel my isolation.

The courses in architecture at the Technische Hochschule bored me to tears. Instead of giving me a taste for harmony, the instructors tortured me with the theory of statics of rigid bodies, equations, the use of vectors, and so on, and I have always been a hopeless mathematician. Very soon I began to cut classes, and finally I did not go there for months at a time. I was too ignorant to enjoy either a concert or the theater. With the exception, perhaps, of a few operettas starring Fritzi Massary, I saw nothing of the good theater in Vienna of that time. My grandmother still kept a seat at the opera and never went there herself, so I drowsed through *Rheingold* and *La Traviata,* wondering why people sometimes sighed with delight and sometimes expressed their disapproval. But I walked a lot. I crisscrossed Vienna from one end to the other, sometimes walking as far as from Döbling to Hietzing, and then taking the tramway back. I walked, preferably at night, through the inner city, watching the swarms of whores on the Kärntnerstrasse. During the day, it was the most elegant of all Viennese streets, and at night it turned into something like the Canebière in Marseille. Or I would stand and marvel at the beauty of the empty Josefsplatz and Fischer von Erlach's National-Bibliothek, wondering why my grandfather had never achieved this perfection. Nobody cared that I came home at four o'clock in the morning, and old Marie had long since given up trying to wake me, knowing that I usually slept till noon.

But of course I was too proud to admit my solitude to anybody. I spent most of my money on clothes, and when I set out for a stroll in the afternoon I would be most elegantly dressed, like some young dandy who is just about to get into his car and drive out to the golf course at Lainz or to the five o'clock tea dance at Hübner's Park Hotel in Hietzing. In the evening, I never left the house except in a very smart dinner jacket or sometimes even, when I felt like it, in tails, with a silk hat on my well-brushed head. After a couple of hours of lonesome walking through empty streets and somber parks, along the tracks of railways or the banks of the Danube Canal, I would sit down for a coffee and a brandy in the lounge of the Hotel Imperial, slipping off my patent-leather pumps under the table to ease my sore feet. One would have thought I was a young man with an exquisite social life.

Once, well after midnight, I came home to my grandmother's house in tails and silk hat and found Minka at the door, fumbling in her handbag for the key she had either forgotten or lost.

She was amused at the misfortune of having no key, and at my arriving just in time to open the door. She was a little drunk. Her eyes sparkled, and her teeth shone moist between those provoking red lips. But, of course, I behaved like a well-bred young man. I unlocked the door and held it open for her with the particular politeness of a certain reserve, and she smiled at me and said I looked splendid. Where had I been, so elegantly clad? At a dance, I said. Where and with whom? With people she would certainly not know. What was their name? she asked. Oh, Rumanians, I said stiffly. It was typically Jewish, I thought, to be so insistent and to ask such personal questions, and I did not like it. The Rumanians were passing through Vienna, I said, on their way to Paris.

She knew frightfully amusing Rumanians in Paris, she said. Had I been there lately? Not lately, I said, following her up the stairs. The steps were flat and easy to mount, but she had a little difficulty with her lame hip and the one drink too many she might have had, so I offered her my arm, and she leaned against it freely. My elbow registered that she was not so bony as the fashion of the early 1930s demanded. It was delightful, and a little embarrassing, so when we reached my grandmother's floor, I stood still, and she let go of my arm and smiled again. "Thank you," she said. "You are charming."

"Would you like me to accompany you to your floor?" I asked, and then bit my lip at my own clumsiness.

She laughed. "Does it show that I'm drunk? I never realize it myself unless I have to get up these stairs on all fours. Come on, then, my young dandy, give me your arm again. . . . I once broke that silly left hip of mine," she said, leaning trustfully against the length of my body. "Because I was in love—imagine! If I had gone on that way, I wouldn't have a sound bone in my body. How are you making out with the girls?"

"Well . . . ," I said, and smiled shyly, as if I were too modest to tell her the full truth.

She laughed. I said nothing more. I wasn't quite sure she hadn't seen through me and just been teasing me. "Would you like to come inside for a nightcap?" she asked when we arrived at her door.

"Thank you very much."

"Thank you, yes, or thank you, no?" She looked straight into my eyes.

"Yes," I said, and felt that I was blushing.

She handed me a key and said, "Fortunately, I haven't lost this one."

Again I unlocked the door and held it open, and she went in, dropping her fur coat on the floor. I picked it up and put it on a chair. "What nice manners you have," she said. "It must be lovely to have you around. How old are you?"

It seemed too silly to say "I'm going to be eighteen next May," so I lied. "Twenty-three."

"Just my cup of tea. There is a phonograph in the corner. Put on a record if you want some music. What will you drink? Whiskey, or a brandy?"

"A whiskey with soda, please." The flat did not look at all as I had imagined it would. She must have redecorated it since the death of the old Raubitscheks. With the exception of a huge library with black carved-wood bookcases that could have belonged to the chamber-music-loving Professor Raubitschek, there was no trace of the particular Jewish-middle-class stuffiness I had had glimpses of through open windows at home in the Bukovina. There were flowers all over the place—her lovers seemed to be quite generous, I thought. Through an open door I could see into her bedroom, gay and feminine, the huge bed covered with a soft, flowery comforter. While she fixed the drinks, I had a look at the records. There were masses of them, piled up carelessly around the phonograph. I put one on with the label "Star Dust," hoping it was Mozart and not as violent as Beethoven's "Allergique." With the first sweet sounds, she came toward me with the drinks. "Here's yours," she said, putting a glass in my hand. "Let's see how you dance." I did not know what to do with my glass, but finally took it in my left hand and put my other arm around her, and we danced a few steps. I could not feel that she limped. "All right," she said, and moved away from me. "A little stiff, but there is hope. I can't dance long, because of my hip, but I love it."

I took a gulp of my whiskey. She dropped down on the couch, leaned back, and shut her eyes. Suddenly she yawned, her beautiful mouth wide open. She yawned with a melodious cry that sounded like a happy weeping and that faded away in a sigh of utter relaxation, at the end of which she opened her eyes and said, "You are sweet. Now go downstairs to your grandma and sleep well." She got up with an unexpected swiftness and went to her bedroom, already unbuttoning her dress in the back.

I stood still in bewilderment, not knowing what to think of all this, not even knowing whether I had imagined something else would happen or what—just simply not knowing how to put my glass down and say "Good night" and "See you soon." She turned and looked at me, still fumbling with buttons at her back. "If you don't want to go," she said, "you can listen to a few more records, if you like. But don't mind if I fall asleep. I'm dog-tired."

I felt humiliated to the core. The situation was totally out of my control, and I wished I'd never accepted her invitation to come in for a nightcap. But, on the other hand, she was so kind, and sweet, and pretty. Her mouth had excited me.

She had turned round fully and stood watching me. Then she came toward me, smiling, and before I could say anything she took my head in both hands and kissed me softly and affectionately. Then she smiled again, close to me, under my eyes, and said, "What's all this? Do you want to stay with me?" I didn't answer. Still looking into my face, she said softly, "Then come!"

She very soon found out the full truth about my worldliness, and it seemed to touch her. She was all sweet understanding, treating me with a tenderness and intimacy I had never known before or even been able to imagine. If it had been possible for me to think such a monstrous thought, I should have called it gay and tender lovemaking with a sister.

I put "Star Dust" on the phonograph again, and we lay in the dark and listened till it came to an end. She laughed and said, "Won't your grandma be upset when she finds out that you've been with me in the middle of the night?"

"She doesn't necessarily need to know."

"Well, certainly not. But she will find out sooner or later. I want to have you around, you are so cozy."

I said, "May I put on that record once more?"

"You do like it, don't you? Well, it's yours. You can take it with you and play it till you can't stand it anymore."

"Thank you."

"I wish I had a little more money, so I could buy you things you like. I have always longed for a little brother to spoil. What is your name?"

"Arnulf."

"What?" she cried, with an outburst of her delightful laughter. "It can't be true. Arnulf! Who ever thought of such a dreadful name?"

"My father," I said, smiling against my will. "It comes from his mother's family; they're Bavarians. I think he thought it would oblige me to behave like a good knight." I sighed. Yet I was very much amused myself.

"But you can't possibly expect me to call you Arnulf," she said.

"Well, I have a few more Christian names. I have about half a dozen. Other people I know have up to fifteen."

"Don't tell me. I expect your other names are even worse. No, I shall call you Brommy—that fits you very well."

"Why, and how?"

"Oh, I don't know. It simply fits you."

"Did you have a pet dog with that name?"

"No. I don't know where I got it from—there was an admiral, I think."

"What have I to do with an admiral?"

"Lots. You are very much like a young cadet who will become an admiral someday. And you don't want me to call you Wilhelm von Tegetthoff."

I laughed. The totally illogical jump was typically Jewish. It sounded like one of the surrealistic jokes that were told in the Bukovina about the merry rabbis of the Hasidim and their shrewdly twisted logic. I could not help feeling very much at home with Minka.

"Now, come," she said. "Be a good boy and let's get some sleep."

She did not send me away. She simply put her arms around me and curled close to me, and instantly fell into a deep and innocent sleep, smelling of well-groomed feminine hair and skin, good perfume, and a little whiskey. I lay for a while with open eyes, listening to the fading sounds of "Star Dust," which was now mine, and thinking how funny it was that at the very moment you got mixed up with Jews you changed your name. Soon I, too, fell asleep, my arms around her.

I have often wondered since whether I had an affair with Minka. Whatever it was, it did not interfere in the slightest with her amorous life, and though it altered my life completely, there seemed not the faintest tie that would have given me the impression that I couldn't do whatever I pleased. From that first morning—when I woke in her arms and watched her face, so fresh and well rested, and she opened her dark eyes and, with joyful laughter, said, "Now, who are *you?* Surely not the boy from downstairs?"—we were together day and night. "I am getting so accustomed to having him in my bed," she would explain to her friends—among whom some were even a little more than friends. "Like a child with its teddy bear. He doesn't kick or snore. He's just sweet and appetizing." And, turning to the nearest female in the circle, "If you really want a good night's sleep, I'll lend him to you."

Of course, there were also moments when she said to me, "Listen, my dear Brommy, there is a certain gentleman who is arriving from Paris, so would you do me a great favor and go skiing with Bobby? He's treating, so you needn't spend your pocket money on that. And please don't show up around here before next Friday."

Bobby was her official lover—the fair, athletic chap who skied and played ice hockey and swam and rode horseback. We had become great friends. "You know, my boy," he would explain to me, "if it were any other girl, you'd become jealous. But not with Minka. First, it would be pointless. Second, she wouldn't let you. She makes it quite clear to you that it's not you who possess her, it's she who possesses you. Now, since she is not jealous of you, what right have you to be jealous of her? It's as simple as that."

There was no use trying to explain to him, or anybody else, that our relationship was, in fact, relatively—and even in great proportion—innocent. When Minka and I went to bed together, it was mainly to curl up in one another's arms and fall asleep. It gave her comfort to have someone near. I have sometimes thought that it may have been an atavism or, let us say, a tradition that she had inherited, like the passion for hunting and shooting among our kind. After all, many of her ancestors must have slept six in one bed, like most of the poor Jews in Galicia and in the Bukovina. But certainly such an explanation would not have helped my grandmother or aunts to understand my affection for Minka; in their eyes it would have made things even worse. In fact, it was all rather scandalous, and I was afraid my father would hear about it—particularly as neither my grandmother nor my aunts gave the slightest sign of knowing what was going on. That they knew perfectly well I could detect from old Marie's trembling resentment whenever I went up to Minka's flat or came down from it, and the resentment increased when the hours I spent downstairs in my room became short intervals between the sojourns upstairs at Minka's. I could only pray to God that the hatred of my mother's relatives for my father would not allow them to give him the satisfaction of saying that it was not surprising I got involved with Jews while staying in their house. He had always warned my mother against her own family, and he would no doubt say that it was her fault for letting me go to Vienna, instead of—as he had wished—sending me to Graz, the capital of Styria, where there were fewer Jews.

There is an old saying that when you change your life you also change your ideas. This is not necessarily so. You can very well change your life and in the meantime send your ideas, so to speak, on a holiday. My life had changed entirely, and though I kept right on disliking Jews, I lived among them—for most of Minka's friends were Jews—from then on. One of them, a monstrously fat and ugly yet highly amusing journalist from Prague, who regularly came to Vienna as a theater critic, gave me the password. Once, after a brief encounter with a well-known actor who was not a Jew and who had treated him with special friendliness, he turned toward me and said, "My mother used to say, 'More than of an anti-Semite, my boy, beware of people who just love Jews.'" Right she was, I thought, laughing heartily. For disliking Jews was not something you could change. It was an inborn reaction that did not hinder you from even liking them in a certain way. I liked Minka tremendously, and if she hadn't been a Jewess, I would have fallen madly in love with her and, in spite of my eighteen years (and to her utter amusement, I presume), probably have asked her to marry me. But even when she woke up in my arms and I in hers, after an innocent night's sleep, there was a taboo that controlled my feelings and made everything even more delightful. I felt so free and unburdened with her. As she said, she liked having me around. She could not take me seriously as a lover. I was her toy, and everything was light and nice and uncomplicated. She could summon me and send me away whenever she wanted. I asked no questions, and she could tell me everything. We would both laugh at our particular adventures and misfortunes, share our joys, our money, our problems. Her girlfriends were sweet and of a charming libertinage. I can't remember a time in my life since when I have had such pleasures. She was the queen of a little kingdom that for a while became my universe, and I served her as a page. The day began with her morning bath and toilet, and I either came up to her flat for it or was already there, ready to wait on her. She was severe and not at all patient. Very soon I learned everything a young man can be taught about a lady's boudoir. I accompanied her to her dressmaker, her hairdresser, her shopping, her brief luncheon at the Café Rebhuhn, where the artists and intellectuals who had chosen it for their head-quarters were great friends of hers. She took me to museums, to concerts, to the theater, to dinner parties, and to the *Heurigen*—the tasting of the new wine in the vineyards of the nearby village of Grinzing. That little kingdom of hers, which became my uni-verse, was composed of all that was best in Vienna in the early 1930s, the most intellectual and most amusing. Her friends came to her home as birds fly in and out of the foliage of a tree. Among them was Karl Kraus, who at that time was considered merely a satirist but whose life stands as an example of moral uprightness and courage which should be put before anyone who writes, in no matter what language. Thanks to Minka, I had, at the age of eighteen, the privilege of listening to his con-versation and watching his face, lit up by the pale fire of his fanatic love for the miracle of the German language and by his holy hatred for those who used it badly. There was also a young man, not a Jew, who was a gifted musician. "Come on, Herbert," Minka would say, "play something on the piano." Many years later, I remembered that his name was von Karajan.

What gave me the right to stand my ground among those people was a rather strange talent Minka had discovered in me. Not for nothing had I passed a great part of my childhood and adolescence amidst Polish Jews. While walking through the streets of Czernowitz and Sadagura and Lvov, I had kept my ears open, and I spoke better Yiddish and knew more of the cus-toms and behavior of the so-called Polish Jews than most of the refined Jews of Vienna or even Prague. I was an expert in all shades of Jewish slang and the way Jews spoke when they wanted to speak select German. And when somebody told a Jewish story, which at that time, and especially among Jewish intellec-tuals, was cultivated as an art, and told it badly, Minka would impatiently interrupt him, saying, "Come on, don't bore us. Tell your story in a low voice to Brommy, and he'll tell it to us much better than you do." If for some reason she chose not to interrupt the imperfect storyteller, she and I would exchange a short, vague, yet significant look, very much in the way that my eyes would meet those of my mother or father, my grandmother or my aunts, when somebody who was not of our kind committed some lapse of manners or language. If, on the other hand, some master told a Jewish story to perfection, then Minka would pull my sleeve and say, "Pay attention, Brommy!"

Brommy. . . . It was a name of quite another form of existence, which ran parallel to my existence as son, grandson, and nephew—very much as Guru Malik within the esoteric community of my aunts led a life parallel to that of brave engineer Weingruber, who lived his petit bourgeois life as an employee of the Styria Motor Company. Once, when someone called me on the telephone, one of my aunts answered, and afterward she asked me with an expression of amazement, "What do your . . . friends call you? 'Brommy'? But you have such nice other Christian names. What a regrettable lack of taste."

Furious, without knowing why, I said, "You mind your own business!"

"Now, really!" she exclaimed. "Have we come to the point where boys of your age speak to adults in such a way? Don't forget, you're only eighteen, after all."

I certainly did not forget it. It weighed on me that I had lied to Minka about my age. One day I could bear it no longer. We had been talking about some of her troubles, and she said, "It's astonishing how understanding you are for your age, my boy."

"Minka," I said, "there's something I have to confess. I lied to you."

"What about?" she said and smiled. "Oh, I see. You want to tell me that in fact there *is* a drop of Jewish blood in you."

"No," I said. "I am sorry there isn't. But I'm not twenty-three. I am only eighteen."

"What? But you're not serious?"

From then on, she treated me as a sort of wonder child. "Would you believe it? He's only eighteen!" They probably all thought I was Jewish, and were proud of my precocity.

Well, it did not go on forever, alas. Very soon I was nineteen, and at twenty I had to do my military service in Rumania, and my gay time in Vienna was over. But it was soon replaced by another fascinating experience. I now became aware that I knew almost nothing about the country I belonged to, the Rumanian people, or their language. In order to fill that gap, a young Rumanian student was hired to teach me Rumanian and something of Rumanian literature and history, and I not only formed friendships with my tutor and some other young Rumanians which have lasted till today but also learned the historical past of the three Rumanian principalities—Moldova (to which the Bukovina had once belonged), Muntenia, and Oltenia—and their struggle to unite against their Turkish oppressors and Phanariot rulers and become a nation and the kingdom of Rumania. By tracing some rather remote lineage of my pedigree until it found root in Rumania, I was able to justify my newly discovered love for that country and my claim to belong there not merely as part of a former Austrian minority but by inheritance. Then I exchanged my first name, Arnulf, for the third of my Christian names, Gregor, which also happened to be the Christian name of some half-Greek, half-Russian ancestor originating in Bessarabia and beautifully outfitted with a Turkish wife. My father watched with intense disapproval my Rumanian friendships and my attempts to tie myself genealogically to Rumania, but by that time I had—thanks to Minka Raubitschek—acquired a certain independence of mind, and when my father said that he loathed the Bukovina and if it hadn't been for the Carpathians would long since have left it, I said boldly that, according to my taste, it was better to have a free outlook over a lovely rolling country with a vast horizon than to be always running your nose against some stone wall, as in Styria. Whereupon my father turned his back, and did not speak to me for a couple of weeks.

I came back to Vienna in the summer of 1937 as Gregor, sporting an enormous Phanariot mustache. I hurried upstairs to embrace Minka and break the news that I was in love. It was not a very happy love story, though, for the lady in question was married, and, to make matters worse, I liked her husband very much. Minka, as usual, was full of understanding, comfort, and good advice. We passed a few gay days together, but no night. I had outgrown my teddy-bear stage and, besides, would have considered it treason to my love to sleep soundly in another woman's bed instead of lying alone, sighing for her. I was going to meet her shortly in Salzburg, where she wanted to attend the festival. Minka took me to the station. Looking up at me while I looked down at her from the open window of my compartment in the train, she saw my excited happiness. Her eyes shone tenderly, with a strange, more profound tenderness than ever. "If you were wise," she said, "you would now get off this train and never see that girl again."

"What do you mean?"

"Everything you have had with her so far is beautiful—all promise and expectation. Now come the troubles."

"Oh, don't talk rot. We are going to be very happy."

"I do hope so," she said. "I am very, very fond of you, you know."

The train started up, and I sat back in my seat in a state of bewilderment. It could not be that Minka was in love with me, could it? No, that was impossible. Yet the thought flattered my vanity, and, rather the prouder for it, I looked forward to meeting my adored one.

Minka was right. Things became frightfully complicated, and Salzburg in the summer of 1937 was just awful. It was overrun with Jews. The worst of them had come from Germany as refugees and, in spite of their luggage-laden Mercedes cars, behaved as if they were the victims of a cruel persecution and therefore had the right to hang around in hundreds at the Café Mozart, criticize everything, and get whatever they wanted faster and cheaper—if not for nothing—than anybody else. They spoke with that particular Berlin snottiness that so got on the nerves of anyone brought up in Austria, and my sharp ears could all too easily detect the background of Jewish slang. My Turkish blood revolted. I could have slaughtered them all. I fled to Styria, for a visit to my old boarding school, and then followed my ladylove back to Rumania.

When I came back to Vienna again, it was February 1938, and what I found was chaos. Minka had come to fetch me at the station. She merely said, "Poor boy, I am afraid that your aunts' guru is right and the Weingrubers and Schicklgrubers and Schweingrubers will soon potentialize the world." Most of her friends—Bobby among them—had already gone to Switzerland, she said, or England, or France, or were preparing to leave Austria even at the price of their material existence.

"Oh, don't exaggerate," I said. "You Jews are always making a fuss about something. What in the world is going on, anyway?"

"Poldi will explain it to you. We're having dinner with him. You just listen to what he has to say."

Poldi was the fat journalist from Prague, who, as a theater critic, went regularly not only to Vienna but also to Berlin. He had lost a lot of weight and was not half so amusing as he used to be. What irritated me most of all was the self-complacent way he treated me—and I could not rise to the occasion, because he resolutely kept aiming at my cultural gaps. "I understand that we have sworn off allegiance to the ancestor of the Carolingians," he greeted me, "even though the mustache is downright Merovingian." And when I shook my head uncomprehendingly, he went on, "I mean, we are no longer calling ourselves Arnulf, now, but Gregor. Good, very good. Gregory the Great, as we all know, was a protector of the Jews."

I dryly answered that this was certainly not the reason I had been given this name, and he threw in, "Very well, let's stay with the Carolingians. We are then not far from Bishop Agobard, and we can look forward to a new *De insolentia Judaeorum* or, even worse, a new *De Judaicis superstitionibus* with a few blood libels. Today, you see, there are two schools of thought—two camps, I must involuntarily say: one outside and one inside the concentration camps. And uncomfortable as the latter may be, it is, still and all, the only one for decent people."

"And I would rather end up there myself than let Brommy get in," said Minka. "But just tell him seriously how things look politically. He's straight out of the Middle Ages, you know. That's where his father lives, in the Carpathians."

Now I realized that Poldi's irony was put on in order to conceal an enormous fear. Most of the things he told us, in a whisper, looking around to make sure he wasn't overheard, did not make much sense to me. In the landscape of my mind, politics had not figured prominently. As a subject of Rumania—that is, of His Majesty King Carol II—I knew, and was expected to know, that he was the sovereign of a constitutional monarchy, and that in Bucharest there was a parliament where deputies represented the party of the peasants and the party of the liberals and whatnot, and that they were a bunch of crooks who did nothing but steal the money of the state. There were also some Jews, who were Communists, and therefore, rightly, were treated as such—that is, as Russian spies and agents provocateurs. But fortunately there were also some young Rumanians who, under their leader, a certain Mr. Cuza—which was a good and noble name, though only adopted by that gentleman—beat up those Jews from time to time, thus keeping them in a hell of a fright, and preventing them from spreading more Communist propaganda and provocation. I knew, too, that in Austria there were many socialists, called Reds, who were beaten up by or beat up the Heimwehr, which was a national guard defending the ethical values—such as the cleanliness of mind guaranteed by the fresh mountain air, and the love for shooting goats and plucking edelweiss—of Styria, Tirol, Carinthia, and others of the old Austrian lands. With the help of the Heimwehr, Chancellor Dollfuss had cannonaded the Reds, only to be shot down later by a Nazi. Nazis, in Austria, were rowdies who dynamited telephone booths, but that was not necessarily true of German Nazis, who, after all, had done very well. They had built up a state of order, and justice, and genuine social welfare, in spite of the fact that Adolf Hitler was a frightful proletarian, as my father said, and looked exactly like a Bohemian footman my grandmother had once employed, against his advice. The footman turned out to be a thief and stole my father's cuff links and some other items, including a very nice hunting knife. Only people like my mother's family could be wrong about somebody with such a face, my father said.

The Reds were bad because they were proletarians and wanted to do away with people of our kind, as had happened in Russia. Jews had a fatal inclination for Reds; therefore they ought to be kept in a hell of a fright, so they would keep quiet. Nazis were also proletarians, but they had some very sound ideas, like the theory of breeding, and some exemplary laws about hunting only in season, which gave the game the chance to regenerate and even improve in number as well as in size. And on the whole they were against Jews and Reds, so it was quite obvious that we had to stick with them. I really did not think there was much more to the subject, and I got rather bored with Poldi's Cassandra-like whispering, so I proposed that we go to the Kärntnerbar for a whiskey. If, as Poldi said, the Germans wanted to conquer Austria, so much the better. The German-speaking peoples would be united again, as they had been in the Holy Roman Empire of Charlemagne. And if the Jews were frightened, it served them right. It would keep them from becoming Russian spies and propagandists of Communism and also make them behave a little more decently at the Salzburg Festival. As for the reaction of the English and French and so on, they should mind their own business. I did not see any reason to start a war just because the German-speaking peoples did what the Czechs and Poles and Rumanians had been encouraged to do by the very same French and English. Of course, I did not say any of this to Poldi and Minka, because they were friends and it would have hurt their feelings. So we went to the Kärntnerbar.

When Minka went to the Kärntnerbar, it was the crest of the wave. We let her down to the ladies' room by a rope and pulled her up again, and Poldi became his old self and was highly amusing. At three o'clock in the morning, we found ourselves in the beer cellar of the Paulanerbräu, sitting between a stone-drunk chap—who shouted in a loud voice that he was a former cavalry officer with a golden decoration for bravery and the official title of the Hero of Zaleszczyki—and a shy little tart I knew fairly well from midnight strolls on the Kärntnerstrasse. We had hardly had a spoonful of our goulash soup and a sip of beer when a huge, rather shabby-looking young man roared in our faces, *"Juden raus!"* "Jews out!"

The former cavalry officer got up in stiff dignity and said that he felt offended by having been called a Jew, and would the gentleman instantly follow him to the men's room in the basement in order to fix the place and conditions of the duel. Poldi pushed him back on his stool. The rowdy then, surprisingly, sat down on the other side of the little tart and stared with a dull expression at the wooden table. Suddenly he lifted his head and looked at me. "Don't you remember me, you swine?" he roared. "Arnulf! I'm Oskar. Oskar Koloman."

I could scarcely believe my eyes. He was one of the boys at the boarding school in Styria, a good deal older than I but in the same class. "Where the hell have you come from?" I asked.

He rose to his full height and volume. "You really want to know?" He nearly fell over the table in the attempt to grasp my shoulder. "Come with me to the men's room in the basement. I'll *tell* you where I've come from."

"I think you'd better go," Minka said, in a low voice. "It'll give Poldi and me a chance to disappear."

I followed my schoolmate past a row of gentlemen standing against a tarred wall, showing us their backs, till he found a gap where we could stand next to one another. He had that very day been released from Steinhausen, the Austrian concentration camp for Nazis under the regime of Chancellor Schuschnigg. As one of a group of Nazi students, he had blown up a telephone booth in Graz and had been caught doing it. He had spent three years in the camp. "For a cigarette butt no bigger than this," he howled into my face, showing as well as he could with his thick fingers how small, "for such a tiny little butt, they made me clean the latrines for a week!" Then, hammering his fists against the tarred wall, "They have forsaken us! They have betrayed us—our brethren of the Reich! They left us in the mire while they became great and mighty. Now they will come and take over here, too!" He leaned his forehead against the wall and wept.

So that was Austria. Hadn't my father been right to keep out of it? Again I fled to the clean mountains of Styria to ski for a couple of weeks. I had nothing to do anyway but wait for the lady I still loved. We had made an appointment to meet in Vienna on the eleventh of March. I was there a day earlier, and felt as if I had wandered into a madhouse. A sort of regimented revolution was going on under the watchful eyes of fat Viennese policemen in long bottle-green coats. On one side of the Kärntnerstrasse, people with swastikas in their buttonholes promenaded, shouted *"Heil!"* and sneered at the people on the other side. The people on the other side, young workers—many Jews among them—shook their fists at the Nazis and shouted *"Rotfront!"* I could not get hold of Minka, who was helping relatives in Mödling prepare their departure, somebody in the Café Rebhuhn told me. So I went home to my grandmother's flat, where I found that my beloved had already arrived in Vienna and would be waiting for me next evening at ten o'clock in an apartment house on the Opernring. I did not go out all the next day but spent the day in great uneasiness waiting for the telephone to ring. The cable with that precise information could only mean that something had gone wrong. But no call came. When I left the house at a quarter to ten, the streets were strangely dark and empty. I walked the short distance from the Florianigasse to the Rathaus, and through the Rathaus arcade—

one of my grandfather's dubious architectural masterpieces. Coming out, I found myself in the middle of an uncanny procession. In blocks that in their disciplined compactness seemed made of cast iron, people marched by thousands, men only, in total silence. The morbid, rhythmic stamping of their feet hung like a gigantic swinging cord in the silence that had fallen on Vienna. This cord seemed to originate somewhere in the outskirts. I could detect it through the length of the Alserstrasse, then winding round toward the Rathaus and leading down the Ringstrasse. Parades of all kinds were not rare in Vienna. They were nearly always led by a detachment of streetcar conductors and were in protest against something or other—unemployment, or the rise in the price of milk, or the pollution of the city water, brought in from the clean mountains of Styria by aqueducts. But this was different. It had an uncomfortably decisive character. I tried to break through between the blocks, but I did not succeed. Two or three times I asked a bystander what was going on, and got no answer. Impatient, fearing I would be late for the appointment with my beloved, I squeezed myself into the last row of a marching block and marched with them.

"What the hell are we marching for?" I asked the man beside me.

"*Anschluss,*" he barked.

Well, that literally meant "connection," and that was exactly what I was looking for. If I could march with them down to the Opernring and get out of the parade there, I'd be in time for my appointment. But they wouldn't let me. I was pushed out. I had come far enough to see the full height of the tower of the Rathaus, toward which the marchers turned their heads, starry-eyed. The tower was surmounted by the statue of a knight in armor, a statue I had loved as a child, so I turned my head, too, and saw a huge flag hanging down from the tower's peak, attached to my knight's armored feet—a red flag with a white circle, in which there was a black swastika. "So that's it. It's come, finally," I said to myself. "Austria has united with the German Reich."

It was not unexpected. For weeks people had spoken of little else. Yet how did all these people know that it would happen this very night? And how, for heaven's sake, did they know their place in the serried ranks? They must have been drilled for months—but where? In cellars? Austrian Nazis had been underground up to this moment, an underground everybody knew about and spoke about quite openly and—with the exception of Jews and Reds, of course—with a certain sympathy. And now here it was. The whole male population of Vienna seemed to be marching in that silent parade. I felt a sudden resentment at being left out. After all, I was an Austrian myself; I had been born under the flag of the double-headed eagle as well as they, and though I was a subject of Rumania, it seemed unjust to deny me a place in one of their marching blocks as if I were a Red, or even a Jew. Politically, too, I wasn't much different from them. Anyway, the event in itself was something I welcomed, even if I didn't much care for the *Pieffkes* (as we Austrians called Germans). These people probably didn't care for them either. Oskar Koloman had already expressed his disillusion. In any case, the unity of the Reich was restored. The dream of a century had come true. Such a political reversal would change many things, perhaps even the decision of my beloved to get a divorce from her husband, whom, unfortunately, I liked so much. There was a promise of hope in the atmosphere. In spite of that uncanny silence all over Vienna, something was happening, something important, and not merely a protest against the diminishing size of *Wiener Kipfeln*—the beloved Viennese croissants—and the pollution of the city water. Again and again I inserted myself into the marching blocks, trying to keep step so it wouldn't be too obvious that I did not belong, and was pushed out of the ranks each time. At last, I came to the Opernring and hurried up the staircase of a certain house, and there she was. We both burst into hysterical laughter. "Can you imagine!" we said. "What an effort to celebrate our union!"

It wasn't a union, though; it was the opposite. With great emotion, and not without tears, she had to tell me that in spite of all her love for me she couldn't divorce the man whom we both liked so much. She had been married to him for too many years. It was the old story of an engagement more or less arranged by their parents; then, suddenly, she had felt that she could not marry him, and was about to tell him so when he went on a trip, and while she was waiting for him to come back so she could tell him how she really felt, he wrote her such charming, loving letters that—well, she finally married him. And he had been sweet to her and decent, and everything I knew so well, too, and—well, that was that. I had to accept it.

Next morning, we stood at the windows and looked down at the Opernring, now empty, where all the night through there had been ecstasy—a sudden ecstasy that had its source in the silent marching blocks, and that drew people out of their houses and made them run toward the marchers, shouting, roaring, embracing one another, swinging flags with swastikas, throwing their arms to heaven, jumping and dancing in delirium. It was an icy-cold yet gloriously sunny day, quite unusual for the middle of March. It was so cold that you would not allow your dog to stay outdoors for longer than five minutes. There was nobody as far as you could see except two or three of the old hags, wrapped, onionlike, in layers of frocks and coats, who sold flowers in the New Market. They were running across the Ring and throwing their roses and carnations in the air, yelling *"Heil!"* What did they have to do with it, anyway? Over the radio we had learned that Austria was about to unite with the German Reich, and the Germans were expected to come here triumphantly, as our brethren, in a huge parade, under a rain of flowers. And that the great unifier and renewer of the German-speaking peoples, Adolf Hitler, was also about to arrive in Austria any moment and would come down the Danube, the old stream of the Nibelungen, to Vienna, the former capital of the Holy Roman Empire.

She stood at one window, I at another. I turned my head toward her and saw her face, pale and suffering. I knew it was not only because we had to part but also for that clear, icy-cold emptiness outside. Out of a sudden intuition, without even thinking about how cruel it was, I said, "I know how you feel about what happened out there last night." She swung her head round and looked coldly at me. "You feel," I said, "precisely the way you did on the day of your marriage." She covered her face with both her hands. "I can't help feeling the same," I said. "We are at a wedding day of sad promise."

I could have gone back to Rumania or somewhere else. But I felt that, at last, I should do something properly. I had wasted so much time, never finishing—if you could say I had ever seriously begun—my studies. Also, there was promise in the air, even if the appearance in Vienna of the great Führer of the now Greater Germany had turned out to be sort of a flop. His voice blared through the loudspeakers, over the heads of some million ecstatic listeners who were crammed together in a compact mass that covered the Heldenplatz. But the voice was choked by emotion (or by the rhythmic uproar of some million voices' *"Sieg Heil! Sieg Heil! Sieg Heil!"*) and could only stutter, "I—I—I—I—I am just so happy!" In spite of all that, as I say, there seemed to be born a new reality, clearer, more transparent, more energetic, more dynamic. It felt as if the fresh mountain air of Styria were blowing through Vienna. Then several divisions of the German Army came down the Danube, in marching blocks that were even more solid, more resolute, more dangerous, in their silence and gray metallic hats, than the ones on the night of *Anschluss*. After that, German civilians swarmed in and took everything into their administering hands. They filled that mountain air with their snotty Berlin slang and, to our utmost surprise, cynically mocked the great Führer and the Nazi Party, so that the Austrians had to take over the task of enthusiastic confirmation that everything was wonderful, really great, marvelous—particularly my aunts, who had now interrupted their *Anschluss* with the world beyond and entirely devoted themselves to the Nazi Women's Union. Mr. Malik, I learned, not only had become the leader of his department at the Styria Motor Company (which very soon united with a German company and disappeared) but also was a *Sturmbannführer* of the SS—a very mighty position, so I had better make friends with him and stop saying that his real name was Schweingruber. Old Marie, for whose senile eyes the victorious symbol "SS" read "44," insisted that he would be made a colonel of the 44th Regiment of the Imperial Infantry, which, as a young girl, she had very much admired. My grandmother shut herself in her rooms and received nobody. Coming back from Mass, she had been laughed at and shouted at in the open street, and nearly manhandled, by a handful of young rowdies who were forcing a group of Jews to wash slogans for the Schuschnigg regime off the wall of a house. Among those Jews, my grandmother recognized a physician who had once cured one of my aunts of a painful otitis media, and she interfered, attacking the young rowdies with her umbrella and shouting that this was going too far. Only the interference of Sturmbannführer Guru Malik saved her from serious trouble.

As for Minka, she was in despair. Of course, I had seen her immediately after the first big events. We were together a few days later when *Anschluss* was officially declared, in an impressive ceremony that we followed on the radio. And there was a rather embarrassing moment when, for the first time, we heard the "Deutschland, Deutschland über Alles" and she burst into tears. "Listen, old girl," I said to her, "it's not all that bad. It's just the first letting out of an old hatred that will soon calm down. Don't be afraid. It appears they really want to build discipline and order."

She turned to me and shouted, "Don't you realize, you imbecile, that it's the 'Gott Erhalte,' our old Imperial Austrian anthem, composed by our Haydn, that they've embezzled for their dirty anthem of Greater Germany? Why, it's a breach of . . . troth!"

Troth. She must have used it quite unconsciously, without a second thought as to the word's immeasurable profundity. This made me rather pensive for a couple of days. She was right: an incredible breach of troth was taking place all around us, but which troth was actually being broken? One already sensed that the faith, the pure enthusiasm with which this transformation had been yearned for and then greeted, was being betrayed. Troth itself was betrayed, I thought. For instance, the troth to the old empire. This Reich had no more to do with my dream of the Holy Roman Empire than with the glorious dream of the Habsburg Dual Monarchy. But I was soon tired of brooding about it. After all, I was a Rumanian, and even if I had been an Austrian, how could I have prevented what all the other Austrians obviously welcomed? I felt frightfully sorry for Minka and all our friends, but it was not my fault that they happened to be Jews, and in the event that they got into serious trouble I could use my connections with the SS to help them out again.

These connections were by no means limited to Sturmbann-führer Malik. I had run into my old schoolmate Oskar Koloman again, and this time he looked prim and tidy, in a splendid black uniform, with the insignia of an even higher rank than that of *Sturmbannführer.* "*Heil,* Arnulf," he greeted me. "How is it you're in civilian clothes? Don't you want to join us?"

"I am Rumanian, you know."

"That means nothing. You were born an Austrian. Sooner or later, all German-speaking people will come home to the Reich. I can easily arrange for you to change your nationality."

"I'll think it over," I said. "Thank you anyhow."

"You were a fairly good skater, and not bad at horseback riding, as I recall. We need sporting types, you know. We have some excellent horses at the Mounted SS. Come and ride them, if you want. What are you doing otherwise?"

"Well, I'm trying to get on with architecture. But it bores me stiff."

"You see! Studying bored me, too. That's why I amused myself blowing up a telephone booth. It cost me three years, all right, but look what I've become now. Not bad, hey? You can have the same if you want. But tell me"—he looked at me mistrustfully—"don't you have contact with Jews? I remember that dark girl you were with when we met again for the first time."

"Oh, she's a Turk," I said, and laughed.

"A Turk. I understand." He laughed, too. "However, a Jewess is no Jew, and a Turkish girl even less. I do understand, you old swine. Now, don't be a fool, and come riding one of these days?"

I did. They had excellent horses. I rode one that had belonged to the Rothschilds, and was very good indeed. The cavalrymen were fantastic yokels. They clicked their heels and threw up their arms and shouted *"Heil Hitler!"* every time they saw me. Sometimes I had the impression they did not take it seriously themselves, because they tried so hard to *do* it seriously. On the whole, they seemed quite harmless, happy with their uniforms and their obsolete importance. Oskar, in order to avoid silly questions about my riding there without being a member of the SS (also, perhaps, in order to give himself an air of clandestine importance), had told them that I was a Rumanian engaged in some special intelligence work, and I did nothing to destroy this legend, so I was treated as if I were the bearer of top secrets that would soon enable Adolf Hitler to unite the Carpathians with the Styrian Alps. I knew I could certainly count on Oskar, because, in a drunken moment, he had confessed to me that his group of Austrian Nazis had been deceived by the men of the Reich. He and his friends had not at all wanted *Anschluss* but a separate Nazi Austria under their own leader, Dr. Rintelen. The next day, he came to me and implored me never to mention what he had told me. I grasped his arm and said, "Well, Oskar, after all, we have always been friends. Let's not fuss about how reliable we are," whereupon he grasped my arm and said, "Arnulf, I always knew you were a fine fellow, though you sometimes"—and here he laughed heartily—"have a trifle too much to do with the Turks. However, I would very much like to meet that Turkish girl of yours. She has something that appeals to my particular taste. If you don't mind."

Of course, Minka knew about all this, and laughed when I told her that she had only to smile at Oskar and he'd immediately make her an honorary Aryan. "Aryans," she said. "I can't stand the sight of them any longer. The sooner I get my affidavit the better. I want to get out of here. It breaks my heart, but I simply have to." She was waiting for her affidavit for England, as most of our friends were. It was not easy to get an affidavit. The English would take only people who wanted to be employed as servants, so very soon some clever man opened a butlers' school on the Praterstrasse, where Jewish bankers and intellectuals were taught how to wait on the British. I once went there with Minka, and we laughed our heads off. Old stockbrokers were waddling around with aprons about their hips, balancing trays and opening bottles of champagne. My talent for imitating Jews made me invent a sketch in which a Scottish laird, reading in the newspapers about the sad destiny of the Viennese Jews, decides to dismiss all his wonderful Highland servants and replace them with Dr. Pisko-Bettelheim, Jacques Pallinker, Yehudo Nagoschiner, and such. Minka's house had become a sort of center for the few Jews left in Vienna and some Aryans unfaithful to their new flag, like myself. My sketch was a great success.

During that summer and autumn of 1938, most of the Jews I knew went away. Some of them were arrested and locked up for a while, and came home with some rather gruesome stories about what was going on in the prisons of the Rossauerlände. Some disappeared, and we did not know whether they had been put in jail or had just fled at the last moment. All this was pretty awful, I had to admit. But one knew, after all, how people were—some being horrid, others really very nice—and those who got arrested were not always entirely innocent. A Jewish lawyer, telling about his cruel treatment at the hands of the SS, said proudly, "But I was not arrested for just being a Jew. I am a criminal." However, I was becoming bored with the Nazi attitude of promise, hope, and expectation, as nothing really happened, and the whole thing was nothing but a great mess with some sordid highlights. Vienna had become a dreary place. Even Oskar complained; he didn't enjoy the *Heurigen* anymore,

God knows why. Then he said, "Do you remember our school library? Well, there was a book called *The City Without Jews*. Actually, I never read it. Have you? Anyway, I sometimes have the feeling that Vienna is just that. There's nobody left to hate."

There was a young boy of great musical talent around Minka in those days—not Herbert von Karajan but a little Jew by the name of Walter, whom I had come to like very much. He was intelligent, and funny, and extremely well read. Minka protected him, as, in happier times, she had protected me, and he showed me a touching affection and confidence that I could not resist. Since he had relatives in America, he got an affidavit rather quickly, and we decided to give him a farewell party. We chose an out-of-the-way place—a small winegrower's cottage behind the Kobenzl—with the poetic name, in the Viennese dialect, of Häusl am Roan (Cottage at the Edge of the Vineyard). We were a party of sixteen, and there were some pretty girls. Someone still had a car, and it took two trips to get us all out there, and we were gay as in the old days. Walter played the nice old Viennese *Heurigenlieder* on the piano. I performed the butler Yehudo Nagoschiner, serving the wine and the fried chicken. Below us, beyond the hills that smelled of mown hay, lay the sparkling lights of Vienna. Suddenly this idyllic happiness was interrupted by a voice that roared, "I've finally caught you in the very act, you scoundrel!" I felt the marrow of my bones freeze. In the door stood Oskar, with a group of sturdy men in civilian clothes behind him. My poor Jewish friends stood or sat motionless as he came toward me, followed by his silent men. Then he threw his arms up and said, "But don't let me interrupt your good time. I'm a schoolmate of Arnulf's, and I wanted to show a few friends from the Reich what a true Viennese *Heurigen* looks like."

It was true. He had not come to arrest me, or anything of the kind. When I asked him how he knew where I was, he said with a smile, "Old boy, there are very few things we don't know."

"Come on, don't give me that. Who told you, really?"

"Your grandmother."

"My *grandmother?*"

"Well, that old witch with the trembling voice who answers the telephone at your house."

Old Marie, then. I was a fool. For months I had told her where I could be reached when I went out, hoping that a call might come through from Bucharest to tell me that things had changed again and that my beloved was getting a divorce. I was more than a fool; I was blind to what was going on around me. I felt this very strongly when Oskar poked his elbow into my side and said, in a loud voice, with a glance toward his companions, "Now, how about introducing me to your beautiful *Turkish* girlfriend?"

"She is my wife," I said. "We are celebrating our wedding."

The Germans were very pleased to hear this, and clicked their heels and congratulated us, shaking our hands so hard they almost pulled our arms out of their sockets. One of them sat down next to Minka in order to tell her about a cousin who lived in Istanbul. Oskar clapped my shoulder and said with a wink, "Don't look so frightened. Tell that little Jew there at the piano to play some *Heurigenlieder*."

The Germans soon got very drunk. The one with the cousin in Istanbul flirted with Minka, in competition with Oskar. The others danced with the pretty girls, and finally one of them performed a most courageous jump over a small stone wall in the garden, misjudged the distance to the ground, fell, and broke his leg. The Germans made a stretcher for him, so they could carry him to the nearest hospital, and then, in a great hurry, they shook our hands, clicked their heels, threw their arms up, shouting *"Heil Hitler!"* and "Long live Kemal Pasha Atatürk!" and disappeared as spookily as they had come, with Oskar waving and calling good-bye.

"You bastard," Minka said to me. She went out into the vineyard and sat down on a stone. I followed her.

"I'm sorry, Minka. I know I am a mindless ass."

"Never mind. After all, it was funny. Did you see darling little Walter playing the piano as if the devils were standing over him?" She laughed her enchanting laugh. "But still . . ." She sank back with a deep sigh.

It was dawn. Out of a mist in the valley Vienna rose, the peaks of its towers first, then the Riesenrad, the Ferris wheel, in the Prater, the monuments, the roofs, the streets. I sat beside Minka, looking down at all this. Suddenly I heard a strange sound coming out of Minka's throat, and thought she was going to cry, but she was laughing instead. "Do you know what happened to Friedel Süssmann?" she asked. "I told you that in order to get her affidavit she got married at the British Consulate to an English sailor she had never seen before? Well, when she got to England, she was met by some gentlemen in black. They had come to break the news to her that her husband had fallen from the mast and broken his neck. She now has a widow's pension—one pound a month."

"Listen, Minka," I said. "After all, I am a Rumanian. My hands are not tied. I need not tell you what it would mean to my parents, and you know that I love somebody else, but if it would help you—I mean, just in order to get you a passport that would enable you to get out of here, and, of course, with an immediate divorce afterward—if you want to, we could bloody well go and get married. You won't get a pension, though, if I break my neck."

She drew herself up slowly till she was looking into my face. Then she took it in both her hands, as she had done when I first came to her flat, and kissed me. "You know, my darling Brommy," she said, "that you are the dearest person on earth to me. I could never have felt closer to a brother, if I'd had one. You are a bastard, it's true, but I am more fond of you than of anybody else. Just kiss me, once—and kiss me tenderly." Her mouth was as beautiful as ever, and I could even feel more than the tenderness I would have felt for a sister. In that moment, it appeared to me that if she had not been a Jew, I could have loved her even in the same way, or perhaps more than, I loved the one I had lost. Still, I felt a twinge of bad conscience, as if I were being a traitor to my flag.

"All right," she said. "That's that. And now don't be afraid that I'll say yes to your kind offer. I couldn't possibly marry you. Apart from the fact that it would hurt your parents and that you love somebody else—we could certainly get an immediate divorce, but that is not the point—I would not want to marry you, if you understand what I mean. Because of certain goyish qualities of your soul. But still, you are the dearest to me. Come, let's see how the party is getting on."

A few days later, she got her affidavit, and within a fortnight she had sold her things, even Professor Raubitschek's carved-wood bookcases, and gone to London.

There I saw her once more, in the year 1947. God knows how she had found out where I was living—near Hamburg at that time. Anyway, I got a letter from her saying that she was all right, and married to a man—not a Jew, by the way—who had left Austria in 1938 and who was as sweet and decent as could be, a professor of philology and a great admirer of Karl Kraus. They were about to emigrate to America, and she would very much like to see me once more. She enclosed in the letter a ticket to London and all the papers necessary to get me, as a former Rumanian, a visa for Great Britain. I accepted all this more than gratefully. I was as penniless, as starved, as miserable as any displaced person could be in the rubble of Germany in early 1947. As she had known how—and where—to trace me, she must also have known that my father had fired his last shot into his temple when the Russians took the Bukovina in 1940, and that, two years later, my grandmother had died in Vienna. I had not had a chance to build up a life or settle in a place for all those years.

There was only one difficulty: I had no valid passport. But Minka had even thought of that. A friend who was with the British Military Government arranged to get me a travel document. It defined me as an "individual of doubtful nationality" but brought me to England, all right. Her husband fetched me at Victoria Station, took a closer look at me, and said, "Let us go to have lunch first. She doesn't know that you are arriving today. I have not told her, in order not to excite her too much."

"Why?" I asked. "Is there anything wrong with her?"

"That trouble with her hip seems to have affected her spine. She is in great pain, and you will have to be very patient with her."

They lived in a nice house in Cadogan Square. Minka's husband showed me in, fixed me a drink, and then called up the stairwell, "Oh, Minka, would you mind coming down? There is a friend of yours." She came down the stairs, a middle-aged woman with gray hair, bent and torn by the atrocious pains of cancer of the bone. "Who is it?" she asked sharply. Then she saw me. "Brommy!" she said, and covered her face with her hands, her poor, tortured body shaken by her sobbing.

On the evening before their departure for America, all of our old friends who had managed to emigrate to Britain came to their house to bid them good-bye. Even though they had been told I would be there, they marveled at seeing me, as if I were a creature from another star. They could not stop asking about Vienna during the war, and how it had looked when I last saw it. They remembered things I had long since forgotten. Had Oskar survived? Oh, he had been hanged in Poland? Poor chap. And Guru Malik, the spiritualist I had told so many funny stories about? No! Had he really been dematerialized by a bomb? Great success, that one. Every one of the guests had brought me a gift, things I badly needed at that time—mostly secondhand clothes. And when, at the end of the evening, I had kissed Minka good-bye—forever, as we both knew—and had shaken hands with everybody, I went back to my hotel carrying two large suitcases full of old clothes that I hoped to sell in Hamburg like a *handalé,* to make enough money to follow Minka to America.

She died there a few months later. ⌣

INTERPRETIVE QUESTIONS
FOR DISCUSSION

Why does Gregor remain an anti-Semite even though he is intimately involved with Minka and her Jewish friends?

1. Why does Gregor suggest that his and his grandmother's anti-Semitism is different from his father's "ancient, traditional, and deep-rooted hatred" of Jews? (113)

2. Why does Gregor report without criticism that the educated classes of Europe amused themselves with "the most absurd justifications" for their anti-Semitism? (114)

3. Why doesn't the young Gregor tell the boys at the skating rink that he cannot play with them because they are Jews? (124–125)

4. What makes Gregor abandon his solitude and his distant behavior with Jews when Minka invites him to stay for a nightcap, and then for the night? (131–133)

5. Why do Gregor and Poldi, the Jewish journalist from Prague, agree that "people who just love Jews" are more dangerous than the typical anti-Semite? (137)

6. Why does Gregor say that his ideas about Jews merely went "on a holiday" while he lived among Minka and her friends? Why does Gregor believe that disliking Jews was not something one could change? (137)

7. Why does Gregor compare his life as "Brommy" to that of Mr. Malik when he poses as a guru? (139)

8. Why doesn't Gregor see the contradiction between thinking that the Nazis must be supported because of their policy toward Jews, and being friends with Minka and her crowd? Why does Gregor think that "if the Jews were frightened, it served them right"? (142–144)

9. Why is Gregor blind to the dangers of Nazi rule until Oskar barges in on Walter's going-away party? (155)

10. When he tenderly kisses Minka after proposing to her, why does Gregor feel "a twinge of bad conscience, as if I were being a traitor to my flag"? (157–158; cf. 122–123)

Suggested textual analyses

Pages 135–139: beginning, "I have often wondered since," and ending, "and were proud of my precocity."

Pages 142–144: beginning, "When I came back to Vienna again," and ending, "So we went to the Kärntnerbar."

Why do Minka and her friends accept Gregor into their circle?

1. Why does Minka find the distant and unworldly young Gregor "cozy" and decide that she wants him around all the time? (134) Why does Gregor eventually become dearer than anyone else to her? (157–158)

2. Why does Gregor see his affair with Minka as "innocent"? (136) Why is it an impossible affair with a married woman that separates Gregor from the love he shared with Minka?

3. Why can Minka possess others, but not be possessed herself? (136)

4. Why does Gregor end up serving Minka like a page in the tradition of his ancestors, knights of the Holy Roman Empire? Why does Minka's "kingdom" of all that was intellectual and amusing in Vienna become Gregor's "universe"? (138)

5. Why does Gregor's sketch featuring dignified Jewish intellectuals and businessmen serving a Scottish laird become a great success in Minka's circle? (154)

6. Why does Minka, who eventually marries a non-Jew, refuse Gregor's offer of marriage "because of certain goyish qualities" of his soul? (158)

7. Why isn't Minka offended or angry when Gregor says that she is exaggerating the danger to the Jews? (142)

8. Why is it suggested that Minka's fall from the window for the sake of love was the cause of her premature death?

9. Why does the story end with Minka giving Gregor old clothes to sell like a Jewish *handalé*? Why does Gregor plan to use the money he makes to follow Minka to America? (159; cf. 114)

10. Did Gregor violate or preserve troth in his relationship with Minka?

Suggested textual analysis
Pages 122–123: beginning, "The majority of the young skaters," and ending, "I had good reason to be ashamed."

Why does Gregor need Minka to tell him that the *Anschluss* represents a breach of troth?

1. Why does Gregor's father perceive his "exile" to Rumania as being forced into a breach of troth? Why does he see Gregor's passion for the Bukovina as an indication that Gregor has no character? (114–115)

2. Why does Gregor embrace the idea that the Holy Roman Empire, the Empire of the German Nation, "was the epitome of order" and that his family was needed to combat the chaos of the East? (119)

3. Why is it easier for Gregor to understand troth than his father's notion of character? (115–116, 118–120)

4. Why does Gregor resent being left out of the "connection" of the German and Austrian peoples, as if he were a Communist "or even a Jew"? (148) Why do both Gregor and his lover feel that the *Anschluss* is "a wedding day of sad promise"? (150)

5. Why does Gregor feel a "promise of hope" in the uniting of the German-speaking peoples, even though he dislikes Germans, knows Austrian Nazis are already disillusioned with Hitler, and is struck by an uncanny silence hanging over Vienna? (148)

6. Why does Gregor think that Minka's and Poldi's fears in February and March of 1938 are exaggerated? (143, 151) Why does he callously complain that the Jews at the Salzburg Festival "behaved as if they were the victims of a cruel persecution" when in fact they were fleeing for their lives? (141–142)

7. Why is the *Anschluss* made the backdrop for the end of Gregor's love affair?

8. Why is Minka furious at Gregor for not seeing that "our old Imperial Austrian anthem, composed by our Haydn," had been embezzled by Germany? (151)

9. Why is Gregor's ultimate feeling about the *Anschluss*—the German Reich's breach of troth—that of boredom? (154)

10. Why are we told that the Jewish émigrés were saddened to hear that Oskar had been hanged? Why are we told that the spiritualist fraud, Mr. Malik, turned out to be an important member of the SS who was "dematerialized" by a bomb during the war? (159)

Suggested textual analyses
Pages 114–121: beginning, "He felt exiled," and ending, "where he had no hunting ground to defend."

Pages 150–152: beginning, "I could have gone back to Rumania," and ending, "I could use my connections with the SS to help them out again."

FOR FURTHER REFLECTION

1. Is the concept of troth all but dead? If not, should it be?

2. Does "Troth" shed light on the essence of European anti-Semitism, or is it merely the story of the prejudices of "a most complicated family"?

3. Is Gregor's ability to have affection for particular individuals while maintaining deep-rooted prejudice toward their ethnicity typical or atypical?

4. Would there be more or less order in the world if individuals and nations lived their lives in accordance with a sense of troth?

5. Are Jews still as hated as they were in prewar Europe? Is anti-Semitism fundamentally an expression of profound jealousy of Jewish learning and accomplishment?

6. Is the fragmentation of empires into smaller nationalist states a positive development in achieving peaceful and orderly international relations?

THE BACCHAE

Euripides

EURIPIDES (484?–406 B.C.) was born in
Phyla, a village north of the ancient city of
Athens, but lived most of his life in Athens.
The youngest of the three great Greek
tragedians, following Aeschylus and
Sophocles, Euripides authored more than
ninety plays, of which fewer than twenty
survive. In the fifty years of his dramatic
career, he won only a few first prizes in the
competition held at the annual spring festival
of Dionysus in Athens. This small number
of awards was perhaps due to his penchant
for raising questions that his audiences found
disturbing. Two years before his death,
Euripides left Athens to live in Macedonia—
a move motivated, it is thought, by his
disappointment at the reception of his plays
and perhaps also by his feelings of dismay
at the ruinous effects of the Peloponnesian
War, then in its twenty-third year. It was
during this period of voluntary exile that
Euripides wrote his last two plays,
Iphigeneia at Aulis and *The Bacchae.*

CHARACTERS

DIONYSUS (also called Bromius, Evius, and Bacchus)

CHORUS OF ASIAN BACCHAE (followers of Dionysus)

TEIRESIAS

CADMUS

PENTHEUS

ATTENDANT

FIRST MESSENGER

SECOND MESSENGER

AGAVE

CORYPHAEUS (chorus leader)

SCENE: *Before the royal palace at Thebes. On the left is the way to Cithaeron; on the right, to the city. In the center of the orchestra stands, still smoking, the vine-covered tomb of Semele, mother of Dionysus.*

Enter DIONYSUS. *He is of soft, even effeminate, appearance. His face is beardless; he is dressed in a fawn-skin and carries a thyrsus (i.e., a stalk of fennel tipped with ivy leaves). On his head he wears a wreath of ivy, and his long blond curls ripple down over his shoulders. Throughout the play he wears a smiling mask.*

DIONYSUS: I am Dionysus, the son of Zeus,
   come back to Thebes, this land where I was born.
   My mother was Cadmus' daughter, Semele by name,
   midwived by fire, delivered by the lightning's
   blast.
         And here I stand, a god incognito,
   disguised as man, beside the stream of Dirce
   and the waters of Ismenus. There before the palace
   I see my lightning-married mother's grave,
   and there upon the ruins of her shattered house
   the living fire of Zeus still smolders on
   in deathless witness of Hera's violence and rage
   against my mother. But Cadmus wins my praise:
   he has made this tomb a shrine, sacred to my mother.
   It was I who screened her grave with the green
   of the clustering vine.
               Far behind me lie
   those golden-rivered lands, Lydia and Phrygia,

where my journeying began. Overland I went,
across the steppes of Persia where the sun strikes hotly
down, through Bactrian fastness and the grim waste
of Media. Thence to rich Arabia I came;
and so, along all Asia's swarming littoral
of towered cities where Greeks and foreign nations,
mingling, live, my progress made. There
I taught my dances to the feet of living men,
establishing my mysteries and rites
that I might be revealed on earth for what I am:
a god.
     And thence to Thebes.
                    This city, first
in Hellas, now shrills and echoes to my women's cries,
their ecstasy of joy. Here in Thebes
I bound the fawn-skin to the women's flesh and armed
their hands with shafts of ivy. For I have come
to refute that slander spoken by my mother's sisters—
those who least had right to slander her.
They said that Dionysus was no son of Zeus,
but Semele had slept beside a man in love
and fathered off her shame on Zeus—a fraud, they sneered,
contrived by Cadmus to protect his daughter's name.
They said she lied, and Zeus in anger at that lie
blasted her with lightning.
                Because of that offense
I have stung them with frenzy, hounded them from home
up to the mountains where they wander, crazed of mind,
and compelled to wear my orgies' livery.
Every woman in Thebes—but the women only—
I drove from home, mad. There they sit,
rich and poor alike, even the daughters of Cadmus,
beneath the silver firs on the roofless rocks.
Like it or not, this city must learn its lesson:
it lacks initiation in my mysteries;

that I shall vindicate my mother Semele
and stand revealed to mortal eyes as the god
she bore to Zeus.
                    Cadmus the king has abdicated,
leaving his throne and power to his grandson Pentheus;
who now revolts against divinity, in *me;*
thrusts *me* from his offerings; forgets *my* name
in his prayers. Therefore I shall *prove* to him
and every man in Thebes that I am god
indeed. And when my worship is established here,
and all is well, then I shall go my way
and be revealed to other men in other lands.
But if the men of Thebes attempt to force
my Bacchae from the mountainside by threat of arms,
I shall marshal my Maenads and take the field.
To these ends I have laid my deity aside
and go disguised as man.

                    (*He wheels and calls offstage.*)

                    On, my women,
women who worship me, women whom I led
out of Asia where Tmolus heaves its rampart
over Lydia!
                    On, comrades of my progress here!
Come, and with your native Phrygian drum—
Rhea's drum and mine—pound at the palace doors
of Pentheus! Let the city of Thebes behold you,
while I return among Cithaeron's forest glens
where my Bacchae wait and join their whirling dances.

                    (*Exit* DIONYSUS *as the* CHORUS OF ASIAN BACCHAE
                    *comes dancing in from the right. They are dressed
                    in fawn-skins, crowned with ivy, and carry
                    thyrsi, timbrels, and flutes.*)

CHORUS: Out of the land of Asia,
  down from holy Tmolus,
  speeding the service of god,
  for Bromius we come!
  Hard are the labors of god;
  hard, but his service is sweet.
  Sweet to serve, sweet to cry:
                    Bacchus!   *Evohé!*

You on the streets!
                  You on the roads!
                        Make way!
Let every mouth be hushed. Let no ill-omened words
profane your tongues.
                  Make way! Fall back!
                            Hush.
For now I raise the old, old hymn to Dionysus.

Blessèd, blessèd are those who know the mysteries of god.
Blessèd is he who hallows his life in the worship of god,
  he whom the spirit of god possesseth, who is one
  with those who belong to the holy body of god.
Blessèd are the dancers and those who are purified,
  who dance on the hill in the holy dance of god.
Blessèd are they who keep the rite of Cybele the Mother.
Blessèd are the thyrsus-bearers, those who wield in their hands
  the holy wand of god.
Blessèd are those who wear the crown of the ivy of god.
Blessèd, blessèd are they: Dionysus is their god!

On, Bacchae, on, you Bacchae,
bear your god in triumph home!
Bear on the god, son of god,
escort your Dionysus home!
Bear him down from Phrygian hill,
attend him through the streets of Hellas!

So his mother bore him once
in labor bitter; lightning-struck,
forced by fire that flared from Zeus,
consumed, she died, untimely torn,
in childbed dead by blow of light!
Of light the son was born!

Zeus it was who saved his son;
with speed outrunning mortal eye,
bore him to a private place,
bound the boy with clasps of gold;
in his thigh as in a womb,
concealed his son from Hera's eyes.

And when the weaving Fates fulfilled the time,
the bull-horned god was born of Zeus. In joy
he crowned his son, set serpents on his head—
wherefrom, in piety, descends to us
the Maenad's writhing crown, her chevelure of snakes.

O Thebes, nurse of Semele,
crown your hair with ivy!
Grow green with bryony!
Redden with berries! O city,
with boughs of oak and fir,
come dance the dance of god!
Fringe your skins of dappled fawn
with tufts of twisted wool!
Handle with holy care
the violent wand of god!
And let the dance begin!
He is Bromius who runs
to the mountain!
to the mountain!
where the throng of women waits,

driven from shuttle and loom,
possessed by Dionysus!

And I praise the holies of Crete,
the caves of the dancing Curetes,
there where Zeus was born,
where helmed in triple tier
around the primal drum
the Corybantes danced. They,
they were the first of all
whose whirling feet kept time
to the strict beat of the taut hide
and the squeal of the wailing flute.
Then from them to Rhea's hands
the holy drum was handed down;
but, stolen by the raving Satyrs,
fell at last to me and now
accompanies the dance
which every other year
celebrates your name:
    Dionysus!

He is sweet upon the mountains. He drops to the earth
    from the running packs.
He wears the holy fawn-skin. He hunts the wild goat
    and kills it.
He delights in the raw flesh.
He runs to the mountains of Phrygia, to the mountains
    of Lydia he runs!
He is Bromius who leads us! *Evohé!*

With milk the earth flows! It flows with wine!
It runs with the nectar of bees!

Like frankincense in its fragrance
is the blaze of the torch he bears.
Flames float out from his trailing wand
   as he runs, as he dances,
    kindling the stragglers,
    spurring with cries,
and his long curls stream to the wind!

And he cries, as they cry, *Evohé!*—
   On, Bacchae!
   On, Bacchae!
Follow, glory of golden Tmolus,
   hymning god
   with a rumble of drums,
with a cry, *Evohé!* to the Evian god,
with a cry of Phrygian cries,
when the holy flute like honey plays
the sacred song of those who go
to the mountain!
              to the mountain!

Then, in ecstasy, like a colt by its grazing mother,
the Bacchante runs with flying feet, she leaps!

(*The* CHORUS *remains grouped in two semicircles about
the orchestra as* TEIRESIAS *makes his entrance. He is
incongruously dressed in the bacchant's fawn-skin
and is crowned with ivy. Old and blind,
he uses his thyrsus to tap his way.*)

TEIRESIAS: Ho there, who keeps the gates?
                    Summon Cadmus—
Cadmus, Agenor's son, the stranger from Sidon
who built the towers of our Thebes.
                  Go, someone.

Say Teiresias wants him. He will know what errand
brings me, that agreement, age with age, we made
to deck our wands, to dress in skins of fawn
and crown our heads with ivy.

(*Enter* CADMUS *from the palace. Dressed in Dionysiac
costume and bent almost double with age, he is an
incongruous and pathetic figure.*)

CADMUS: My old friend,
  I knew it must be you when I heard your summons.
  For there's a wisdom in his voice that makes
  the man of wisdom known.
                    But here I am,
  dressed in the costume of the god, prepared to go.
  Insofar as we are able, Teiresias, we must
  do honor to this god, for he was born
  my daughter's son, who has been revealed to men,
  the god, Dionysus.
                    Where shall we go, where
  shall we tread the dance, tossing our white heads
  in the dances of god?
                    Expound to me, Teiresias.
  For in such matters you are wise.
                    Surely
  I could dance night and day, untiringly
  beating the earth with my thyrsus! And how sweet it is
  to forget my old age.

TEIRESIAS: It is the same with me.
  I too feel young, young enough to dance.

CADMUS: Good. Shall we take our chariots to the mountain?

TEIRESIAS: Walking would be better. It shows more honor
  to the god.

CADMUS: So be it. I shall lead, my old age
    conducting yours.

TEIRESIAS: The god will guide us there
    with no effort on our part.

CADMUS: Are we the only men
    who will dance for Bacchus?

TEIRESIAS: They are all blind.
    Only we can see.

CADMUS: But we delay too long.
    Here, take my arm.

TEIRESIAS: Link my hand in yours.

CADMUS: I am a man, nothing more. I do not scoff
    at heaven.

TEIRESIAS: We do not trifle with divinity.
    No, we are the heirs of customs and traditions
    hallowed by age and handed down to us
    by our fathers. No quibbling logic can topple *them*,
    whatever subtleties this clever age invents.
    People may say: "Aren't you ashamed? At your age,
    going dancing, wreathing your head with ivy?"
    Well, I am *not* ashamed. Did the god declare
    that just the young or just the old should dance?
    No, he desires his honor from all mankind.
    He wants no one excluded from his worship.

CADMUS: Because you cannot see, Teiresias, let me be
    interpreter for you this once. Here comes
    the man to whom I left my throne, Echion's son,

Pentheus, hastening toward the palace. He seems
excited and disturbed. Yes, listen to him.

> (*Enter* PENTHEUS *from the right. He is a young man of
> athletic build, dressed in traditional Greek dress;
> like Dionysus, he is beardless. He enters
> excitedly, talking to the attendants
> who accompany him.*)

PENTHEUS: I happened to be away, out of the city,
    but reports reached me of some strange mischief here,
    stories of our women leaving home to frisk
    in mock ecstasies among the thickets on the mountain,
    dancing in honor of the latest divinity,
    a certain Dionysus, whoever he may be!
    In their midst stand bowls brimming with wine.
    And then, one by one, the women wander off
    to hidden nooks where they serve the lusts of men.
    Priestesses of Bacchus they claim they are,
    but it's really Aphrodite they adore.
    I have captured some of them; my jailers
    have locked them away in the safety of our prison.
    Those who run at large shall be hunted down
    out of the mountains like the animals they are—
    yes, my own mother Agave, and Ino
    and Autonoë, the mother of Actaeon.
    In no time at all I shall have them trapped
    in iron nets and stop this obscene disorder.
       I am also told a foreigner has come to Thebes
    from Lydia, one of those charlatan magicians,
    with long yellow curls smelling of perfumes,
    with flushed cheeks and the spells of Aphrodite
    in his eyes. His days and nights he spends
    with women and girls, dangling before them the joys
    of initiation in his mysteries.

But let me bring him underneath that roof
and I'll stop his pounding with his wand and tossing
his head. By god, I'll have his head cut off!
And *this* is the man who claims that Dionysus
is a god and was sewn into the thigh of Zeus,
when, in point of fact, that same blast of lightning
consumed him and his mother both for her lie
that she had lain with Zeus in love. Whoever
this stranger is, aren't such impostures,
such unruliness, worthy of hanging?

(*For the first time he sees* TEIRESIAS *and*
CADMUS *in their Dionysiac costumes.*)

What!
But this is incredible! Teiresias the seer
tricked out in a dappled fawn-skin!
                    And *you,*
you, my own grandfather, playing at the bacchant
with a wand!
            Sir, I shrink to see your old age
so foolish. Shake that ivy off, grandfather!
Now drop that wand. Drop it, I say.

(*He wheels on* TEIRESIAS.)

                    Aha,
I see: this is *your* doing, Teiresias.
Yes, you want still another god revealed to men
so you can pocket the profits from burnt offerings
and bird-watching. By heaven, only your age
restrains me now from sending you to prison
with those Bacchic women for importing here to Thebes
these filthy mysteries. When once you see
the glint of wine shining at the feasts of women,
then you may be sure the festival is rotten.

CORYPHAEUS: What blasphemy! Stranger, have you no respect
for heaven? For Cadmus who sowed the dragon teeth?
Will the son of Echion disgrace his house?

TEIRESIAS: Give a wise man an honest brief to plead
and his eloquence is no remarkable achievement.
But you are glib; your phrases come rolling out
smoothly on the tongue, as though your words were wise
instead of foolish. The man whose glibness flows
from his conceit of speech declares the thing he is:
a worthless and a stupid citizen.
                                        I tell you,
this god whom you ridicule shall someday have
enormous power and prestige throughout Hellas.
Mankind, young man, possesses two supreme blessings.
First of these is the goddess Demeter, or Earth—
whichever name you choose to call her by.
It was she who gave to man his nourishment of grain.
But after her there came the son of Semele,
who matched her present by inventing liquid wine
as his gift to man. For filled with that good gift,
suffering mankind forgets its grief; from it
comes sleep; with it oblivion of the troubles
of the day. There is no other medicine
for misery. And when we pour libations
to the gods, we pour the god of wine himself
that through his intercession man may win
the favor of heaven.
                            You sneer, do you, at that story
that Dionysus was sewed into the thigh of Zeus?
Let me teach you what that really means. When Zeus
rescued from the thunderbolt his infant son,
he brought him to Olympus. Hera, however,
plotted at heart to hurl the child from heaven.
Like the god he is, Zeus countered her. Breaking off
a tiny fragment of that ether which surrounds the world,

he molded from it a dummy Dionysus.
This he *showed* to Hera, but with time men garbled
the word and said that Dionysus had been *sewed*
into the thigh of Zeus. This was their story,
whereas, in fact, Zeus *showed* the dummy to Hera
and gave it as a hostage for his son.

         Moreover,
this is a god of prophecy. His worshippers,
like madmen, are endowed with mantic powers.
For when the god enters the body of a man
he fills him with the breath of prophecy.

         Besides,
he has usurped even the functions of warlike Ares.
Thus, at times, you see an army mustered under arms
stricken with panic before it lifts a spear.
This panic comes from Dionysus.

        Someday
you shall even see him bounding with his torches
among the crags at Delphi, leaping the pastures
that stretch between the peaks, whirling and waving
his thyrsus: great throughout Hellas.

        Mark my words,
Pentheus. Do not be so certain that power
is what matters in the life of man; do not mistake
for wisdom the fantasies of your sick mind.
Welcome the god to Thebes; crown your head;
pour him libations and join his revels.

  Dionysus does not, I admit, *compel* a woman
to be chaste. Always and in every case
it is her character and nature that keeps
a woman chaste. But even in the rites of Dionysus,
the chaste woman will not be corrupted.

         Think:
you are pleased when men stand outside your doors
and the city glorifies the name of Pentheus.
And so the god: he too delights in glory.

But Cadmus and I, whom you ridicule, will crown
our heads with ivy and join the dances of the god—
an ancient foolish pair perhaps, but dance
we must. Nothing you have said would make me
change my mind or flout the will of heaven.
You are mad, grievously mad, beyond the power
of any drugs to cure, for you are drugged
with madness.

CORYPHAEUS: Apollo would approve your words.
Wisely you honor Bromius: a great god.

CADMUS: My boy,
Teiresias advises well. Your home is here
with us, with our customs and traditions, not
outside, alone. Your mind is distracted now,
and what you think is sheer delirium.
Even if this Dionysus is no god,
as you assert, persuade yourself that he is.
The fiction is a noble one, for Semele will seem
to be the mother of a god, and this confers
no small distinction on our family.
                              You saw
that dreadful death your cousin Actaeon died
when those man-eating hounds he had raised himself
savaged him and tore his body limb from limb
because he boasted that his prowess in the hunt surpassed
the skill of Artemis.
                    Do not let his fate be yours.
Here, let me wreathe your head with leaves of ivy.
Then come with us and glorify the god.

PENTHEUS: Take your hands off me! Go worship your Bacchus,
but do not wipe your madness off on me.
By god, I'll make him pay, the man who taught you
this folly of yours.

(*He turns to his attendants.*)

Go, someone, this instant,
to the place where this prophet prophesies.
Pry it up with crowbars, heave it over,
upside down; demolish everything you see.
Throw his fillets out to wind and weather.
That will provoke him more than anything.
As for the rest of you, go and scour the city
for that effeminate stranger, the man who infects our women
with this strange disease and pollutes our beds.
And when you take him, clap him in chains
and march him here. He shall die as he deserves—
by being stoned to death. He shall come to rue
his merrymaking here in Thebes.

(*Exeunt attendants.*)

TEIRESIAS: Reckless fool,
you do not know the consequences of your words.
You talked madness before, but this is raving
lunacy!
          Cadmus, let us go and pray
for this raving fool and for this city too,
pray to the god that no awful vengeance strike
from heaven.
               Take your staff and follow me.
Support me with your hands, and I shall help you too
lest we stumble and fall, a sight of shame,
two old men together.
                       But go we must,
acknowledging the service that we owe to god,
Bacchus, the son of Zeus.
                           And yet take care
lest someday your house repent of Pentheus

in its sufferings. I speak not prophecy
but fact. The words of fools finish in folly.

(*Exeunt* TEIRESIAS *and* CADMUS.
PENTHEUS *retires into the palace.*)

CHORUS: Holiness, queen of heaven,
   Holiness on golden wing
   who hover over earth,
   do you hear what Pentheus says?
   Do you hear his blasphemy
   against the prince of the blessèd,
   the god of garlands and banquets,
   Bromius, Semele's son?
   These blessings he gave:
   laughter to the flute
   and the loosing of cares
   when the shining wine is spilled
   at the feast of the gods,
   and the wine-bowl casts its sleep
   on feasters crowned with ivy.

   A tongue without reins,
   defiance, unwisdom—
   their end is disaster.
   But the life of quiet good,
   the wisdom that accepts—
   these abide unshaken,
   preserving, sustaining
   the houses of men.
   Far in the air of heaven,
   the sons of heaven live.
   But they watch the lives of men.
   And what passes for wisdom is not;
   unwise are those who aspire,

who outrange the limits of man.
Briefly, we live. Briefly,
then die. Wherefore, I say,
he who hunts a glory, he who tracks
some boundless, superhuman dream,
may lose his harvest here and now
and garner death. Such men are mad,
    their counsels evil.

O let me come to Cyprus,
island of Aphrodite,
homes of the loves that cast
their spells on the hearts of men!
Or Paphos where the hundred-
mouthed barbarian river
brings ripeness without rain!
To Pieria, haunt of the Muses,
and the holy hill of Olympus!
O Bromius, leader, god of joy,
Bromius, take me there!
There the lovely Graces go,
and there Desire, and there
the right is mine to worship
    as I please.

The deity, the son of Zeus,
in feast, in festival, delights.
He loves the goddess Peace,
generous of good,
preserver of the young.
To rich and poor he gives
the simple gift of wine,
the gladness of the grape.
But him who scoffs he hates,
and him who mocks his life,
the happiness of those

for whom the day is blessed
but doubly blessed the night;
whose simple wisdom shuns the thoughts
of proud, uncommon men and all
their god-encroaching dreams.
But what the common people do,
the things that simple men believe,
    I too believe and do.

> (*As* PENTHEUS *reappears from the palace,
> enter from the left several attendants
> leading* DIONYSUS *captive.*)

ATTENDANT: Pentheus, here we are; not empty-handed either.
We captured the quarry you sent us out to catch.
But our prey here was tame: refused to run
or hide, held out his hands as willing as you please,
completely unafraid. His ruddy cheeks were flushed
as though with wine, and he stood there smiling,
making no objection when we roped his hands
and marched him here. It made me feel ashamed.
"Listen, stranger," I said, "I am not to blame.
We act under orders from Pentheus. He ordered
your arrest."
            As for those women you clapped in chains
and sent to the dungeon, they're gone, clean away,
went skipping off to the fields crying on their god
Bromius. The chains on their legs snapped apart
by themselves. Untouched by any human hand,
the doors swung wide, opening of their own accord.
Sir, this stranger who has come to Thebes is full
of many miracles. I know no more than that.
The rest is your affair.

PENTHEUS: Untie his hands.
We have him in our net. He may be quick,
but he cannot escape us now, I think.

> (*While the servants untie* DIONYSUS' *hands,* PENTHEUS
> *attentively scrutinizes his prisoner. Then*
> *the servants step back, leaving* PENTHEUS
> *and* DIONYSUS *face to face.*)

                              So,
you *are* attractive, stranger, at least to women—
which explains, I think, your presence here in Thebes.
Your curls are long. You do not wrestle, I take it.
And what fair skin you have—you must take care of it—
no daylight complexion; no, it comes from the night
when you hunt Aphrodite with your beauty.
                                        Now then,
who are you and from where?

DIONYSUS: It is nothing
to boast of and easily told. You have heard, I suppose,
of Mount Tmolus and her flowers?

PENTHEUS: I know the place.
It rings the city of Sardis.

DIONYSUS: I come from there.
My country is Lydia.

PENTHEUS: Who is this god whose worship
you have imported into Hellas?

DIONYSUS: Dionysus, the son of Zeus.
He initiated me.

PENTHEUS: You have some local Zeus

who spawns new gods?

DIONYSUS: He is the same as yours—
the Zeus who married Semele.

PENTHEUS: How did you see him?
In a dream or face to face?

DIONYSUS: Face to face.
He gave me his rites.

PENTHEUS: What form do they take,
these mysteries of yours?

DIONYSUS: It is forbidden
to tell the uninitiate.

PENTHEUS: Tell me the benefits
that those who know your mysteries enjoy.

DIONYSUS: I am forbidden to say. But they are worth knowing.

PENTHEUS: Your answers are designed to make me curious.

DIONYSUS: No:
our mysteries abhor an unbelieving man.

PENTHEUS: You say you saw the god. What form did he assume?

DIONYSUS: Whatever form he wished. The choice was his,
not mine.

PENTHEUS: You evade the question.

DIONYSUS: Talk sense to a fool
and he calls you foolish.

PENTHEUS: Have you introduced your rites
in other cities too? Or is Thebes the first?

DIONYSUS: Foreigners everywhere now dance for Dionysus.

PENTHEUS: They are more ignorant than Greeks.

DIONYSUS: In this matter
they are not. Customs differ.

PENTHEUS: Do you hold your rites
during the day or night?

DIONYSUS: Mostly by night.
The darkness is well suited to devotion.

PENTHEUS: Better suited to lechery and seducing women.

DIONYSUS: You can find debauchery by daylight too.

PENTHEUS: You shall regret these clever answers.

DIONYSUS: And you,
your stupid blasphemies.

PENTHEUS: What a bold bacchant!
You wrestle well—when it comes to words.

DIONYSUS: Tell me,
what punishment do you propose?

PENTHEUS: First of all,
I shall cut off your girlish curls.

DIONYSUS: My hair is holy.
My curls belong to god.

(PENTHEUS *shears away the god's curls.*)

PENTHEUS: Second, you will surrender
your wand.

DIONYSUS: *You* take it. It belongs to Dionysus.

(PENTHEUS *takes the thyrsus.*)

PENTHEUS: Last, I shall place you under guard and confine you
in the palace.

DIONYSUS: The god himself will set me free
whenever I wish.

PENTHEUS: You will be with your women in prison
when you call on him for help.

DIONYSUS: He is here now
and sees what I endure from you.

PENTHEUS: Where is he?
I cannot see him.

DIONYSUS: With me. Your blasphemies
have made you blind.

PENTHEUS (*to attendants*): Seize him. He is mocking me
and Thebes.

DIONYSUS: I give you sober warnings, fools:
place no chains on *me*.

PENTHEUS: But *I* say: chain him.
And I am the stronger here.

DIONYSUS: You do not know
the limits of your strength. You do not know
what you do. You do not know who you are.

PENTHEUS: I am Pentheus, the son of Echion and Agave.

DIONYSUS: Pentheus: you shall repent that name.

PENTHEUS: Off with him.
Chain his hands; lock him in the stables by the palace.
Since he desires the darkness, give him what he wants.
Let him dance down there in the dark.

(*As the attendants bind* DIONYSUS' *hands, the* CHORUS
*beats on its drums with increasing agitation
as though to emphasize the sacrilege.*)

As for these women,
your accomplices in making trouble here,
I shall have them sold as slaves or put to work
at my looms. That will silence their drums.

(*Exit* PENTHEUS.)

DIONYSUS: I go,
though not to suffer, since that cannot be.
But Dionysus whom you outrage by your acts,
who you deny is god, will call you to account.
When you set chains on me, you manacle the god.

(*Exeunt attendants with* DIONYSUS *captive.*)

CHORUS: O Dirce, holy river,
child of Achelöus' water,
yours the springs that welcomed once
divinity, the son of Zeus!

For Zeus the father snatched his son
from deathless flame, crying:
Dithyrambus, come!
Enter my male womb.
I name you Bacchus and to Thebes
proclaim you by that name.
But now, O blessèd Dirce,
you banish me when to your banks I come,
crowned with ivy, bringing revels.
O Dirce, why am I rejected?
By the clustered grapes I swear,
by Dionysus' wine,
someday you shall come to know
    the name of *Bromius!*

With fury, with fury, he rages,
Pentheus, son of Echion,
born of the breed of Earth,
spawned by the dragon, whelped by Earth!
Inhuman, a rabid beast,
a giant in wildness raging,
storming, defying the children of heaven.
He has threatened me with bonds
though my body is bound to god.
He cages my comrades with chains;
he has cast them in prison darkness.
O lord, son of Zeus, do you see?
O Dionysus, do you see
how in shackles we are held
unbreakably, in the bonds of oppressors?
Descend from Olympus, lord!
Come, whirl your wand of gold
and quell with death this beast of blood
whose violence abuses man and god
    outrageously.

O lord, where do you wave your wand
among the running companies of god?
There on Nysa, mother of beasts?
There on the ridges of Corycia?
Or there among the forests of Olympus
where Orpheus fingered his lyre
and mustered with music the trees,
mustered the wilderness beasts?
O Pieria, you are blessed!
Evius honors you. He comes to dance,
bringing his Bacchae, fording the race
where Axios runs, bringing his Maenads
whirling over Lydias,
generous father of rivers
and famed for his lovely waters
that fatten a land of good horses.

(*Thunder and lightning. The earth trembles.*
The CHORUS *is crazed with fear.*)

DIONYSUS (*from within*): Ho!
    Hear me! Ho, Bacchae!
    Ho, Bacchae! Hear my cry!

CHORUS: Who cries?
    Who calls me with that cry
    of Evius? Where are you, lord?

DIONYSUS: Ho! Again I cry—
    the son of Zeus and Semele!

CHORUS: O lord, lord Bromius!
    Bromius, come to us now!

DIONYSUS: *Let the earthquake come! Shatter the floor of the*
    world!

CHORUS: Look there, how the palace of Pentheus totters.
Look, the palace is collapsing!
Dionysus is within. Adore him!
We adore him!
Look there!
        Above the pillars, how the great stones
gape and crack!
          Listen. Bromius cries his victory!

DIONYSUS: *Launch the blazing thunderbolt of god! O lightnings,*
come! Consume with flame the palace of Pentheus!

    (*A burst of lightning flares across the façade of the palace*
        and tongues of flame spurt up from the tomb of
           Semele. Then a great crash of thunder.)

CHORUS: Ah,
look how the fire leaps up
on the holy tomb of Semele,
the flame of Zeus of Thunders,
his lightnings, still alive,
blazing where they fell!
Down, Maenads,
fall to the ground in awe! He walks
among the ruins he has made!
He has brought the high house low!
He comes, our god, the son of Zeus!

    (*The* CHORUS *falls to the ground in oriental fashion, bowing*
        their heads in the direction of the palace. A hush;
        then DIONYSUS *appears, lightly picking his way*
        among the rubble. Calm and smiling still,
        he speaks to the CHORUS *with a*
        solicitude approaching banter.)

DIONYSUS: What, women of Asia? Were you so overcome with
    fright
  you fell to the ground? I think then you must have seen
  how Bacchus jostled the palace of Pentheus. But come, rise.
  Do not be afraid.

CORYPHAEUS: O greatest light of our holy revels,
  how glad I am to see your face! Without you I was lost.

DIONYSUS: Did you despair when they led me away to cast me
    down
  in the darkness of Pentheus' prison?

CORYPHAEUS: What else could I do?
  Where would I turn for help if something happened to you?
  But how did you escape that godless man?

DIONYSUS: With ease.
  No effort was required.

CORYPHAEUS: But the manacles on your wrists?

DIONYSUS: There I, in turn, humiliated him, outrage for outrage.
  He seemed to think that he was chaining me but never once
  so much as touched my hands. He fed on his desires.
  Inside the stable he intended as my jail, instead of me,
  he found a bull and tried to rope its knees and hooves.
  He was panting desperately, biting his lips with his teeth,
  his whole body drenched with sweat, while I sat nearby,
  quietly watching. But at that moment Bacchus came,
  shook the palace and touched his mother's grave with tongues
  of fire. Imagining the palace was in flames,
  Pentheus went rushing here and there, shouting to his slaves
  to bring him water. Every hand was put to work: in vain.
  Then, afraid I might escape, he suddenly stopped short,
  drew his sword and rushed to the palace. There, it seems,

Bromius had made a shape, a phantom which resembled me,
within the court. Bursting in, Pentheus thrust and stabbed
at that thing of gleaming air as though he thought it me.
And then, once again, the god humiliated him.
He razed the palace to the ground where it lies, shattered
in utter ruin—his reward for my imprisonment.
At that bitter sight, Pentheus dropped his sword, exhausted
by the struggle. A man, a man, and nothing more,
yet he presumed to wage a war with god.

                                   For my part,
I left the palace quietly and made my way outside.
For Pentheus I care nothing.

                         But judging from the sound
of tramping feet inside the court, I think our man
will soon be here. What, I wonder, will he have to say?
But let him bluster. I shall not be touched to rage.
Wise men know constraint: our passions are controlled.

(*Enter* PENTHEUS, *stamping heavily, from the ruined palace.*)

PENTHEUS: But this is mortifying. That stranger, that man
I clapped in irons, has escaped.

                        (*He catches sight of* DIONYSUS.)

                    What! *You?*
Well, what do you have to say for yourself?
How did you escape? Answer me.

DIONYSUS: Your anger
walks too heavily. Tread lightly here.

PENTHEUS: *How did you escape?*

DIONYSUS: Don't you remember?
Someone, I said, would set me free.

PENTHEUS: Someone?
But who? Who is this mysterious someone?

DIONYSUS: [He who makes the grape grow its clusters
for mankind.]

PENTHEUS: A splendid contribution, that.

DIONYSUS: You disparage the gift that is his chiefest glory.

PENTHEUS: [If I catch him here, he will not escape my anger.]
I shall order every gate in every tower
to be bolted tight.

DIONYSUS: And so? Could not a god
hurdle your city walls?

PENTHEUS: You are clever—very—
but not where it counts.

DIONYSUS: Where it counts the most,
there I *am* clever.

(*Enter a* MESSENGER, *a herdsman from Mount Cithaeron.*)

                    But hear this messenger
who brings you news from the mountain of Cithaeron.
We shall remain where we are. Do not fear:
we will not run away.

MESSENGER: Pentheus, king of Thebes,
I come from Cithaeron where the gleaming flakes of snow
fall on and on forever—

PENTHEUS: Get to the point.
What is your message, man?

MESSENGER: Sir, I have seen
the holy Maenads, the women who ran barefoot
and crazy from the city, and I wanted to report
to you and Thebes what weird fantastic things,
what miracles and more than miracles,
these women do. But may I speak freely
in my own way and words, or make it short?
I fear the harsh impatience of your nature, sire,
too kingly and too quick to anger.

PENTHEUS: Speak freely.
You have my promise: I shall not punish you.
Displeasure with a man who speaks the truth is wrong.
However, the more terrible this tale of yours,
that much more terrible will be the punishment
I impose upon that man who taught our womenfolk
this strange new magic.

MESSENGER: About that hour
when the sun lets loose its light to warm the earth,
our grazing herds of cows had just begun to climb
the path along the mountain ridge. Suddenly
I saw three companies of dancing women,
one led by Autonoë, the second captained
by your mother Agave, while Ino led the third.
There they lay in the deep sleep of exhaustion,
some resting on boughs of fir, others sleeping
where they fell, here and there among the oak leaves—
but all modestly and soberly, not, as you think,
drunk with wine, nor wandering, led astray
by the music of the flute, to hunt their Aphrodite
through the woods.
                    But your mother heard the lowing
of our horned herds, and springing to her feet,
gave a great cry to waken them from sleep.
And they too, rubbing the bloom of soft sleep

from their eyes, rose up lightly and straight—
a lovely sight to see: all as one,
the old women and the young and the unmarried girls.
First they let their hair fall loose, down
over their shoulders, and those whose straps had slipped
fastened their skins of fawn with writhing snakes
that licked their cheeks. Breasts swollen with milk,
new mothers who had left their babies behind at home
nestled gazelles and young wolves in their arms,
suckling them. Then they crowned their hair with leaves,
ivy and oak and flowering bryony. One woman
struck her thyrsus against a rock and a fountain
of cool water came bubbling up. Another drove
her fennel in the ground, and where it struck the earth,
at the touch of god, a spring of wine poured out.
Those who wanted milk scratched at the soil
with bare fingers and the white milk came welling up.
Pure honey spurted, streaming, from their wands.
If you had been there and seen these wonders for yourself,
you would have gone down on your knees and prayed
to the god you now deny.
              We cowherds and shepherds
gathered in small groups, wondering and arguing
among ourselves at these fantastic things,
the awful miracles those women did.
But then a city fellow with the knack of words
rose to his feet and said: "All you who live
upon the pastures of the mountain, what do you say?
Shall we earn a little favor with King Pentheus
by hunting his mother Agave out of the revels?"
Falling in with his suggestion, we withdrew
and set ourselves in ambush, hidden by the leaves
among the undergrowth. Then at a signal
all the Bacchae whirled their wands for the revels
to begin. With one voice they cried aloud:
"O Iacchus! Son of Zeus!" "O Bromius!" they cried

until the beasts and all the mountain seemed
wild with divinity. And when they ran,
everything ran with them.

     It happened, however,
that Agave ran near the ambush where I lay
concealed. Leaping up, I tried to seize her,
but she gave a cry: "Hounds who run with me,
men are hunting us down! Follow, follow me!
Use your wands for weapons."

      At this we fled
and barely missed being torn to pieces by the women.
Unarmed, they swooped down upon the herds of cattle
grazing there on the green of the meadow. And then
you could have seen a single woman with bare hands
tear a fat calf, still bellowing with fright,
in two, while others clawed the heifers to pieces.
There were ribs and cloven hooves scattered everywhere,
and scraps smeared with blood hung from the fir trees.
And bulls, their raging fury gathered in their horns,
lowered their heads to charge, then fell, stumbling
to the earth, pulled down by hordes of women
and stripped of flesh and skin more quickly, sire,
than you could blink your royal eyes. Then,
carried up by their own speed, they flew like birds
across the spreading fields along Asopus' stream
where most of all the ground is good for harvesting.
Like invaders they swooped on Hysiae
and on Erythrae in the foothills of Cithaeron.
Everything in sight they pillaged and destroyed.
They snatched the children from their homes. And when
they piled their plunder on their backs, it stayed in place,
untied. Nothing, neither bronze nor iron,
fell to the dark earth. Flames flickered
in their curls and did not burn them. Then the villagers,
furious at what the women did, took to arms.
And *there,* sire, was something terrible to see.

For the men's spears were pointed and sharp, and yet
drew no blood, whereas the wands the women threw
inflicted wounds. And then the men *ran,*
routed by women! Some god, I say, was with them.
The Bacchae then returned where they had started,
by the springs the god had made, and washed their hands
while the snakes licked away the drops of blood
that dabbled their cheeks.
                      Whoever this god may be,
sire, welcome him to Thebes. For he is great
in many other ways as well. It was he,
or so they say, who gave to mortal men
the gift of lovely wine by which our suffering
is stopped. And if there is no god of wine,
there is no love, no Aphrodite either,
nor other pleasure left to men.

                                     (*Exit* MESSENGER.)

CORYPHAEUS: I tremble
  to speak the words of freedom before the tyrant.
  But let the truth be told: there is no god
  greater than Dionysus.

PENTHEUS: Like a blazing fire
  this Bacchic violence spreads. It comes too close.
  We are disgraced, humiliated in the eyes
  of Hellas. This is no time for hesitation.

                          (*He turns to an* ATTENDANT.)

You there. Go down quickly to the Electran gates
and order out all heavy-armored infantry;
call up the fastest troops among our cavalry,
the mobile squadrons and the archers. We march

against the Bacchae! Affairs are out of hand
when we tamely endure such conduct in our women.

(*Exit* ATTENDANT.)

DIONYSUS: Pentheus, you do not hear, or else you disregard
my words of warning. You have done me wrong,
and yet, in spite of that, I warn you once
again: do not take arms against a god.
Stay quiet here. Bromius will not let you
drive his women from their revels on the mountain.

PENTHEUS: Don't you lecture me. You escaped from prison.
Or shall I punish you again?

DIONYSUS: If I were you,
I would offer him a sacrifice, not rage
and kick against necessity, a man defying
god.

PENTHEUS: I shall give your god the sacrifice
that he deserves. His victims will be his women.
I shall make a great slaughter in the woods of Cithaeron.

DIONYSUS: You will all be routed, shamefully defeated,
when their wands of ivy turn back your shields
of bronze.

PENTHEUS: It is hopeless to wrestle with this man.
Nothing on earth will make him hold his tongue.

DIONYSUS: Friend,
you can still save the situation.

PENTHEUS: How?
By accepting orders from my own slaves?

DIONYSUS: No.
I undertake to lead the women back to Thebes.
Without bloodshed.

PENTHEUS: This is some trap.

DIONYSUS: A trap?
How so, if I save you by my own devices?

PENTHEUS: I know.
You and they have conspired to establish your rites
forever.

DIONYSUS: True, I *have* conspired—with god.

PENTHEUS: Bring my armor, someone. And *you* stop talking.

> (PENTHEUS *strides toward the left, but when he is almost
> offstage,* DIONYSUS *calls imperiously to him.*)

DIONYSUS: *Wait!*
Would you like to *see* their revels on the mountain?

PENTHEUS: I would pay a great sum to see that sight.

DIONYSUS: Why are you so passionately curious?

PENTHEUS: Of course
I'd be sorry to see them drunk—

DIONYSUS: But for all your sorrow,
you'd like very much to see them?

PENTHEUS: Yes, very much.
I could crouch beneath the fir trees, out of sight.

DIONYSUS: But if you try to hide, they may track you down.

PENTHEUS: Your point is well taken. I will go openly.

DIONYSUS: Shall I lead you there now? Are you ready to go?

PENTHEUS: The sooner the better. The loss of even a moment
would be disappointing now.

DIONYSUS: First, however,
you must dress yourself in women's clothes.

PENTHEUS: *What?*
You want *me*, a man, to wear a woman's dress. But why?

DIONYSUS: If they knew you were a man, they would kill you
instantly.

PENTHEUS: True. You are an old hand at cunning, I see.

DIONYSUS: Dionysus taught me everything I know.

PENTHEUS: Your advice is to the point. What I fail to see
is what we do.

DIONYSUS: I shall go inside with you
and help you dress.

PENTHEUS: Dress? In a *woman's* dress,
you mean? I would die of shame.

DIONYSUS: Very well.
Then you no longer hanker to see the Maenads?

PENTHEUS: What is this costume I must wear?

DIONYSUS: On your head
I shall set a wig with long curls.

PENTHEUS: And then?

DIONYSUS: Next, robes to your feet and a net for your hair.

PENTHEUS: Yes? Go on.

DIONYSUS: Then a thyrsus for your hand
and a skin of dappled fawn.

PENTHEUS: I could not bear it.
I *cannot* bring myself to dress in women's clothes.

DIONYSUS: Then you must fight the Bacchae. That means
bloodshed.

PENTHEUS: Right. First we must go and reconnoiter.

DIONYSUS: Surely a wiser course than that of hunting bad
with worse.

PENTHEUS: But how can we pass through the city
without being seen?

DIONYSUS: We shall take deserted streets.
I will lead the way.

PENTHEUS: Any way you like,
provided those women of Bacchus don't jeer at me.
First, however, I shall ponder your advice,
whether to go or not.

DIONYSUS: Do as you please.

I am ready, whatever you decide.

PENTHEUS: Yes.
   Either I shall march with my army to the mountain
   or act on your advice.

                    (*Exit* PENTHEUS *into the palace.*)

DIONYSUS: Women, our prey now thrashes
   in the net we threw. He shall see the Bacchae
   and pay the price with death.
                         O Dionysus,
   now action rests with you. And you are near.
   Punish this man. But first distract his wits;
   bewilder him with madness. For sane of mind
   this man would never wear a woman's dress;
   but obsess his soul and he will not refuse.
   After those threats with which he was so fierce,
   I want him made the laughingstock of Thebes,
   paraded through the streets, a woman.
                                Now
   I shall go and costume Pentheus in the clothes
   which he must wear to Hades when he dies, butchered
   by the hands of his mother. He shall come to know
   Dionysus, son of Zeus, consummate god,
   most terrible, and yet most gentle, to mankind.

                    (*Exit* DIONYSUS *into the palace.*)

CHORUS: When shall I dance once more
   with bare feet the all-night dances,
   tossing my head for joy
   in the damp air, in the dew,
   as a running fawn might frisk
   for the green joy of the wide fields,

free from fear of the hunt,
free from the circling beaters
and the nets of woven mesh
and the hunters hallooing on
their yelping packs? And then, hard pressed,
she sprints with the quickness of wind,
bounding over the marsh, leaping
to frisk, leaping for joy,
gay with the green of the leaves,
to dance for joy in the forest,
to dance where the darkness is deepest,
   where no man is.

What is wisdom? What gift of the gods
is held in honor like this:
to hold your hand victorious
over the heads of those you hate?
Honor is precious forever.

Slow but unmistakable
the might of the gods moves on.
It punishes that man,
infatuate of soul
and hardened in his pride,
who disregards the gods.
The gods are crafty:
they lie in ambush
a long step of time
to hunt the unholy.
Beyond the old beliefs,
no thought, no act shall go.
Small, small is the cost
to believe in this:
whatever is god is strong;
whatever long time has sanctioned,

that is a law forever;
the law tradition makes
is the law of nature.

What is wisdom? What gift of the gods
is held in honor like this:
to hold your hand victorious
over the heads of those you hate?
Honor is precious forever.

Blessèd is he who escapes a storm at sea,
    who comes home to his harbor.
Blessèd is he who emerges from under affliction.
In various ways one man outraces another in the
    race for wealth and power.
Ten thousand men possess ten thousand hopes.
A few bear fruit in happiness; the others go awry.
But he who garners day by day the good of life,
    he is happiest. Blessèd is he.

> (*Re-enter* DIONYSUS *from the palace. At the threshold
> he turns and calls back to* PENTHEUS.)

DIONYSUS: Pentheus, if you are still so curious to see
    forbidden sights, so bent on evil still,
    come out. Let us see you in your woman's dress,
    disguised in Maenad clothes so you may go and spy
    upon your mother and her company.

(*Enter* PENTHEUS *from the palace. He wears a long linen dress
    which partially conceals his fawn-skin. He carries a thyrsus
    in his hand; on his head he wears a wig with long blond
    curls bound by a snood. He is dazed and completely in
    the power of the god who has now possessed him.*)

Why,
you look exactly like one of the daughters of Cadmus.

PENTHEUS: I seem to see two suns blazing in the heavens.
And now two Thebes, two cities, and each
with seven gates. And you—you are a bull
who walks before me there. Horns have sprouted
from your head. Have you always been a beast?
But now I see a bull.

DIONYSUS: It is the god you see.
Though hostile formerly, he now declares a truce
and goes with us. You see what you could not
when you were blind.

PENTHEUS (*coyly primping*): Do I look like anyone?
Like Ino or my mother Agave?

DIONYSUS: So much alike
I almost might be seeing one of them. But look:
one of your curls has come loose from under the snood
where I tucked it.

PENTHEUS: It must have worked loose
when I was dancing for joy and shaking my head.

DIONYSUS: Then let me be your maid and tuck it back.
Hold still.

PENTHEUS: Arrange it. I am in your hands
completely.

                    (DIONYSUS *tucks the curl back under the snood*.)

DIONYSUS: And now your strap has slipped. Yes,
and your robe hangs askew at the ankles.

PENTHEUS (*bending backward to look*):   I think so.
  At least on my right leg. But on the left the hem
  lies straight.

DIONYSUS: You will think me the best of friends
  when you see to your surprise how chaste the Bacchae are.

PENTHEUS: But to be a real Bacchante, should I hold
  the wand in my right hand? Or this way?

DIONYSUS: No.
  In your right hand. And raise it as you raise
  your right foot. I commend your change of heart.

PENTHEUS: Could I lift Cithaeron up, do you think?
  Shoulder the cliffs, Bacchae and all?

DIONYSUS: If you wanted.
  Your mind was once unsound, but now you think
  as sane men do.

PENTHEUS: Should we take crowbars with us?
  Or should I put my shoulder to the cliffs
  and heave them up?

DIONYSUS: What? And destroy the haunts
  of the nymphs, the holy groves where Pan plays
  his woodland pipe?

PENTHEUS: You are right. In any case,
  women should not be mastered by brute strength.
  I will hide myself beneath the firs instead.

DIONYSUS: You will find all the ambush you deserve,
  creeping up to spy on the Maenads.

PENTHEUS: Think.
I can see them already, there among the bushes,
mating like birds, caught in the toils of love.

DIONYSUS: Exactly. This is your mission: you go to watch.
You may surprise them—or they may surprise you.

PENTHEUS: Then lead me through the very heart of Thebes,
since I, alone of all this city, dare to go.

DIONYSUS: You and you alone will suffer for your city.
A great ordeal awaits you. But you are worthy
of your fate. I shall lead you safely there;
someone else shall bring you back.

PENTHEUS: Yes, my mother.

DIONYSUS: An example to all men.

PENTHEUS: It is for that I go.

DIONYSUS: You will be carried home—

PENTHEUS: O luxury!

DIONYSUS: cradled in your mother's arms.

PENTHEUS: You will spoil me.

DIONYSUS: I *mean* to spoil you.

PENTHEUS: I go to my reward.

DIONYSUS: You are an extraordinary young man, and you go
to an extraordinary experience. You shall win
a glory towering to heaven and usurping
god's.

(*Exit* PENTHEUS.)

Agave and you daughters of Cadmus,
reach out your hands! I bring this young man
to a great ordeal. The victor? Bromius.
Bromius—and I. The rest the event shall show.

(*Exit* DIONYSUS.)

CHORUS: Run to the mountain, fleet hounds of madness!
    Run, run to the revels of Cadmus' daughters!
    Sting them against the man in women's clothes,
    the madman who spies on the Maenads, who peers
    from behind the rocks, who spies from a vantage!
    His mother shall see him first. She will cry
    to the Maenads: "Who is this spy who has come
    to the mountains to peer at the mountain-revels
    of the women of Thebes? What bore him, Bacchae?
    This man was born of no woman. Some lioness
    give him birth, some one of the Libyan gorgons!"

    O Justice, principle of order, spirit of custom,
    come! Be manifest; reveal yourself with a sword!
    Stab through the throat that godless man,
    the mocker who goes, flouting custom and outraging god!
    O Justice, stab the evil earth-born spawn of Echion!

    Uncontrollable, the unbeliever goes,
    in spitting rage, rebellious and amok,
    madly assaulting the mysteries of god,
    profaning the rites of the mother of god.
    Against the unassailable he runs, with rage
    obsessed. Headlong he runs to death.
    For death the gods exact, curbing by that bit
    the mouths of men. They humble us with death
    that we remember what we are who are not god,

but men. We run to death. Wherefore, I say,
accept, accept:
humility is wise; humility is blest.
But what the world calls wise I do not want.
Elsewhere the chase. I hunt another game,
those great, those manifest, those certain goals,
achieving which, our mortal lives are blest.
Let these things be the quarry of my chase:
purity; humility; an unrebellious soul,
accepting all. Let me go the customary way,
the timeless, honored, beaten path of those who walk
with reverence and awe beneath the sons of heaven.

O Justice, principle of order, spirit of custom,
come! Be manifest; reveal yourself with a sword!
Stab through the throat that godless man,
the mocker who goes, flouting custom and outraging god!
O Justice, destroy the evil earth-born spawn of Echion!

O Dionysus, reveal yourself a bull! Be manifest,
a snake with darting heads, a lion breathing fire!
O Bacchus, come! Come with your smile!
Cast your noose about this man who hunts
your Bacchae! Bring him down, trampled
underfoot by the murderous herd of your Maenads!

(*Enter a* MESSENGER *from Cithaeron.*)

MESSENGER: How prosperous in Hellas these halls once were,
this house founded by Cadmus, the stranger from Sidon
who sowed the dragon seed in the land of the snake!
I am a slave and nothing more, yet even so
I mourn the fortunes of this fallen house.

CORYPHAEUS: What is it?
Is there news of the Bacchae?

MESSENGER: This is my news:
Pentheus, the son of Echion, is dead.

CORYPHAEUS: All hail to Bromius! Our god is a great god!

MESSENGER: What is this you say, women? You dare to rejoice
at these disasters which destroy this house?

CORYPHAEUS: I am no Greek. I hail my god
in my own way. No longer need I
shrink with fear of prison.

MESSENGER: If you suppose this city is so short of men—

CORYPHAEUS: Dionysus, Dionysus, not Thebes,
has power over me.

MESSENGER: Your feelings might be forgiven, then. But this,
this exultation in disaster—it is not right.

CORYPHAEUS: Tell us how the mocker died.
How was he killed?

MESSENGER: There were three of us in all: Pentheus and I,
attending my master, and that stranger who volunteered
his services as guide. Leaving behind us
the last outlying farms of Thebes, we forded
the Asopus and struck into the barren scrubland
of Cithaeron.
　　　　　　There in a grassy glen we halted,
unmoving, silent, without a word,
so we might see but not be seen. From that vantage,
in a hollow cut from the sheer rock of the cliffs,
a place where water ran and the pines grew dense
with shade, we saw the Maenads sitting, their hands
busily moving at their happy tasks. Some

wound the stalks of their tattered wands with tendrils
of fresh ivy; others, frisking like fillies
newly freed from the painted bridles, chanted
in Bacchic songs, responsively.

But Pentheus—
unhappy man—could not quite see the companies
of women. "Stranger," he said, "from where I stand,
I cannot see these counterfeited Maenads.
But if I climbed that towering fir that overhangs
the banks, then I could see their shameless orgies
better."

And now the stranger worked a miracle.
Reaching for the highest branch of a great fir,
he bent it down, down, down to the dark earth,
till it was curved the way a taut bow bends
or like a rim of wood when forced about the circle
of a wheel. Like that he forced that mountain fir
down to the ground. No mortal could have done it.
Then he seated Pentheus at the highest tip
and with his hands let the trunk rise straightly up,
slowly and gently, lest it throw its rider.
And the tree rose, towering to heaven, with my master
huddled at the top. And now the Maenads saw him
more clearly than he saw them. But barely had they seen,
when the stranger vanished and there came a great voice
out of heaven—Dionysus', it must have been—
crying: "Women, I bring you the man who has mocked
at you and me and at our holy mysteries.
Take vengeance upon him." And as he spoke
a flash of awful fire bound earth and heaven.
The high air hushed, and along the forest glen
the leaves hung still; you could hear no cry of beasts.
The Bacchae heard that voice but missed its words,
and leaping up, they stared, peering everywhere.
Again that voice. And now they knew his cry,
the clear command of god. And breaking loose

like startled doves, through grove and torrent,
over jagged rocks, they flew, their feet maddened
by the breath of god. And when they saw my master
perching in his tree, they climbed a great stone
that towered opposite his perch and showered him
with stones and javelins of fir, while the others
hurled their wands. And yet they missed their target,
poor Pentheus in his perch, barely out of reach
of their eager hands, treed, unable to escape.
Finally they splintered branches from the oaks
and with those bars of wood tried to lever up the tree
by prying at the roots. But every effort failed.
Then Agave cried out: "Maenads, make a circle
about the trunk and grip it with your hands.
Unless we take this climbing beast, he will reveal
the secrets of the god." With that, thousands of hands
tore the fir tree from the earth, and down, down
from his high perch fell Pentheus, tumbling
to the ground, sobbing and screaming as he fell,
for he knew his end was near. His own mother,
like a priestess with her victim, fell upon him
first. But snatching off his wig and snood
so she would recognize his face, he touched her cheeks,
screaming, *"No, no, Mother! I am Pentheus,*
your own son, the child you bore to Echion!
Pity me, spare me, Mother! I have done a wrong,
but do not kill your own son for my offense."
But she was foaming at the mouth, and her crazed eyes
rolling with frenzy. She was mad, stark mad,
possessed by Bacchus. Ignoring his cries of pity,
she seized his left arm at the wrist; then, planting
her foot upon his chest, she pulled, wrenching away
the arm at the shoulder—not by her own strength,
for the god had put inhuman power in her hands.
Ino, meanwhile, on the other side, was scratching off
his flesh. Then Autonoë and the whole horde

of Bacchae swarmed upon him. Shouts everywhere,
he screaming with what little breath was left,
they shrieking in triumph. One tore off an arm,
another a foot still warm in its shoe. His ribs
were clawed clean of flesh and every hand
was smeared with blood as they played ball with scraps
of Pentheus' body.

          The pitiful remains lie scattered,
one piece among the sharp rocks, others
lying lost among the leaves in the depths
of the forest. His mother, picking up his head,
impaled it on her wand. She seems to think it is
some mountain lion's head which she carries in triumph
through the thick of Cithaeron. Leaving her sisters
at the Maenad dances, she is coming here, gloating
over her grisly prize. She calls upon Bacchus:
he is her "fellow-huntsman," "comrade of the chase,
crowned with victory." But all the victory
she carries home is her own grief.

                    Now,
before Agave returns, let me leave
this scene of sorrow. Humility,
a sense of reverence before the sons of heaven—
of all the prizes that a mortal man might win,
these, I say, are wisest; these are best.

                    (*Exit* MESSENGER.)

CHORUS: We dance to the glory of Bacchus!
   We dance to the death of Pentheus,
   the death of the spawn of the dragon!
     He dressed in woman's dress;
     he took the lovely thyrsus;
     it waved him down to death,
       led by a bull to Hades.
  Hail, Bacchae! Hail, women of Thebes!

Your victory is fair, fair the prize,
  this famous prize of grief!
Glorious the game! To fold your child
in your arms, streaming with his blood!

CORYPHAEUS: But look: there comes Pentheus' mother, Agave,
running wild-eyed toward the palace.
                                    —Welcome,
welcome to the reveling band of the god of joy!

(*Enter* AGAVE *with other Bacchantes. She is covered with blood
and carries the head of* PENTHEUS *impaled upon her thyrsus.*)

AGAVE: Bacchae of Asia—

CHORUS: Speak, speak.

AGAVE: We bring this branch to the palace,
  this fresh-cut spray from the mountains.
  Happy was the hunting.

CHORUS: I see.
  I welcome our fellow-reveler of god.

AGAVE: The whelp of a wild mountain lion,
  and snared by me without a noose.
  Look, look at the prize I bring.

CHORUS: Where was he caught?

AGAVE: On Cithaeron—

CHORUS: On Cithaeron?

AGAVE: Our prize was killed.

CHORUS: Who killed him?

AGAVE: I struck him first.
  The Maenads call me "Agave the blest."

CHORUS: And then?

AGAVE: Cadmus'—

CHORUS: Cadmus'?

AGAVE: Daughters.
  After me, they reached the prey.
  After me. Happy was the hunting.

CHORUS: Happy indeed.

AGAVE: Then share my glory,
  share the feast.

CHORUS: Share, unhappy woman?

AGAVE: See, the whelp is young and tender.
  Beneath the soft mane of its hair,
  the down is blooming on the cheeks.

CHORUS: With that mane he *looks* a beast.

AGAVE: Our god is wise. Cunningly, cleverly,
  Bacchus the hunter lashed the Maenads
  against his prey.

CHORUS: Our king is a hunter.

AGAVE: You praise me now?

CHORUS: I praise you.

AGAVE: The men of Thebes—

CHORUS: And Pentheus, your son?

AGAVE: Will praise his mother. She caught
   a great quarry, this lion's cub.

CHORUS: Extraordinary catch.

AGAVE: Extraordinary skill.

CHORUS: You are proud?

AGAVE: Proud and happy.
   I have won the trophy of the chase,
   a great prize, manifest to all.

CORYPHAEUS: Then, poor woman, show the citizens of Thebes
   this great prize, this trophy you have won
   in the hunt.

   (AGAVE *proudly exhibits her thyrsus with the head*
                 of PENTHEUS *impaled upon the point.*)

AGAVE: You citizens of this towered city,
   men of Thebes, behold the trophy of your women's
   hunting! *This* is the quarry of our chase, taken
   not with nets nor spears of bronze but by the white
   and delicate hands of women. What are they worth,
   your boastings now and all that uselessness
   your armor is, since we, with our bare hands,
   captured this quarry and tore its bleeding body
   limb from limb?
                    —But where is my father, Cadmus?

He should come. And my son. Where is Pentheus?
Fetch him. I will have him set his ladder up
against the wall and, there upon the beam,
nail the head of this wild lion I have killed
as a trophy of my hunt.

(*Enter* CADMUS, *followed by attendants who bear upon
a bier the dismembered body of* PENTHEUS.)

CADMUS: Follow me, attendants.
Bear your dreadful burden in and set it down,
there before the palace.

(*The attendants set down the bier.*)

                    This was Pentheus
whose body, after long and weary searchings
I painfully assembled from Cithaeron's glens
where it lay, scattered in shreds, dismembered
throughout the forest, no two pieces
in a single place.
                    Old Teiresias and I
had returned to Thebes from the orgies on the mountain
before I learned of this atrocious crime
my daughters did. And so I hurried back
to the mountain to recover the body of this boy
murdered by the Maenads. There among the oaks
I found Aristaeus' wife, the mother of Actaeon,
Autonoë, and with her Ino, both
still stung with madness. But Agave, they said,
was on her way to Thebes, still possessed.
And what they said was true, for there she is,
and not a happy sight.

AGAVE: Now, Father,
yours can be the proudest boast of living men.

For you are now the father of the bravest daughters
in the world. All of your daughters are brave,
but I above the rest. I have left my shuttle
at the loom; I raised my sight to higher things—
to hunting animals with my bare hands.

                                            You see?
Here in my hands I hold the quarry of my chase,
a trophy for our house. Take it, Father, take it.
Glory in my kill and invite your friends to share
the feast of triumph. For you are blest, Father,
by this great deed I have done.

CADMUS: This is a grief
so great it knows no size. I cannot look.
This is the awful murder your hands have done.
This, this is the noble victim you have slaughtered
to the gods. And to share a feast like this
you now invite all Thebes and me?

                                    O gods,
how terribly I pity you and then myself.
Justly—too, too justly—has lord Bromius,
this god of our own blood, destroyed us all,
every one.

AGAVE: How scowling and crabbed is old age
in men. I hope my son takes after his mother
and wins, as she has done, the laurels of the chase
when he goes hunting with the younger men of Thebes.
But all my son can do is quarrel with god.
He should be scolded, Father, and you are the one
who should scold him. Yes, someone call him out
so he can see his mother's triumph.

CADMUS: Enough. No more.
When you realize the horror you have done,
you shall suffer terribly. But if with luck

your present madness lasts until you die,
you will seem to have, not having, happiness.

AGAVE: Why do you reproach me? Is there something wrong?

CADMUS: First raise your eyes to the heavens.

AGAVE: There.
But why?

CADMUS: Does it look the same as it did before?
Or has it changed?

AGAVE: It seems—somehow—clearer,
brighter than it was before.

CADMUS: Do you still feel
the same flurry inside you?

AGAVE: The same—flurry?
No, I feel—somehow—calmer. I feel as though—
my mind were somehow—changing.

CADMUS: Can you still hear me?
Can you answer clearly?

AGAVE: No. I have forgotten
what we were saying, Father.

CADMUS: Who was your husband?

AGAVE: Echion—a man, they said, born of the dragon seed.

CADMUS: What was the name of the child you bore your
husband?

AGAVE: Pentheus.

CADMUS: And whose head do you hold in your hands?

AGAVE (*averting her eyes*): A lion's head—or so the hunters told me.

CADMUS: Look directly at it. Just a quick glance.

AGAVE: What is it? What am I holding in my hands?

CADMUS: Look more closely still. Study it carefully.

AGAVE: *No!* O gods, I see the greatest grief there is.

CADMUS: Does it look like a lion now?

AGAVE: No, no. It is—
    Pentheus' head—I hold—

CADMUS: And mourned by me
    before you ever knew.

AGAVE: But *who* killed him?
    Why am *I* holding him?

CADMUS: O savage truth,
    what a time to come!

AGAVE: For god's sake, speak.
    My heart is beating with terror.

CADMUS: *You* killed him.
    You and your sisters.

AGAVE: But where was he killed?

Here at home? Where?

CADMUS: He was killed on Cithaeron,
    there where the hounds tore Actaeon to pieces.

AGAVE: But why? Why had Pentheus gone to Cithaeron?

CADMUS: He went to your revels to mock the god.

AGAVE: But *we*—
    what were we doing on the mountain?

CADMUS: You were mad.
    The whole city was possessed.

AGAVE: Now, now I see:
    Dionysus has destroyed us all.

CADMUS: You outraged him.
    You denied that he was truly god.

AGAVE: Father,
    where is my poor boy's body now?

CADMUS: There it is.
    I gathered the pieces with great difficulty.

AGAVE: Is his body entire? Has he been laid out well?

CADMUS: [All but the head. The rest is mutilated
    horribly.]

AGAVE: But why should Pentheus suffer for my crime?

CADMUS: He, like you, blasphemed the god. And so
    the god has brought us all to ruin at one blow,

you, your sisters, and this boy. All our house
the god has utterly destroyed and, with it,
me. For I have no sons left, no male heir;
and I have lived only to see this boy,
this branch of your own body, most horribly
and foully killed.

(*He turns and addresses the corpse.*)

—To you my house looked up.
Child, you were the stay of my house; you were
my daughter's son. Of you this city stood in awe.
No one who once had seen your face dared outrage
the old man, or if he did, you punished him.
Now I must go, a banished and dishonored man—
I, Cadmus the great, who sowed the soldiery
of Thebes and harvested a great harvest. My son,
dearest to me of all men—for even dead,
I count you still the man I love the most—
never again will your hand touch my chin;
no more, child, will you hug me and call me
"Grandfather" and say, "Who is wronging you?
Does anyone trouble you or vex your heart, old man?
Tell me, Grandfather, and I will punish him."
No, now there is grief for me; the mourning
for you; pity for your mother; and for her sisters,
sorrow.
            If there is still any mortal man
who despises or defies the gods, let him look
on this boy's death and believe in the gods.

CORYPHAEUS: Cadmus, I pity you. Your daughter's son
has died as he deserved, and yet his death
bears hard on you.

[At this point there is a break in the manuscript of nearly fifty lines. The following speeches of Agave and Coryphaeus and the first part of Dionysus' speech have been conjecturally reconstructed from fragments and later material which made use of *The Bacchae*. Lines which can plausibly be assigned to the lacuna are otherwise not indicated. My own inventions are designed not to complete the speeches, but to effect a transition between the fragments, and are bracketed. —TRANS.]

AGAVE: O Father, now you can see
how everything has changed. I am in anguish now,
tormented, who walked in triumph minutes past,
exulting in my kill. And that prize I carried home
with such pride was my own curse. Upon these hands
I bear the curse of my son's blood. How then
with these accursed hands may I touch his body?
How can I, accursed with such a curse, hold him
to my breast? O gods, what dirge can I sing
[that there might be] a dirge [for every]
broken limb? . . .
              Where is a shroud to cover up his corpse?
O my child, what hands will give you proper care
unless with my own hands I lift my curse?

(*She lifts up one of* PENTHEUS' *limbs and asks the help of*
CADMUS *in piecing the body together. She mourns each
piece separately before replacing it on the bier.*)

Come, Father. We must restore his head
to this unhappy boy. As best we can, we shall make
him whole again.
            —O dearest, dearest face!
Pretty boyish mouth! Now with this veil
I shroud your head, gathering with loving care
these mangled bloody limbs, this flesh I brought
to birth . . .

CORYPHAEUS: Let this scene teach those [who see these things:
    Dionysus is the son] of Zeus.

    (*Above the palace* DIONYSUS *appears in epiphany.*)

DIONYSUS: [I am Dionysus,
    the son of Zeus, returned to Thebes, revealed,
    a god to men.] But the men [of Thebes] blasphemed me.
    They slandered me; they said I came of mortal man,
    and not content with speaking blasphemies,
    [they dared to threaten my person with violence.]
    These crimes this people whom I cherished well
    did from malice to their benefactor. Therefore,
    I now disclose the sufferings in store for them.
    Like [enemies], they shall be driven from this city
    to other lands; there, submitting to the yoke
    of slavery, they shall wear out wretched lives,
    captives of war, enduring much indignity.

    (*He turns to the corpse of* PENTHEUS.)

    This man has found the death which he deserved,
    torn to pieces among the jagged rocks.
    You are my witnesses: he came with outrage;
    he attempted to chain my hands, abusing me
    [and doing what he should least of all have done.]
    And therefore he has rightly perished by the hands
    of those who should the least of all have murdered him.
    What he suffers, he suffers justly.
                        Upon you,
    Agave, and on your sisters I pronounce this doom:
    you shall leave this city in expiation
    of the murder you have done. You are unclean,
    and it would be a sacrilege that murderers
    should remain at peace beside the graves [of those
    whom they have killed]. . . .

(*He turns to* CADMUS.)

[Manuscript resumes here.]

          Next I shall disclose the trials
which await this man. You, Cadmus, shall be changed
to a serpent, and your wife, the child of Ares,
immortal Harmonia, shall undergo your doom,
a serpent too. With her, it is your fate
to go a journey in a car drawn on by oxen,
leading behind you a great barbarian host.
For thus decrees the oracle of Zeus.
With a host so huge its numbers cannot be counted,
you shall ravage many cities; but when your army
plunders the shrine of Apollo, its homecoming
shall be perilous and hard. Yet in the end
the god Ares shall save Harmonia and you
and bring you both to live among the blest.
   So say I, born of no mortal father,
Dionysus, true son of Zeus. If then,
when you would not, you had muzzled your madness,
you should have an ally now in the son of Zeus.

CADMUS: We implore you, Dionysus. We have done wrong.

DIONYSUS: Too late. When there was time, you did not know me.

CADMUS: We have learned. But your sentence is too harsh.

DIONYSUS: I am a god. I was blasphemed by you.

CADMUS: Gods should be exempt from human passions.

DIONYSUS: Long ago my father Zeus ordained these things.

AGAVE: It is fated, Father. We must go.

DIONYSUS: Why then delay?
  For you must go.

CADMUS: Child, to what a dreadful end
  have we all come, you and your wretched sisters
  and my unhappy self. An old man, I must go
  to live a stranger among barbarian peoples, doomed
  to lead against Hellas a motley foreign army.
  Transformed to serpents, I and my wife,
  Harmonia, the child of Ares, we must captain
  spearsmen against the tombs and shrines of Hellas.
  Never shall my sufferings end; not even
  over Acheron shall I have peace.

AGAVE (*embracing* CADMUS):   O Father,
  to be banished, to live without you!

CADMUS: Poor child,
  like a white swan warding its weak old father,
  why do you clasp those white arms about my neck?

AGAVE: But banished! Where shall I go?

CADMUS: I do not know,
  my child. Your father can no longer help you.

AGAVE: Farewell, my home! City, farewell.
  O bridal bed, banished I go,
  in misery, I leave you now.

CADMUS: Go, poor child, seek shelter in Aristaeus' house.

AGAVE: I pity you, Father.

CADMUS: And I pity you, my child,
  and I grieve for your poor sisters. I pity them.

AGAVE: Terribly has Dionysus brought
    disaster down upon this house.

DIONYSUS: I was terribly blasphemed,
    my name dishonored in Thebes.

AGAVE: Farewell, Father.

CADMUS: Farewell to you, unhappy child.
    Fare well. But you shall find your faring hard.

(Exit CADMUS.*)*

AGAVE: Lead me, guides, where my sisters wait,
    poor sisters of my exile. Let me go
    where I shall never see Cithaeron more,
    where that accursed hill may not see me,
    where I shall find no trace of thyrsus!
        That I leave to other Bacchae.

(Exit AGAVE *with attendants.)*

CHORUS: The gods have many shapes.
    The gods bring many things
    to their accomplishment.
    And what was most expected
    has not been accomplished.
    But god has found his way
    for what no man expected.
        So ends the play. ⌒

INTERPRETIVE QUESTIONS
FOR DISCUSSION

Why is Pentheus so intent upon capturing and punishing the Bacchae?

1. Why does Pentheus regard the religious rites of the Maenads as an "obscene disorder"—mock ecstasies serving the lusts of men? (179)

2. Why does Pentheus rage that Thebes is "humiliated in the eyes of Hellas" by the conduct of its women? (202)

3. Why does Pentheus cut off Dionysus' "girlish curls"? (190–191) Why does he respond immediately to Dionysus' beauty yet mock the effeminate stranger? (188)

4. Why does Euripides have the Bacchae warn us against hunting "a glory" or tracking "some boundless, superhuman dream"? Are we meant to see Pentheus as one who aspires to "outrange the limits of man"? (186)

5. Why does Pentheus ignore Dionysus' warning to place no chains on him, boldly asserting, "But *I* say: chain him. / And I am the stronger here"? (191) Does Pentheus understand that he is waging war against a god?

6. Why does Dionysus respond to Pentheus' threat of chains by telling him, "You do not know who you are"? (192)

7. Why is Pentheus so "passionately curious" to observe the revels of the Bacchae? (204)

8. Why does Euripides have Dionysus and Pentheus share a common ancestry through Cadmus? (170–172) Why does Euripides have Pentheus disguise himself with a wig that has long curls like those of Dionysus? (205–206, 210)

9. What does Dionysus mean when he says that Pentheus is "worthy" of the "great ordeal" that is his fate? (212)

10. Why must Pentheus pay such a horrible price—dismemberment by his own mother—for having mocked Dionysus, the Maenads, and their mysteries?

Suggested textual analyses

Pages 179–180: beginning, "(*Enter* PENTHEUS *from the right. He is a young man of athletic build,*" and ending, "then you may be sure the festival is rotten."

Pages 187–192: beginning, "Pentheus, here we are; not empty-handed either," and ending, "(*Exeunt attendants with* DIONYSUS *captive.*)"

Why do both Pentheus and the Bacchae see themselves as being on the side of order?

1. Why do the Bacchae call on the "principle of order" to savage Pentheus, the "mocker who goes, flouting custom"? (213)

2. Why do the Bacchae proclaim that "whatever long time has sanctioned,/ that is a law forever;/ the law tradition makes/ is the law of nature"? (208–209) Is Euripides saying that the law of nature is separate from the law of the state?

3. Why are we told that Pentheus plans a great slaughter in order to stop the spread of Bacchic violence? (203)

4. Why do the Maenads identify with wild animals, wearing fawn-skins and suckling young wolves and gazelles? (200) Why are we told that on Mt. Cithaeron the Maenads pillaged

and destroyed everything in sight and snatched children from their homes? (201)

5. Why is Dionysus the "consummate god, / most terrible, and yet most gentle, to mankind"? (207) Why do his gifts include raw flesh torn from living animals, as well as milk, honey, and wine? (175, 200)

6. Why does Euripides have Dionysus claim that wisdom lies in constraint and the control of passions? (197)

7. Why does Dionysus offer to lead the Bacchae back to Thebes without bloodshed? (204) Is this offer made in good faith?

8. Why does Dionysus say that Pentheus "has *rightly* perished by the hands / of those who should the least of all have murdered him" (italics added)? (229)

9. Why does Dionysus insist that Agave and her sisters expiate the murder he has caused them to commit? Why would it be a "sacrilege" for them to remain at peace beside the grave of the murdered Pentheus? (229)

10. Is Cadmus speaking for Euripides when he says that "gods should be exempt from human passions"? (230)

Suggested textual analyses

Pages 207–209: beginning, "Women, our prey now thrashes," and ending, "he is happiest. Blessèd is he."

Pages 213–214: beginning, "Run to the mountain, fleet hounds of madness!" and ending, "trampled / underfoot by the murderous herd of your Maenads!"

Why does Euripides have Agave fail in her aspirations to manly glory?

1. Why is it only the women of Thebes that Dionysus has driven from home to wander mad in the mountains? (171)

2. Why does the worship of Dionysus bring liberation from "shuttle and loom"? (175) Why does Euripides have Pentheus threaten to sell the Asian Bacchae as slaves or put them to work at his looms? (192)

3. Why does Agave say that in hunting animals with her bare hands she has turned her sight to "higher things" than her shuttle and loom? (223)

4. Why does Euripides have Teiresias tell Pentheus that "even in the rites of Dionysus,/the chaste woman will not be corrupted"? (182)

5. Why does Dionysus turn women into fierce hunters of men? Why are we told of the women routing the men of Hysiae and Erythrae? (201)

6. Why are we told that Agave attacked her son "like a priestess with her victim"? (217) Why is Pentheus destroyed by being torn apart, like a sacrificial victim?

7. Why does Euripides have Agave attack Pentheus in a maddened state, so that she kills her son without realizing what she is doing? (217–218)

8. Why is Agave made to boast of her triumphant "women's hunting" before the men of Thebes? Why does she deride the "uselessness" of men's armor compared to the "white and delicate hands" of women? (221)

9. Why does Euripides make Agave, through the murder of her son, the agent of destruction of the royal house of Thebes? (227)

10. Are we meant to view the worship of Dionysus as liberation or servitude?

Suggested textual analyses

Pages 200–202: beginning, "We cowherds and shepherds," and ending, "nor other pleasure left to men."

Pages 219–223: beginning, "(*Enter* AGAVE *with other Bacchantes,*" and ending, "this god of our own blood, destroyed us all, / every one."

Why does Euripides have Asian mysteries triumph over Greek rationality?

1. Why is Pentheus made to experience Bacchic madness before he is punished for his defiance of the god?

2. Why does Dionysus allow Pentheus to think that he has succeeded in imprisoning the effeminate stranger when he has really only chained a bull? Why does Dionysus allow a phantom of himself to be stabbed by Pentheus? (196–197)

3. Why does Dionysus' revenge include humiliating Pentheus by dressing him like a woman and parading him through the streets of Thebes? (207)

4. When in the possession of Dionysus, why does Pentheus become childlike, eagerly anticipating his return to Thebes cradled in his mother's arms? (212)

5. Why does Cadmus try to persuade Pentheus to worship Dionysus by telling him, "Your home is here / with us, with our customs and traditions, not / outside, alone"? (183)

6. Are Teiresias and Cadmus sincere in their devotion to Dionysus, or are they just worshipping him out of expediency? (184)

7. Why do the Asian Bacchae align themselves with the common people, asserting that "what the common people do,/the things that simple men believe,/I too believe and do"? (187) Is Euripides suggesting that Hellas needs a new infusion of democratic principles?

8. Why do the Asian Bacchae call Pentheus "inhuman, a rabid beast"? Why are we repeatedly reminded that, as the son of Echion, Pentheus was "born of the breed of Earth,/spawned by the dragon"? (193, 218)

9. Is the messenger who witnesses Pentheus' death speaking for Euripides when he says, "Humility,/a sense of reverence before the sons of heaven—/of all the prizes that a mortal man might win,/these, I say, are wisest"? (218)

10. Why does the play end with images and events—dismemberment, exile, and slavery—that signify a complete collapse of human order?

Suggested textual analysis
Pages 216–218: beginning, "And now the stranger worked a miracle," and ending, "these, I say, are wisest; these are best."

FOR FURTHER REFLECTION

1. Are reason and religion in conflict? Is religion allied with madness?

2. Why does religion often demand sacrifice, whether literal or sacramental?

3. Does civilization depend on a periodic, controlled indulgence in violence?

4. Is Euripides suggesting that Greek culture is fatally flawed by its oppression of women?

5. Is psychic androgyny an ideal that we should aspire to?

6. Should human beings attempt to embrace the Dionysian force? How can we best do so without losing control?

EVERYTHING THAT RISES MUST CONVERGE

Flannery O'Connor

FLANNERY O'CONNOR (1925–1964)
was born in Savannah, Georgia. During her
short life she produced two novels, *Wise
Blood* and *The Violent Bear It Away,* and
two collections of short stories, *A Good
Man Is Hard to Find* and *Everything That
Rises Must Converge.* O'Connor's brutal,
comic fiction focuses on life in the South
and reflects her strong Roman Catholic
faith. Suffering from a form of lupus,
she spent the last ten years of her life as
an invalid, writing and raising peacocks
on her mother's farm in Georgia.

H ER DOCTOR had told Julian's mother that she must lose twenty pounds on account of her blood pressure, so on Wednesday nights Julian had to take her downtown on the bus for a reducing class at the Y. The reducing class was designed for working girls over fifty, who weighed from 165 to 200 pounds. His mother was one of the slimmer ones, but she said ladies did not tell their age or weight. She would not ride the buses by herself at night since they had been integrated, and because the reducing class was one of her few pleasures, necessary for her health, and *free,* she said Julian could at least put himself out to take her, considering all she did for him. Julian did not like to consider all she did for him, but every Wednesday night he braced himself and took her.

She was almost ready to go, standing before the hall mirror, putting on her hat, while he, his hands behind him, appeared pinned to the door frame, waiting like Saint Sebastian for the arrows to begin piercing him. The hat was new and had cost her seven dollars and a half. She kept saying, "Maybe I shouldn't have paid that for it. No, I shouldn't have. I'll take it off and return it tomorrow. I shouldn't have bought it."

Julian raised his eyes to heaven. "Yes, you should have bought it," he said. "Put it on and let's go." It was a hideous hat. A purple velvet flap came down on one side of it and stood up on the other; the rest of it was green and looked like a cushion with the stuffing out. He decided it was less comical than jaunty and pathetic. Everything that gave her pleasure was small and depressed him.

She lifted the hat one more time and set it down slowly on top of her head. Two wings of gray hair protruded on either side of her florid face, but her eyes, sky-blue, were as innocent and untouched by experience as they must have been when she was ten. Were it not that she was a widow who had struggled fiercely to feed and clothe and put him through school and who was supporting him still, "until he got on his feet," she might have been a little girl that he had to take to town.

"It's all right, it's all right," he said. "Let's go." He opened the door himself and started down the walk to get her going. The sky was a dying violet and the houses stood out darkly against it, bulbous liver-colored monstrosities of a uniform ugliness though no two were alike. Since this had been a fashionable neighborhood forty years ago, his mother persisted in thinking they did well to have an apartment in it. Each house had a narrow collar of dirt around it in which sat, usually, a grubby child. Julian walked with his hands in his pockets, his head down and thrust forward and his eyes glazed with the determination to make himself completely numb during the time he would be sacrificed to her pleasure.

The door closed and he turned to find the dumpy figure, surmounted by the atrocious hat, coming toward him. "Well," she said, "you only live once and paying a little more for it, I at least won't meet myself coming and going."

"Some day I'll start making money," Julian said gloomily— he knew he never would—"and you can have one of those jokes whenever you take the fit." But first they would move. He visualized a place where the nearest neighbors would be three miles away on either side.

"I think you're doing fine," she said, drawing on her gloves. "You've only been out of school a year. Rome wasn't built in a day."

She was one of the few members of the Y reducing class who arrived in hat and gloves and who had a son who had been to college. "It takes time," she said, "and the world is in such a mess. This hat looked better on me than any of the others, though when she brought it out I said, 'Take that thing back. I wouldn't have it on my head,' and she said, 'Now wait till you see it on,' and when she put it on me, I said, 'We-ull,' and she said, 'If you ask me, that hat does something for you and you do something for the hat, and besides,' she said, 'with that hat, you won't meet yourself coming and going.'"

Julian thought he could have stood his lot better if she had been selfish, if she had been an old hag who drank and screamed at him. He walked along, saturated in depression, as if in the midst of his martyrdom he had lost his faith. Catching sight of his long, hopeless, irritated face, she stopped suddenly with a grief-stricken look, and pulled back on his arm. "Wait on me," she said. "I'm going back to the house and take this thing off and tomorrow I'm going to return it. I was out of my head. I can pay the gas bill with that seven-fifty."

He caught her arm in a vicious grip. "You are not going to take it back," he said. "I like it."

"Well," she said, "I don't think I ought . . ."

"Shut up and enjoy it," he muttered, more depressed than ever.

"With the world in the mess it's in," she said, "it's a wonder we can enjoy anything. I tell you, the bottom rail is on the top."

Julian sighed.

"Of course," she said, "if you know who you are, you can go anywhere." She said this every time he took her to the reducing class. "Most of them in it are not our kind of people," she said, "but I can be gracious to anybody. I know who I am."

"They don't give a damn for your graciousness," Julian said savagely. "Knowing who you are is good for one generation only. You haven't the foggiest idea where you stand now or who you are."

She stopped and allowed her eyes to flash at him. "I most certainly do know who I am," she said, "and if you don't know who you are, I'm ashamed of you."

"Oh hell," Julian said.

"Your great-grandfather was a former governor of this state," she said. "Your grandfather was a prosperous landowner. Your grandmother was a Godhigh."

"Will you look around you," he said tensely, "and see where you are now?" and he swept his arm jerkily out to indicate the neighborhood, which the growing darkness at least made less dingy.

"You remain what you are," she said. "Your great-grandfather had a plantation and two hundred slaves."

"There are no more slaves," he said irritably.

"They were better off when they were," she said. He groaned to see that she was off on that topic. She rolled onto it every few days like a train on an open track. He knew every stop, every junction, every swamp along the way, and knew the exact point at which her conclusion would roll majestically into the station: "It's ridiculous. It's simply not realistic. They should rise, yes, but on their own side of the fence."

"Let's skip it," Julian said.

"The ones I feel sorry for," she said, "are the ones that are half white. They're tragic."

"Will you skip it?"

"Suppose we were half white. We would certainly have mixed feelings."

"I have mixed feelings now," he groaned.

"Well let's talk about something pleasant," she said. "I remember going to Grandpa's when I was a little girl. Then the house had double stairways that went up to what was really the second floor—all the cooking was done on the first. I used to like to stay down in the kitchen on account of the way the walls smelled. I would sit with my nose pressed against the plaster and take deep breaths. Actually the place belonged to the Godhighs but your grandfather Chestny paid the mortgage and saved it for them. They were in reduced circumstances," she said, "but reduced or not, they never forgot who they were."

"Doubtless that decayed mansion reminded them," Julian muttered. He never spoke of it without contempt or thought of it without longing. He had seen it once when he was a child before it had been sold. The double stairways had rotted and been torn down. Negroes were living in it. But it remained in his mind as his mother had known it. It appeared in his dreams regularly. He would stand on the wide porch, listening to the rustle of oak leaves, then wander through the high-ceilinged hall into the parlor that opened onto it and gaze at the worn rugs and faded draperies. It occurred to him that it was he, not she, who could have appreciated it. He preferred its threadbare elegance to anything he could name and it was because of it that all the neighborhoods they had lived in had been a torment to him—whereas she had hardly known the difference. She called her insensitivity "being adjustable."

"And I remember the old darky who was my nurse, Caroline. There was no better person in the world. I've always had a great respect for my colored friends," she said. "I'd do anything in the world for them and they'd . . ."

"Will you for God's sake get off that subject?" Julian said. When he got on a bus by himself, he made it a point to sit down beside a Negro, in reparation as it were for his mother's sins.

"You're mighty touchy tonight," she said. "Do you feel all right?"

"Yes I feel all right," he said. "Now lay off."

She pursed her lips. "Well, you certainly are in a vile humor," she observed. "I just won't speak to you at all."

They had reached the bus stop. There was no bus in sight and Julian, his hands still jammed in his pockets and his head thrust forward, scowled down the empty street. The frustration of having to wait on the bus as well as ride on it began to creep up his neck like a hot hand. The presence of his mother was borne in upon him as she gave a pained sigh. He looked at her bleakly. She was holding herself very erect under the preposterous hat, wearing it like a banner of her imaginary dignity. There was in him an evil urge to break her spirit. He suddenly unloosened his tie and pulled it off and put it in his pocket.

She stiffened. "Why must you look like *that* when you take me to town?" she said. "Why must you deliberately embarrass me?"

"If you'll never learn where you are," he said, "you can at least learn where I am."

"You look like a—thug," she said.

"Then I must be one," he murmured.

"I'll just go home," she said. "I will not bother you. If you can't do a little thing like that for me . . ."

Rolling his eyes upward, he put his tie back on. "Restored to my class," he muttered. He thrust his face toward her and hissed, "True culture is in the mind, the *mind*," he said, and tapped his head, "the mind."

"It's in the heart," she said, "and in how you do things and how you do things is because of who you *are*."

"Nobody in the damn bus cares who you are."

"I care who I am," she said icily.

The lighted bus appeared on top of the next hill and as it approached, they moved out into the street to meet it. He put his hand under her elbow and hoisted her up on the creaking step. She entered with a little smile, as if she were going into a drawing room where everyone had been waiting for her. While he put in the tokens, she sat down on one of the broad front seats for three which faced the aisle. A thin woman with protruding teeth and long yellow hair was sitting on the end of it. His mother moved up beside her and left room for Julian beside herself. He sat down and looked at the floor across the aisle where a pair of thin feet in red and white canvas sandals were planted.

His mother immediately began a general conversation meant to attract anyone who felt like talking. "Can it get any hotter?" she said and removed from her purse a folding fan, black with a Japanese scene on it, which she began to flutter before her.

"I reckon it might could," the woman with the protruding teeth said, "but I know for a fact my apartment couldn't get no hotter."

"It must get the afternoon sun," his mother said. She sat forward and looked up and down the bus. It was half filled. Everybody was white. "I see we have the bus to ourselves," she said. Julian cringed.

"For a change," said the woman across the aisle, the owner of the red and white canvas sandals. "I come on one the other day and they were thick as fleas—up front and all through."

"The world is in a mess everywhere," his mother said. "I don't know how we've let it get in this fix."

"What gets my goat is all those boys from good families stealing automobile tires," the woman with the protruding teeth said. "I told my boy, I said you may not be rich but you been raised right and if I ever catch you in any such mess, they can send you on to the reformatory. Be exactly where you belong."

"Training tells," his mother said. "Is your boy in high school?"

"Ninth grade," the woman said.

"My son just finished college last year. He wants to write but he's selling typewriters until he gets started," his mother said.

The woman leaned forward and peered at Julian. He threw her such a malevolent look that she subsided against the seat. On the floor across the aisle there was an abandoned newspaper. He got up and got it and opened it out in front of him. His mother discreetly continued the conversation in a lower tone but the woman across the aisle said in a loud voice, "Well that's nice. Selling typewriters is close to writing. He can go right from one to the other."

"I tell him," his mother said, "that Rome wasn't built in a day."

Behind the newspaper Julian was withdrawing into the inner compartment of his mind where he spent most of his time. This was a kind of mental bubble in which he established himself when he could not bear to be a part of what was going on around him. From it he could see out and judge but in it he was safe from any kind of penetration from without. It was the only place where he felt free of the general idiocy of his fellows. His mother had never entered it but from it he could see her with absolute clarity.

The old lady was clever enough and he thought that if she had started from any of the right premises, more might have been expected of her. She lived according to the laws of her own fantasy world, outside of which he had never seen her set foot. The law of it was to sacrifice herself for him after she had first created the necessity to do so by making a mess of things. If he had permitted her sacrifices, it was only because her lack of foresight had made them necessary. All of her life had been a struggle to act like a Chestny without the Chestny goods, and to give him everything she thought a Chestny ought to have; but since, said she, it was fun to struggle, why complain? And when you had won, as she had won, what fun to look back on the hard times! He could not forgive her that she had enjoyed the struggle and that she thought *she* had won.

What she meant when she said she had won was that she had brought him up successfully and had sent him to college and that he had turned out so well—good looking (her teeth had gone unfilled so that his could be straightened), intelligent (he realized he was too intelligent to be a success), and with a future ahead of him (there was of course no future ahead of him). She excused his gloominess on the grounds that he was still growing up and his radical ideas on his lack of practical experience. She said he didn't yet know a thing about "life," that he hadn't even entered the real world—when already he was as disenchanted with it as a man of fifty.

The further irony of all this was that in spite of her, he had turned out so well. In spite of going to only a third-rate college, he had, on his own initiative, come out with a first-rate education; in spite of growing up dominated by a small mind, he had ended up with a large one; in spite of all her foolish views, he was free of prejudice and unafraid to face facts. Most miraculous of all, instead of being blinded by love for her as she was for him, he had cut himself emotionally free of her and could see her with complete objectivity. He was not dominated by his mother.

The bus stopped with a sudden jerk and shook him from his meditation. A woman from the back lurched forward with little steps and barely escaped falling in his newspaper as she righted herself. She got off and a large Negro got on. Julian kept his paper lowered to watch. It gave him a certain satisfaction to see injustice in daily operation. It confirmed his view that with a few exceptions there was no one worth knowing within a radius of three hundred miles. The Negro was well dressed and carried a briefcase. He looked around and then sat down on the other end of the seat where the woman with the red and white canvas sandals was sitting. He immediately unfolded a newspaper and obscured himself behind it. Julian's mother's elbow at once prodded insistently into his ribs. "Now you see why I won't ride on these buses by myself," she whispered.

The woman with the red and white canvas sandals had risen at the same time the Negro sat down and had gone further back in the bus and taken the seat of the woman who had got off. His mother leaned forward and cast her an approving look.

Julian rose, crossed the aisle, and sat down in the place of the woman with the canvas sandals. From this position, he looked serenely across at his mother. Her face had turned an angry red. He stared at her, making his eyes the eyes of a stranger. He felt his tension suddenly lift as if he had openly declared war on her.

He would have liked to get in conversation with the Negro and to talk with him about art or politics or any subject that would be above the comprehension of those around them, but the man remained entrenched behind his paper. He was either ignoring the change of seating or had never noticed it. There was no way for Julian to convey his sympathy.

His mother kept her eyes fixed reproachfully on his face. The woman with the protruding teeth was looking at him avidly as if he were a type of monster new to her.

"Do you have a light?" he asked the Negro.

Without looking away from his paper, the man reached in his pocket and handed him a packet of matches.

"Thanks," Julian said. For a moment he held the matches foolishly. A NO SMOKING sign looked down upon him from over the door. This alone would not have deterred him; he had no cigarettes. He had quit smoking some months before because he could not afford it. "Sorry," he muttered and handed back the matches. The Negro lowered the paper and gave him an annoyed look. He took the matches and raised the paper again.

His mother continued to gaze at him but she did not take advantage of his momentary discomfort. Her eyes retained their battered look. Her face seemed to be unnaturally red, as if her blood pressure had risen. Julian allowed no glimmer of sympathy to show on his face. Having got the advantage, he wanted desperately to keep it and carry it through. He would have liked to teach her a lesson that would last her a while, but there seemed no way to continue the point. The Negro refused to come out from behind his paper.

Julian folded his arms and looked stolidly before him, facing her but as if he did not see her, as if he had ceased to recognize her existence. He visualized a scene in which, the bus having reached their stop, he would remain in his seat and when she said, "Aren't you going to get off?" he would look at her as at a stranger who had rashly addressed him. The corner they got off on was usually deserted, but it was well lighted and it would not hurt her to walk by herself the four blocks to the Y. He decided to wait until the time came and then decide whether or not he would let her get off by herself. He would have to be at the Y at ten to bring her back, but he could leave her wondering if he was going to show up. There was no reason for her to think she could always depend on him.

He retired again into the high-ceilinged room sparsely settled with large pieces of antique furniture. His soul expanded momentarily but then he became aware of his mother across from him and the vision shriveled. He studied her coldly. Her feet in little pumps dangled like a child's and did not quite reach the floor. She was training on him an exaggerated look of reproach. He felt completely detached from her. At that moment he could with pleasure have slapped her as he would have slapped a particularly obnoxious child in his charge.

He began to imagine various unlikely ways by which he could teach her a lesson. He might make friends with some distinguished Negro professor or lawyer and bring him home to spend the evening. He would be entirely justified but her blood pressure would rise to 300. He could not push her to the extent of making her have a stroke, and moreover, he had never been successful at making any Negro friends. He had tried to strike up an acquaintance on the bus with some of the better types, with ones that looked like professors or ministers or lawyers. One morning he had sat down next to a distinguished-looking dark brown man who had answered his questions with a sonorous solemnity but who had turned out to be an undertaker. Another day he had sat down beside a cigar-smoking Negro with a diamond ring on his finger, but after a few stilted pleasantries, the Negro had rung the buzzer and risen, slipping two lottery tickets into Julian's hand as he climbed over him to leave.

He imagined his mother lying desperately ill and his being able to secure only a Negro doctor for her. He toyed with that idea for a few minutes and then dropped it for a momentary vision of himself participating as a sympathizer in a sit-in demonstration. This was possible but he did not linger with it. Instead, he approached the ultimate horror. He brought home a beautiful suspiciously Negroid woman. Prepare yourself, he said. There is nothing you can do about it. This is the woman I've chosen. She's intelligent, dignified, even good, and she's suffered and she hasn't thought it *fun*. Now persecute us, go ahead and persecute us. Drive her out of here, but remember, you're driving me too. His eyes were narrowed and through the indignation he had generated, he saw his mother across the aisle, purple-faced, shrunken to the dwarf-like proportions of her moral nature, sitting like a mummy beneath the ridiculous banner of her hat.

He was tilted out of his fantasy again as the bus stopped. The door opened with a sucking hiss and out of the dark a large, gaily dressed, sullen-looking colored woman got on with a little boy. The child, who might have been four, had on a short plaid suit and a Tyrolean hat with a blue feather in it. Julian hoped that he would sit down beside him and that the woman would push in beside his mother. He could think of no better arrangement.

As she waited for her tokens, the woman was surveying the seating possibilities—he hoped with the idea of sitting where she was least wanted. There was something familiar-looking about her but Julian could not place what it was. She was a giant of a woman. Her face was set not only to meet opposition but to seek it out. The downward tilt of her large lower lip was like a warning sign: DON'T TAMPER WITH ME. Her bulging figure was encased in a green crepe dress and her feet overflowed in red shoes. She had on a hideous hat. A purple velvet flap came down on one side of it and stood up on the other; the rest of it was green and looked like a cushion with the stuffing out. She carried a mammoth red pocketbook that bulged throughout as if it were stuffed with rocks.

To Julian's disappointment, the little boy climbed up on the empty seat beside his mother. His mother lumped all children, black and white, into the common category, "cute," and she thought little Negroes were on the whole cuter than little white children. She smiled at the little boy as he climbed on the seat.

Meanwhile the woman was bearing down upon the empty seat beside Julian. To his annoyance, she squeezed herself into it. He saw his mother's face change as the woman settled herself next to him and he realized with satisfaction that this was more objectionable to her than it was to him. Her face seemed almost gray and there was a look of dull recognition in her eyes, as if suddenly she had sickened at some awful confrontation. Julian saw that it was because she and the woman had, in a sense, swapped sons. Though his mother would not realize the symbolic significance of this, she would feel it. His amusement showed plainly on his face.

The woman next to him muttered something unintelligible to herself. He was conscious of a kind of bristling next to him, a muted growling like that of an angry cat. He could not see anything but the red pocketbook upright on the bulging green thighs. He visualized the woman as she had stood waiting for her tokens—the ponderous figure, rising from the red shoes upward over the solid hips, the mammoth bosom, the haughty face, to the green and purple hat.

His eyes widened.

The vision of the two hats, identical, broke upon him with the radiance of a brilliant sunrise. His face was suddenly lit with joy. He could not believe that Fate had thrust upon his mother such a lesson. He gave a loud chuckle so that she would look at him and see that he saw. She turned her eyes on him slowly. The blue in them seemed to have turned a bruised purple. For a moment he had an uncomfortable sense of her innocence, but it lasted only a second before principle rescued him. Justice entitled him to laugh. His grin hardened until it said to her as plainly as if he were saying aloud: Your punishment exactly fits your pettiness. This should teach you a permanent lesson.

Her eyes shifted to the woman. She seemed unable to bear looking at him and to find the woman preferable. He became conscious again of the bristling presence at his side. The woman was rumbling like a volcano about to become active. His mother's mouth began to twitch slightly at one corner. With a sinking heart, he saw incipient signs of recovery on her face and realized that this was going to strike her suddenly as funny and was going to be no lesson at all. She kept her eyes on the woman and an amused smile came over her face as if the woman were a monkey that had stolen her hat. The little Negro was looking up at her with large fascinated eyes. He had been trying to attract her attention for some time.

"Carver!" the woman said suddenly. "Come heah!"

When he saw that the spotlight was on him at last, Carver drew his feet up and turned himself toward Julian's mother and giggled.

"Carver!" the woman said. "You heah me? Come heah!"

Carver slid down from the seat but remained squatting with his back against the base of it, his head turned slyly around toward Julian's mother, who was smiling at him. The woman reached a hand across the aisle and snatched him to her. He righted himself and hung backwards on her knees, grinning at Julian's mother. "Isn't he cute?" Julian's mother said to the woman with the protruding teeth.

"I reckon he is," the woman said without conviction.

The Negress yanked him upright but he eased out of her grip and shot across the aisle and scrambled, giggling wildly, onto the seat beside his love.

"I think he likes me," Julian's mother said, and smiled at the woman. It was the smile she used when she was being particularly gracious to an inferior. Julian saw everything lost. The lesson had rolled off her like rain on a roof.

The woman stood up and yanked the little boy off the seat as if she were snatching him from contagion. Julian could feel the rage in her at having no weapon like his mother's smile. She gave the child a sharp slap across his leg. He howled once and then thrust his head into her stomach and kicked his feet against her shins. "Be-have," she said vehemently.

The bus stopped and the Negro who had been reading the newspaper got off. The woman moved over and set the little boy down with a thump between herself and Julian. She held him firmly by the knee. In a moment he put his hands in front of his face and peeped at Julian's mother through his fingers.

"I see yoooooooo!" she said and put her hand in front of her face and peeped at him.

The woman slapped his hand down. "Quit yo' foolishness," she said, "before I knock the living Jesus out of you!"

Julian was thankful that the next stop was theirs. He reached up and pulled the cord. The woman reached up and pulled it at the same time. Oh my God, he thought. He had the terrible intuition that when they got off the bus together, his mother would open her purse and give the little boy a nickel. The gesture would be as natural to her as breathing. The bus stopped and the woman got up and lunged to the front, dragging the child, who wished to stay on, after her. Julian and his mother got up and followed. As they neared the door, Julian tried to relieve her of her pocketbook.

"No," she murmured, "I want to give the little boy a nickel."

"No!" Julian hissed. "No!"

She smiled down at the child and opened her bag. The bus door opened and the woman picked him up by the arm and descended with him, hanging at her hip. Once in the street she set him down and shook him.

Julian's mother had to close her purse while she got down the bus step but as soon as her feet were on the ground, she opened it again and began to rummage inside. "I can't find but a penny," she whispered, "but it looks like a new one."

"Don't do it!" Julian said fiercely between his teeth. There was a streetlight on the corner and she hurried to get under it so that she could better see into her pocketbook. The woman was heading off rapidly down the street with the child still hanging backward on her hand.

"Oh little boy!" Julian's mother called and took a few quick steps and caught up with them just beyond the lamppost. "Here's a bright new penny for you," and she held out the coin, which shone bronze in the dim light.

The huge woman turned and for a moment stood, her shoulders lifted and her face frozen with frustrated rage, and stared at Julian's mother. Then all at once she seemed to explode like a piece of machinery that had been given one ounce of pressure too much. Julian saw the black fist swing out with the red pocketbook. He shut his eyes and cringed as he heard the woman shout, "He don't take nobody's pennies!" When he opened his eyes, the woman was disappearing down the street with the little boy staring wide-eyed over her shoulder. Julian's mother was sitting on the sidewalk.

"I told you not to do that," Julian said angrily. "I told you not to do that!"

He stood over her for a minute, gritting his teeth. Her legs were stretched out in front of her and her hat was on her lap. He squatted down and looked her in the face. It was totally expressionless. "You got exactly what you deserved," he said. "Now get up."

He picked up her pocketbook and put what had fallen out back in it. He picked the hat up off her lap. The penny caught his eye on the sidewalk and he picked that up and let it drop before her eyes into the purse. Then he stood up and leaned over and held his hands out to pull her up. She remained immobile. He sighed. Rising above them on either side were black apartment buildings, marked with irregular rectangles of light. At the end of the block a man came out of a door and walked off in the opposite direction. "All right," he said, "suppose somebody happens by and wants to know why you're sitting on the sidewalk?"

She took the hand and, breathing hard, pulled heavily up on it and then stood for a moment, swaying slightly as if the spots of light in the darkness were circling around her. Her eyes, shadowed and confused, finally settled on his face. He did not try to conceal his irritation. "I hope this teaches you a lesson," he said. She leaned forward and her eyes raked his face. She seemed trying to determine his identity. Then, as if she found nothing familiar about him, she started off with a headlong movement in the wrong direction.

"Aren't you going on to the Y?" he asked.

"Home," she muttered.

"Well, are we walking?"

For answer she kept going. Julian followed along, his hands behind him. He saw no reason to let the lesson she had had go without backing it up with an explanation of its meaning. She might as well be made to understand what had happened to her. "Don't think that was just an uppity Negro woman," he said. "That was the whole colored race which will no longer take your condescending pennies. That was your black double. She can wear the same hat as you, and to be sure," he added gratuitously (because he thought it was funny), "it looked better on her than it did on you. What all this means," he said, "is that the old world is gone. The old manners are obsolete and your graciousness is not worth a damn." He thought bitterly of the house that had been lost for him. "You aren't who you think you are," he said.

She continued to plow ahead, paying no attention to him. Her hair had come undone on one side. She dropped her pocketbook and took no notice. He stooped and picked it up and handed it to her but she did not take it.

"You needn't act as if the world had come to an end," he said, "because it hasn't. From now on you've got to live in a new world and face a few realities for a change. Buck up," he said, "it won't kill you."

She was breathing fast.

"Let's wait on the bus," he said.

"Home," she said thickly.

"I hate to see you behave like this," he said. "Just like a child. I should be able to expect more of you." He decided to stop where he was and make her stop and wait for a bus. "I'm not going any farther," he said, stopping. "We're going on the bus."

She continued to go on as if she had not heard him. He took a few steps and caught her arm and stopped her. He looked into her face and caught his breath. He was looking into a face he had never seen before. "Tell Grandpa to come get me," she said.

He stared, stricken.

"Tell Caroline to come get me," she said.

Stunned, he let her go and she lurched forward again, walking as if one leg were shorter than the other. A tide of darkness seemed to be sweeping her from him. "Mother!" he cried. "Darling, sweetheart, wait!" Crumpling, she fell to the pavement. He dashed forward and fell at her side, crying, "Mamma, Mamma!" He turned her over. Her face was fiercely distorted. One eye, large and staring, moved slightly to the left as if it had become unmoored. The other remained fixed on him, raked his face again, found nothing and closed.

"Wait here, wait here!" he cried and jumped up and began to run for help toward a cluster of lights he saw in the distance ahead of him. "Help, help!" he shouted, but his voice was thin, scarcely a thread of sound. The lights drifted farther away the faster he ran and his feet moved numbly as if they carried him nowhere. The tide of darkness seemed to sweep him back to her, postponing from moment to moment his entry into the world of guilt and sorrow. ～

Interpretive Questions
for Discussion

Why does Julian consider himself a failure even though he has received a first-rate education and has otherwise "turned out so well"?

1. Why is Julian depressed by everything that gives his mother pleasure? (246)

2. Why does Julian fantasize about befriending African Americans? Why are all his attempts to do so unsuccessful?

3. Why does Julian speak of his grandfather's plantation mansion with contempt but think of it with longing? (249)

4. Why can Julian emotionally withdraw from his mother and even actively oppose her prejudices, but not become independent from her?

5. Does Julian blame his mother for his sense of failure?

6. Why do both Julian and his mother revert to childhood at the end of the story?

7. Are we meant to admire Julian for feeling the guilt that his mother seems incapable of feeling?

Suggested textual analysis
Pages 252–253: beginning, "Behind the newspaper," and ending, "He was not dominated by his mother."

Why does Julian have an "evil urge" to break his mother's spirit?

1. Why does Julian want to teach his mother a lesson about race relations rather than allow her to live in the "fantasy world" of her past? (252)

2. Why is Julian annoyed by the fact that his mother can put a bright face on her suffering?

3. Does Julian see his mother with "absolute clarity"? (252)

4. Why does Julian's mother, despite her attempts at kindness, end up humiliating both her son and the African American woman?

5. Why does Julian tell his mother that in being hit by the woman, she got exactly what she deserved? (260)

6. Why does his mother's stroke condemn Julian to dwell in a "world of guilt and sorrow"? (262)

7. Why does the African American woman's rebuff devastate Julian's mother in a way that Julian's own attempt to put her in her place does not?

Suggested textual analysis
Pages 254–256: beginning, "Julian folded his arms," and ending, "He could think of no better arrangement."

Why does "converging" with the enraged African American woman cause Julian's mother to suffer a stroke?

1. Why does the author have Julian's mother and the African American woman wear the same hideous hat?

2. Why does Julian imagine that although his mother wouldn't realize the "symbolic significance" of having "in a sense, swapped sons" with the African American woman, she would at least feel it? (257)

3. Why is the child attracted to Julian's mother?

4. Why does Julian's mother smile graciously at the African American woman and say of the little boy, "I think he likes me"? (258) Is Julian's mother oblivious to the woman's feelings or does she think graciousness will overcome the woman's displeasure?

5. Why does Julian's mother play with the child even though this obviously angers his mother? Why does she try to give the child a penny despite Julian's warning not to?

6. Why does Julian see his mother's smile as a "weapon" against which the African American woman has no response but rage? (258)

7. Why does the "convergence" of hats not serve as a "permanent lesson" to Julian's mother? (257)

Suggested textual analysis
Pages 260–262: from "He picked up her pocketbook," to the end of the story.

FOR FURTHER REFLECTION

1. Does Julian owe his mother more respect than he gives her, or does her racism justify his contempt?

2. Was Julian right to try to force his mother to leave her "fantasy world"?

3. Can the attitude of people like Julian's mother be changed?

4. Is Julian in his own way just as racist as his mother?

5. Who is more guilty of failing to "face a few realities," Julian or his mother?

6. Can you ignore ancestry in determining who you are?

POETRY

William Butler Yeats

Wallace Stevens

Robert Frost

Elizabeth Bishop

WILLIAM BUTLER YEATS (1865–1939) had one
of the longest and most productive careers in
the history of letters. In addition to writing
fourteen books of poetry, he composed and
produced nineteen plays, and wrote twenty-three
books of prose on such topics as Celtic mythology
and folklore, mysticism, Irish politics, and poetic
theory. From 1922 to 1928, Yeats served as a
senator of the Irish Free State. He was awarded
the Nobel Prize for literature in 1923. T. S. Eliot
described Yeats as the greatest poet of his time—
"certainly the greatest in this language, and so
far as I am able to judge, in any language."

∾

WALLACE STEVENS (1879–1955) was educated at
Harvard University and New York Law School and
worked for the Hartford Accident and Indemnity
Company, becoming its vice president in 1934.
Stevens' first volume of poetry, *Harmonium,* which
includes "Sunday Morning," was published in
1923. In the last six years of his life, Stevens
received the Bollingen Prize, the National Book
Award (twice), and the Pulitzer Prize.

ROBERT FROST (1874–1963) was born and raised
in San Francisco, moving to New England—his
ancestral home and the setting for much of his
poetry—at the age of eleven. Frost studied at
Dartmouth and Harvard, but dropped out in order
to teach. His first book of poetry, *A Boy's Will*
(1913), was published in England, where he lived
for three years before returning to growing acclaim
in his own country. Frost received a special congres-
sional medal during the Eisenhower administration
and read at the inauguration of John F. Kennedy.
He also won the Pulitzer Prize four times and
received seventeen honorary college degrees.

ELIZABETH BISHOP (1911–1979) was born in
Massachusetts. After graduating from Vassar,
she traveled in Europe and Africa, lived in Mexico
and Key West, and ultimately settled in Brazil for
nearly twenty years. During the 1970s, she taught
writing at Harvard. Bishop was awarded the
Pulitzer Prize for her poetry in 1956. Her *Complete
Poems* (1969) won the National Book Award.

Lapis Lazuli
(for Harry Clifton)

I HAVE heard that hysterical women say
They are sick of the palette and fiddle-bow,
Of poets that are always gay,
For everybody knows or else should know
That if nothing drastic is done
Aeroplane and Zeppelin will come out,
Pitch like King Billy[1] bomb-balls in
Until the town lie beaten flat.

All perform their tragic play,
There struts Hamlet, there is Lear,
That's Ophelia, that Cordelia;
Yet they, should the last scene be there,
The great stage curtain about to drop,
If worthy their prominent part in the play,
Do not break up their lines to weep.
They know that Hamlet and Lear are gay;
Gaiety transfiguring all that dread.
All men have aimed at, found and lost;
Black out; Heaven blazing into the head:
Tragedy wrought to its uttermost.
Though Hamlet rambles and Lear rages,
And all the drop-scenes drop at once
Upon a hundred thousand stages,
It cannot grow by an inch or an ounce.

---

1. [*King Billy:* William of Orange, king of England, used cannon against the Irish in the
Battle of the Boyne in 1690. Yeats may also have in mind Wilhelm II of Germany
("Kaiser Bill"), who sent zeppelins to bomb London during World War I.]

On their own feet they came, or on shipboard,
Camel-back, horse-back, ass-back, mule-back,
Old civilisations put to the sword.
Then they and their wisdom went to rack:
No handiwork of Callimachus,
Who handled marble as if it were bronze,
Made draperies that seemed to rise
When sea-wind swept the corner, stands;
His long lamp-chimney shaped like the stem
Of a slender palm, stood but a day;
All things fall and are built again,
And those that build them again are gay.

Two Chinamen, behind them a third,
Are carved in lapis lazuli,
Over them flies a long-legged bird,
A symbol of longevity;
The third, doubtless a serving-man,
Carries a musical instrument.

Every discoloration of the stone,
Every accidental crack or dent,
Seems a water-course or an avalanche,
Or lofty slope where it still snows
Though doubtless plum or cherry-branch
Sweetens the little half-way house
Those Chinamen climb towards, and I
Delight to imagine them seated there;

There, on the mountain and the sky,
On all the tragic scene they stare.
One asks for mournful melodies;
Accomplished fingers begin to play.
Their eyes mid many wrinkles, their eyes,
Their ancient, glittering eyes, are gay.

William Butler Yeats

Sunday Morning

1

COMPLACENCIES of the peignoir, and late
Coffee and oranges in a sunny chair,
And the green freedom of a cockatoo
Upon a rug mingle to dissipate
The holy hush of ancient sacrifice.
She dreams a little, and she feels the dark
Encroachment of that old catastrophe,
As a calm darkens among water-lights.
The pungent oranges and bright, green wings
Seem things in some procession of the dead,
Winding across wide water, without sound.
The day is like wide water, without sound,
Stilled for the passing of her dreaming feet
Over the seas, to silent Palestine,
Dominion of the blood and sepulchre.

2

Why should she give her bounty to the dead?
What is divinity if it can come
Only in silent shadows and in dreams?
Shall she not find in comforts of the sun,
In pungent fruit and bright, green wings, or else
In any balm or beauty of the earth,
Things to be cherished like the thought of heaven?

Divinity must live within herself:
Passions of rain, or moods in falling snow;
Grievings in loneliness, or unsubdued
Elations when the forest blooms; gusty
Emotions on wet roads on autumn nights;
All pleasures and all pains, remembering
The bough of summer and the winter branch.
These are the measures destined for her soul.

3

Jove in the clouds had his inhuman birth.
No mother suckled him, no sweet land gave
Large-mannered motions to his mythy mind
He moved among us, as a muttering king,
Magnificent, would move among his hinds,
Until our blood, commingling, virginal,
With heaven, brought such requital to desire
The very hinds discerned it, in a star.
Shall our blood fail? Or shall it come to be
The blood of paradise? And shall the earth
Seem all of paradise that we shall know?
The sky will be much friendlier then than now,
A part of labor and a part of pain,
And next in glory to enduring love,
Not this dividing and indifferent blue.

4

She says, "I am content when wakened birds,
Before they fly, test the reality
Of misty fields, by their sweet questionings;
But when the birds are gone, and their warm fields
Return no more, where, then, is paradise?"

There is not any haunt of prophecy,
Nor any old chimera of the grave,
Neither the golden underground, nor isle
Melodious, where spirits gat them home,
Nor visionary south, nor cloudy palm
Remote on heaven's hill, that has endured
As April's green endures; or will endure
Like her remembrance of awakened birds,
Or her desire for June and evening, tipped
By the consummation of the swallow's wings.

5

She says, "But in contentment I still feel
The need of some imperishable bliss."
Death is the mother of beauty; hence from her,
Alone, shall come fulfilment to our dreams
And our desires. Although she strews the leaves
Of sure obliteration on our paths,
The path sick sorrow took, the many paths
Where triumph rang its brassy phrase, or love
Whispered a little out of tenderness,
She makes the willow shiver in the sun
For maidens who were wont to sit and gaze
Upon the grass, relinquished to their feet.
She causes boys to pile new plums and pears
On disregarded plate. The maidens taste
And stray impassioned in the littering leaves.

6

Is there no change of death in paradise?
Does ripe fruit never fall? Or do the boughs
Hang always heavy in that perfect sky,
Unchanging, yet so like our perishing earth,
With rivers like our own that seek for seas
They never find, the same receding shores
That never touch with inarticulate pang?
Why set the pear upon those river-banks
Or spice the shores with odors of the plum?
Alas, that they should wear our colors there,
The silken weavings of our afternoons,
And pick the strings of our insipid lutes!
Death is the mother of beauty, mystical,
Within whose burning bosom we devise
Our earthly mothers waiting, sleeplessly.

7

Supple and turbulent, a ring of men
Shall chant in orgy on a summer morn
Their boisterous devotion to the sun,
Not as a god, but as a god might be,
Naked among them, like a savage source.
Their chant shall be a chant of paradise,
Out of their blood, returning to the sky;
And in their chant shall enter, voice by voice,
The windy lake wherein their lord delights,
The trees, like serafin, and echoing hills,
That choir among themselves long afterward.
They shall know well the heavenly fellowship
Of men that perish and of summer morn.
And whence they came and whither they shall go
The dew upon their feet shall manifest.

8

She hears, upon that water without sound,
A voice that cries, "The tomb in Palestine
Is not the porch of spirits lingering.
It is the grave of Jesus, where he lay."
We live in an old chaos of the sun,
Or old dependency of day and night,
Or island solitude, unsponsored, free,
Of that wide water, inescapable.
Deer walk upon our mountains, and the quail
Whistle about us their spontaneous cries;
Sweet berries ripen in the wilderness;
And, in the isolation of the sky,
At evening, casual flocks of pigeons make
Ambiguous undulations as they sink,
Downward to darkness, on extended wings.

Wallace Stevens

Design

I FOUND a dimpled spider, fat and white,
On a white heal-all, holding up a moth
Like a white piece of rigid satin cloth—
Assorted characters of death and blight
Mixed ready to begin the morning right,
Like the ingredients of a witches' broth—
A snow-drop spider, a flower like a froth,
And dead wings carried like a paper kite.

What had that flower to do with being white,
The wayside blue and innocent heal-all?
What brought the kindred spider to that height,
Then steered the white moth thither in the night?
What but design of darkness to appall?—
If design govern in a thing so small.

Robert Frost

The Armadillo
(for Robert Lowell)

THIS IS the time of year
when almost every night
the frail, illegal fire balloons appear.
Climbing the mountain height,

rising toward a saint
still honored in these parts,
the paper chambers flush and fill with light
that comes and goes, like hearts.

Once up against the sky it's hard
to tell them from the stars—
planets, that is—the tinted ones:
Venus going down, or Mars,

or the pale green one. With a wind,
they flare and falter, wobble and toss;
but if it's still they steer between
the kite sticks of the Southern Cross,

receding, dwindling, solemnly
and steadily forsaking us,
or, in the downdraft from a peak,
suddenly turning dangerous.

Last night another big one fell.
It splattered like an egg of fire
against the cliff behind the house.
The flame ran down. We saw the pair

of owls who nest there flying up
and up, their whirling black-and-white
stained bright pink underneath, until
they shrieked up out of sight.

The ancient owls' nest must have burned.
Hastily, all alone,
a glistening armadillo left the scene,
rose-flecked, head down, tail down,

and then a baby rabbit jumped out,
short-eared, to our surprise.
So soft!—a handful of intangible ash
with fixed, ignited eyes.

Too pretty, dreamlike mimicry!
O falling fire and piercing cry
and panic, and a weak mailed fist
clenched ignorant against the sky!

Elizabeth Bishop

Interpretive Questions
for Discussion

In "Lapis Lazuli," why does the poet suggest that the hysterical women are wrong to abandon art when civilization is threatened by chaos?

1. Why does the prospect of destruction cause the "hysterical women" to become sick of art and artists?

2. Why does the poet think that actors, who "do not break up their lines to weep," are good models for us in dealing with life's tragedies?

3. If this poem is a defense of art, why does the poet suggest that it does not matter that past great works of art and even the cultures of entire civilizations have been destroyed and lost forever?

4. Why, in the eyes of the poet, do the imperfections in the stone of the lapis lazuli carving become lovely embellishments of the scene it depicts?

5. Why does the poet "delight" to imagine the Chinamen seated at the top of the mountain they are climbing? Why does he imagine that one of them might want to hear "mournful" music?

6. Why does the poet seem more interested in the scene he imagines for the Chinamen than in the one actually depicted in the carving?

7. Why are the aged Chinamen "gay" as they look upon the "tragic scene" of life?

8. Is the poet suggesting that we should be indifferent to the world's woes?

According to "Sunday Morning," why are we better off living "in an old chaos of the sun" than in a world ordered by religious faith and observance?

1. Why does the recollection of "that old catastrophe" make the oranges and the cockatoo seem to the woman like "things in some procession of the dead"?

2. Why must divinity "live within" the woman in the poem? Why does the poet suggest that pain as well as pleasure should be recognized as divine?

3. Why will the sky be "much friendlier" when the earth seems "all of paradise that we shall know"?

4. Why, according to the poet, has no otherworldly thing "endured / As April's green endures"?

5. Why is death "the mother of beauty"? Why will the "fulfilment to our dreams / And our desires" come only from death?

6. Why is the poet troubled by the thought of a paradise where nothing changes? Why does he say, "Alas, that they should wear our colors there"?

7. Why does the poet suggest that the best form of worship would be "boisterous devotion to the sun, / Not as a god, but as a god might be, / Naked among them, like a savage source"? Why do "men that perish" constitute a "heavenly fellowship"?

8. Why does the poem conclude with the image of "casual flocks of pigeons" making "ambiguous undulations as they sink, / Downward to darkness, on extended wings"?

In "Design," why is the poet unable to decide whether the spectacle of "death and blight" on the heal-all blossom is the result of design?

1. Why does the scene on the heal-all blossom appear to result from the "design of darkness to appall" rather than from the ordinary workings of nature?

2. Why does the poet choose pretty, delicate things—"satin cloth," "snow-drop," "froth," "paper kite"—to describe the scene on the flower?

3. Why does the poet remark wryly that the "assorted characters of death and blight / Mixed ready to begin the morning right"?

4. Why does the poet choose a heal-all to be the flower on which the spider sits? Why does he ask, "What had that flower to do with being white?"

5. Why is the spider "kindred" to the heal-all?

6. Why does the poet wonder whether design governs in a thing as small as the scene on the heal-all?

7. Is the poet suggesting that the "design" he perceives in the scene on the heal-all exists only in the human imagination?

In "The Armadillo," does the poet believe that the danger of the fire balloons invalidates the meaning and beauty of the ritual of setting them aloft?

1. Why are we told that the fire balloons are illegal? Why are we told that they honor a saint whose popularity is on the wane?

2. Why does the poet compare the transitory light of the "frail" fire balloons to the beating of hearts?

3. Why does the poet point out that if the fire balloons rise and fly successfully, they either forsake us or turn dangerous?

4. Why does the poet stress the danger of the fire balloons to animals and not the danger they present to human life and property?

5. Why are the fire balloons described as *"too pretty, dreamlike mimicry"*?

6. Why does the poet describe the baby rabbit as if it were mimicking fire—"a handful of intangible ash / with fixed, ignited eyes"?

7. Why does the poem conclude with the image of the armadillo's *"weak mailed fist / clenched ignorant against the sky"*?

FOR FURTHER REFLECTION

1. Is art a luxury and a foolish distraction when civilization itself is threatened?

2. Is thinking of ourselves as actors in a tragic play a good way to deal with tragedy?

3. Is death the mother of beauty?

4. Is our earthly life enough or do we need "some imperishable bliss"?

5. Is art an attempt to discover the "design" in all things?

Questions for

THE MASTER
AND MARGARITA

Mikhail Bulgakov

MIKHAIL BULGAKOV (1891–1940) was born
in Kiev, the son of a professor at the Kiev
Theological Academy. He graduated from the
Medical College of Kiev University, but after
two years as a physician abandoned medicine
for literature. Bulgakov was among those
Russian writers who did not emigrate after the
Russian Revolution but nonetheless insisted on
writing in their own way and on their own
choice of subjects. He wrote a number of
important plays that provoked bitter attacks
in the press, and was shut out of the theater
and literature in 1929. Only after making a
direct appeal to Stalin was Bulgakov permitted
to work in the theater, where his tasks included
dramatizing other authors' books. Censors
continued to reject most of his original work.
Bulgakov's depiction of the Master's novel is
prophetic, for *The Master and Margarita* could
not be published until more than a quarter
of a century after his death.

NOTE: All page references are from the Vintage
International edition of *The Master and Margarita*
(first printing 1996).

INTERPRETIVE QUESTIONS
FOR DISCUSSION

**Why does the devil come to Moscow to wreak havoc on the Soviet
literary and theatrical community?**

1. Why does Berlioz criticize the poet Ivan for writing about Jesus
   in such a way as to suggest that he really existed? (6) Why does
   Woland insist that Jesus *did* exist and tell Berlioz and Ivan the
   Master's story of Pontius Pilate? (12)

2. Why does Woland offer a philosophical challenge to Berlioz'
   atheism? (7–8) Why does he implore Berlioz to "at least believe
   that the devil exists"? (34–35)

3. Why does Woland bring his retinue to carry out his mission in
   Moscow? Why do they appear as Korovyov-Fagot, Behemoth,
   and Azazello rather than in their true forms of dark-violet
   knight, demon-page/jester, and demon-killer? (69, 321–322)

4. Why do some people, like Margarita and Natasha, benefit from
   the devil's magic while others, such as Berlioz, Styopa,
   Varenukha, and Nikanor, are harmed or driven crazy by it?

5. At his public performance at the Variety Theater, why does
   Woland make a show of generosity, giving the audience money
   and fine clothes that later disappear? (103, 105)

6. Why are Bengalsky and Sempleyarov punished for demanding
   that Woland provide an exposé of his magic? Why does Woland
   relent and replace Bengalsky's head in response to the audience's
   compassion for and forgiveness of him? (104, 108)

7. Why is Woland the instrument of Margarita's compassion and kindness toward Frieda and the Master, and of Yeshua's toward the Master and Pilate? (241–245, 324–325)

8. Why does Woland punish Berlioz for denying life after death? Why does he affirm the theory that "to each man it will be given according to his beliefs"? (233)

9. Why is the "buccaneer" Archibald Archibaldovich able to recognize Koroviev and Behemoth and escape when they destroy Griboyedev by fire? (303)

10. Why does Ivan Bezdomny give up writing poetry and become a professor, "a fellow of the Institute of History and Philosophy"? Why does he take up the occupation claimed by Woland when Ivan meets him? (332; cf. 11–12)

11. In this story, is the devil an evil spirit, an instrument of justice, or both?

12. Why does the author depict a society that demands socialist realism in the arts being confronted with the undeniable existence of supernatural power?

Suggested textual analyses
Pages 4–12 (from Chapter 1): from "This conversation," to the end of the chapter.

Pages 98–109 (Chapter 12)

Why does the author retell the story of the Passion of Jesus from the point of view of Pontius Pilate?

1. Why is Pilate portrayed as a sympathetic character who is reluctant to condemn Yeshua to death?

2. Why is Yeshua presented as an ordinary human being who courageously confronts Pilate with the conviction that all men

are good? Why is he portrayed as a pacifist and supporter of a nonauthoritarian utopia? (20–22)

3. Why does the author suggest that the Gospel of Matthew is the result of Levi Matvei's misperceptions about the doings and sayings of Jesus? (16)

4. Why is Levi Matvei's one concern during Yeshua's execution to find a way to kill him and spare him torture? Why does Levi curse God when his plan fails? (148–149)

5. Why does Pilate offer Levi a job? Why does Pilate admit to Levi that he had Judas killed, when before he was careful not to speak openly of it even to Afranius? (279–280)

6. Why does Woland dislike Levi, when he seems to have no problem with Yeshua? Why does Woland call Levi "slave"? (305)

7. Why is it so important to save the Master's novel from being lost, if he and Margarita are to leave the world anyway? Why does Margarita make the Master promise that he won't forget a single word? (245, 314)

8. When Woland sees Margarita's compassion for Pilate, why does he tell her, "Everything will be made right, that is what the world is built on"? (323)

9. Why at the end of the novel is Yeshua treated as if he were a divine savior instead of an ordinary mortal? Why is Woland the executor of Yeshua's will? (324)

10. Why does Yeshua, having read the Master's novel, want Woland to reward the Master? Why has the Master earned peace, but not light? (305, 324)

11. Why does Pilate dream that he is involved in an "engaging and endless" dispute with Yeshua, "the philosopher who had conceived the absurd notion that all people were good," and that Yeshua's execution never took place? (271–272) Why does Yeshua free Pilate to walk with him and continue their discussion? (324)

12. Why does Pilate need Yeshua to tell him that the Crucifixion never happened? Why does Yeshua swear that it never did? (334–335)

Suggested textual analyses
Pages 14–24 (from Chapter 2): beginning, "The procurator's cheek twitched," and ending, "and the secretary copied down what Pilate said."

Pages 271–272 (from Chapter 26): beginning, "The couch stood in semidarkness," and ending, "and laughed with joy in his sleep."

Pages 322–325 (from Chapter 32): from "Woland set his horse down," to the end of the chapter.

Why must Margarita become a witch and host the devil's ball in order to accomplish the good deed of helping the Master?

1. Why does Margarita, who has a good and loving husband, need the Master in order to be happy? (185–186)

2. Why does the Master's novel become Margarita's life? Why does she call him Master? (118)

3. Why is Margarita the only one who actually invites the devil into her life? (190)

4. Why does Margarita indulge her urge to be destructive while riding her broom to the meeting? Why does she nonetheless take the time to comfort a scared child? (201–206)

5. As hostess of the devil's ball, why must Margarita notice everyone, but show no partiality for anyone? (223–224)

6. Why does Margarita take pity on Frieda, the woman who killed her baby? Why does Margarita not only free Frieda from her punishment, but forgive her, an act usually associated only with God? (228–229, 241–243)

7. Why must Margarita drink Baron Maigel's blood? Why does that bring the ball to an end? (234)

8. Why does Woland tell Margarita not to ask for anything, and then urge her to show more courage in saying what she wants? Why does Margarita ask for something for Frieda before asking for something for herself? (241)

9. Why must Margarita become a normal person again, even though she likes being a witch? Why must she lose the "witch's squint and the cruelty and wildness of her features"? (309, 312–313)

10. Why, before accompanying Woland on their final journey, must the Master and Margarita be poisoned and then brought back to life with the wine that poisoned them? (313)

Suggested textual analyses
Pages 223–235 (Chapter 23)

Pages 240–243 (from Chapter 24): beginning, "The merry supper continued," and ending, "and a spasm contorted her face."

FOR FURTHER REFLECTION

1. Should society strive for perfect order?

2. Does one have to suffer bouts of chaos to achieve order?

3. What limits should government impose on artistic freedom? Is the best art subversive?

4. Is Jesus an inspiring figure in Bulgakov's reinterpretation of the Passion?

5. Must there be limits to forgiveness?

6. Does belief in God require a power like Woland to explain why there is evil in the world?

7. What would Woland and his retinue do if they came to the United States today?

8. Can art fulfill the same spiritual need as religion?

9. Do you condemn Pilate, or was he a victim of the system?

10. Can an atheistic society survive?

Questions for

THINGS FALL

APART

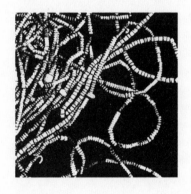

Chinua Achebe

CHINUA ACHEBE (1930–   ), born in the
village of Ogidi in Nigeria, studied medicine
and literature at the University of Ibadan.
His first novel, *Things Fall Apart* (1958),
has been translated into fifty languages.
The novels that followed, *No Longer at
Ease* (1960), *Arrow of God* (1964), *A Man
of the People* (1966), and *Anthills of the
Savannah* (1987), have earned Achebe
numerous international honors and prizes,
including fellowships from the Modern
Language Association and the Scottish Arts
Council and doctorates from universities
in Canada, England, Nigeria, Scotland,
and the United States. Achebe served as
a diplomat for Biafra during the Nigerian
civil war (1967–1970) and wrote poetry
and essays about this experience.
In 1982, he founded the Association
of Nigerian Writers. Achebe has taught
at Bard College and the universities of
Nigeria, Massachusetts, and Connecticut,
and edits the prominent journal *Okike*.

NOTE: All page references are from the
Anchor Books/Doubleday edition of *Things Fall
Apart* (first printing 1994).

INTERPRETIVE QUESTIONS
FOR DISCUSSION

Why does Okonkwo commit suicide, an act his tribe considers an offense against the Earth?

1. Why is Okonkwo's fear of failure and weakness "deeper and more intimate" than his fear of evil and capricious gods, magic, and malevolent forces in nature? (13)

2. Are we meant to admire Okonkwo's achievements—his climb to distinction from a shameful childhood—or to condemn him and his overbearing and violent nature?

3. Why does Okonkwo despise everything about his father, Unoka—his gentleness as well as his laziness? (13) Why is Okonkwo impatient with his father even when Unoka imparts encouragement and wisdom to him? (24–25)

4. Why does fear of being called a coward compel Okonkwo to kill his adopted son, Ikemefuna? (58–61) Why doesn't Okonkwo follow the tribal order forbidding him to have anything to do with the sacrifice? (57)

5. Why does Okonkwo see laziness and weakness in his son Nwoye, a lad who eventually excels in his studies and becomes a teacher?

6. Why does Okonkwo often think to himself that it would have been better for him had his daughter Ezinma been a boy? (66, 173)

7. Why did Okonkwo survive the tragedies of his first year as a farmer without giving up and despairing as others did that year? (24)

8. Why can't Okonkwo control his anger even during the sacred Week of Peace? (29–30)

9. Why does Okonkwo prosper in exile and only come to his ruin once he returns to his fatherland?

10. Are we meant to think that it was the destiny of Okonkwo's *chi* to fail—that Okonkwo was doomed with or without the arrival of colonialism? (131)

11. Why do Okonkwo and his father—men whose lives and spirits differed so dramatically—both die of what the Ibo call "abomination"? (18, 207)

12. Is Okonkwo's suicide an act of despair or one of pride and self-assertion?

Suggested textual analyses

Pages 23–25 (from Chapter 3): from "The year that Okonkwo took eight hundred seed-yams," to the end of the chapter.

Pages 151–153 (from Chapter 17): from "One morning Okonkwo's cousin," to the end of the chapter.

Why do "things fall apart" for the villages of Umuofia?

1. Why does the humane way of punishing the murderer of an Umuofia woman (taking a young man and a virgin as compensation) disintegrate into a senseless act of savagery— the boy's murder by his adopted father? Why is Ikemefuna's sad story told in Umuofia to the present day?

2. Why are we told that Umuofia was feared for its power in both war and magic? (11) Does Umuofia fall apart because white culture changed its system of government and religion, or because it undermined its base of fear?

3. Why does Ibo religion condemn any conflict based on *"a fight of blame"*? (12) Why does Okonkwo reject the idea that Umuofia cannot fight white imperialism because this would constitute a "war of blame"? (200–201)

4. Why do Okonkwo and Obierika disagree about how the Earth will respond to Okonkwo's involvement in Ikemefuna's death? (66–67)

5. Why is the duty of Evil Forest and the other *egwugwu* "not to blame this man or to praise that, but to settle the dispute"? (93) Why is order preserved and respected when the nine judges of the village assume the roles of powerful spirits?

6. Why is the tribe able to serve as a corrective to Okonkwo's pride, anger, and insensitivity toward others? (26, 30–31, 151–152, 158–159)

7. Why is it for the good of the village that Okonkwo spend seven years exiled to his motherland for the inadvertent killing of a clansman? (124–125)

8. Why does Uchendu say that men are fools to kill a person who says nothing, but need not fear killing one who shouts? (140)

9. Why doesn't Obierika allow Okonkwo to thank him for looking after his possessions during his exile? Why does Obierika joke about Okonkwo killing his sons or himself? (142)

10. Why, with the white man's government in place, are prisons and executions necessary to maintain order, whereas with tribal governance none were necessary? (123–125)

11. Why don't Okonkwo's comrades understand why he killed the messenger? Why does the murder diffuse the men's lust for war? (204–205)

12. Why does tribal power come to an end when a Christian convert unmasks one of the *egwugwu*? (186–187)

Suggested textual analysis
Pages 171–177 (Chapter 20)

Does the author mourn the demise of Ibo tribal culture, or does he believe that Christianity offered the Ibo a better way of life?

1. Why does Nwoye, Okonkwo's eldest son, find salvation in Christianity?

2. Are we meant to think that Unoka, Okonkwo's father, would have thrived in a Christian community as his grandson Nwoye did? Did Unoka become an improvident, lazy man because his personality wasn't suited for tribal life, in which agriculture and warfare were the only possible pursuits?

3. Does the author think that Christianity took hold of the Ibo imagination because it had compatible superstitions and beliefs?

4. Why do the Ibo men celebrate the funeral of the great warrior Ezeudu by dashing about in a frenzy and occasionally becoming very violent? Why do they use the occasion of a funeral to act out their impulses and fears in the guise of *egwugwu*? (121–124)

5. Why, to the Ibo, is "the land of the living . . . not far removed from the domain of the ancestors"? (122)

6. Why do both Christianity and Ibo religion believe that it is a sin to despair? (134)

7. Why are the first Ibo converts to Christianity not moved by the "mad logic" of the new religion, but rather stirred by its hymns? (146–147)

8. Why does the first serious trouble between the Mbanta clan and its Christian converts arise from a rumor that one of the outcasts

killed a royal python? (157–158) Why does the situation subside when the outcast dies, proving to the clan that the old gods could "fight their own battles"? (161)

9. Why does the white missionary Mr. Brown, understanding that "a frontal attack" will not convert the Ibo, become successful by joining education with religion? (181)

10. Why are we told that while Mr. Brown runs the church in Umuofia, excesses of zeal are restrained and tribal religion is respected? (178–179) Why does the author have him succeeded by the intolerant Mr. Smith, who sees everything as "black and white"? (184)

11. Why is it the Christians, and not the Ibo, who want to wage a holy war? (184; cf. 158)

12. Why does Obierika attribute the disintegration of Umuofia's power to the fact that his brothers—members of the clan— embraced Christianity? (176)

Suggested textual analysis
Pages 178–183 (Chapter 21)

FOR FURTHER REFLECTION

1. Must any regime, culture, religion, or personal relationship that is built upon fear inevitably "fall apart"?

2. Do you find Okonkwo a universal, tragic figure?

3. How can a society keep from falling apart when the values and self-determination of the individual take precedence over those of the community?

4. Does the rest of life usually become easier or more challenging when a person achieves great success in youth?

5. Does society fall apart when we forget the strength of kinship bonds?

All possible care has been taken to trace ownership and secure permission for each selection in this anthology. The Great Books Foundation wishes to thank the following authors, publishers, and representatives for permission to reprint copyrighted material.

The Overcoat, from THE DIARY OF A MADMAN AND OTHER STORIES, by Nikolai Gogol. Translated by Andrew R. MacAndrew. Translation copyright 1960, renewed 1988 by Andrew R. MacAndrew. Reprinted by permission of Dutton Signet, a division of Penguin Books USA, Inc.

Bhagavad-Gita, from THE SONG OF GOD: BHAGAVAD-GITA. Translated by Swami Prabhavananda and Christopher Isherwood, with introduction by Aldous Huxley. Copyright 1944, 1951, 1972, 1987 by The Vedanta Society of Southern California. Reprinted by permission of Vedanta Press.

Troth, from MEMOIRS OF AN ANTI-SEMITE, by Gregor von Rezzori. Copyright 1969, 1981 by Gregor von Rezzori. Reprinted by permission of Viking Penguin, a division of Penguin Books USA, Inc.

The Bacchae, by Euripides, from THE COMPLETE GREEK TRAGEDIES: EURIPIDES IV, edited by David Grene and Richmond Lattimore. Translated by William Arrowsmith. Copyright 1958, 1959 by The University of Chicago. Reprinted by permission of The University of Chicago Press.